State and Regional Patterns
in
American
Manufacturing
1860-1900

ALBERT W. NIEMI, JR.

Contributions in Economics and Economic History, Number 10

Greenwood Press
Westport, Connecticut • London, England

Library of Congress Cataloging in Publication Data

Niemi, Albert W
    State and regional patterns in American manufacturing, 1860-1900.

    (Contributions in economics and economic history, no. 10)
    Bibliography: p.
    1. United States—Manufactures—History. 2. Indus-
tries, Location of—United States—History. I. Title.
HD9725.N53   338'.0973   73-13289
ISBN 0-8371-7148-2

Library of Congress Catalog Card Number: 73-13289
ISBN: 0-8371-7148-2

First published in 1974

Greenwood Press, a division of Williamhouse-Regency Inc.
51 Riverside Avenue, Westport, Connecticut 06880

Manufactured in the United States of America

To Maria

Contents

List of Tables

List of Appendix Tables

Preface

A major change in the direction of American economic growth took place during the period 1860-1900. The movement toward industrialization which developed in the antebellum era became intensified, and, before the end of the nineteenth century, manufacturing replaced agriculture as the leading source of economic growth. Scarce formal attention has been paid to a close examination of the changing structural patterns within manufacturing that accompanied this rise of industry. This void in the literature can largely be attributed to the data collection procedures followed in the census surveys of manufacturing during the late nineteenth century. The industry stub used in collecting the pertinent information varied from census year to census year. The classification in each census was very detailed, approaching six hundred industries in some census years, and there was no attempt at a meaningful aggregation of the data according to some rigidly defined industry categories. As a result of these problems in the industrial classification system, intertemporal

comparisons of manufacturing developments are virtually impossible to make on the basis of the published census data. In
addition, for given census years, the industry stub varied to some
extent from state to state, thus limiting the possibility of meaningful state and regional comparisons for single time periods.
Another problem in using the published census manufacturing
data is that much nonmanufacturing activity was included as
manufacturing in the original census returns. In particular, the
census included a portion of output produced in mining, construction, and many of the hand trades, such as blacksmithing,
carpentering, and plumbing, as originating in manufacturing.

This treatment attempts to fill this void in the literature and
provides an analysis of national, regional, and state patterns in
manufacturing structure during 1860-1900. In order to solve
the statistical problems resulting from the inadequacy of existing
census data, a conversion of the census figures to the Standard
Industrial Classification (SIC) two-digit industry categories was
performed.[1] This conversion involved the aggregation of the
detailed census data into twenty major manufacturing industry
groups (SIC 20-39): food and kindred products; tobacco and
tobacco products; textile mill products; apparel and related
products; lumber and wood products; furniture and fixtures;
paper and allied products; printing and publishing; chemicals
and allied products; petroleum and coal products; rubber and
plastics products; leather and leather products; stone, clay, and
glass products; primary metals industries; fabricated metals
products; non-electrical machinery; electrical machinery;
transportation equipment; instruments and related products;
and miscellaneous manufacturing. The aggregation was performed separately for all states and census regions[2] in 1860 and
1900. This classification of the census data solves the problem
of making intertemporal comparisons of structural developments and also allows for state and regional analysis.

The national pattern of manufacturing that developed during
the antebellum era and state and regional variation from the
national industry pattern will be highlighted in Chapters 1 and 2.

It will be shown that, generally, manufacturing was concentrated in the Northeast in 1860 but that several important instances of localized production were also evident, particularly in the metals and machinery industries. The heterogeneity of the particular states within census regions will be demonstrated and the appropriateness of describing regional manufacturing development through the traditional three region economy, Northeast, West, and South, will be questioned. In addition, the marked spatial and industrial changes in manufacturing that occurred in the United States during the last half of the nineteenth century will be surveyed in the first two chapters. During the period 1860-1900 there was a general shift from the resource processing type of manufacturing industries toward industries involving more sophisticated stages of production, particularly metals and machinery. It will be demonstrated that locational patterns in the metals and machinery industries became more concentrated spatially, but in most of the other manufacturing industries the trend was toward more localized production.

An analysis of the forces underlying locational patterns in state and regional manufacturing is presented in Chapter 3. The classical comparative cost doctrine is examined by testing the degree of association between relative labor supplies and the labor intensity of production. In addition, the Heckscher-Ohlin hypothesis is analyzed by testing the degree of association between relative supplies of capital and labor and concentration on capital and labor intensive industries. The results suggest that the mobile factors of production, capital and labor, were relatively unimportant in nineteenth century decisions on industrial location. It is hypothesized that relatively immobile factors, such as local demand, resource conditions, economies of scale, and external economies, largely determined state and regional industrial location patterns during this period.

A long-run view (1860-1970) of per capita output trends in state and regional manufacturing is taken in Chapter 4. Several conceptually different measures of state and regional dispersion of industry are used; all indicators point to a general movement toward convergence to national per capita output levels, both in aggregate manufacturing and in most two-digit industries. It appears that there was very little tendency toward convergence in the late nineteenth century and that most of the narrowing of state and regional per capita manufacturing output differences occurred after 1900.

A step toward further understanding of the state and regional variation in structural patterns in American manufacturing during the late nineteenth century has been taken in this work through a rather careful and arduous redefining of the available statistical information. Perhaps the greatest contribution of this study is the collection and presentation of data in a form conducive to analysis. Estimates in two-digit detail of manufacturing value added, total capital invested, employment, average cost per employee, output-labor ratios, capital-labor ratios, and capital-output ratios are provided in the appendix tables for each state and census region. It is hoped that the vast pool of data organized in the appendix tables will serve to stimulate research into other aspects of late nineteenth century American manufacturing.

I am grateful for the advice and critical review provided by my colleagues at the University of Georgia. Robert E. Gallman of the University of North Carolina offered many helpful suggestions in the beginning stages of this research and Stanley L. Engerman of the University of Rochester was responsible for substantial improvement of Chapter 3. The College of Business at the University of Georgia provided an atmosphere conducive to the preparation of this manuscript. Finally, I am indebted to my wife Maria who carefully read the manuscript and offered many helpful suggestions.

NOTES

1. The procedure of converting census data to the SIC two-digit industries was first developed by this author in "The Development of Industrial

Structure in Southern New England," *Journal of Economic History,* September 1970, pp. 657-662; also see "Structural Shifts in Southern Manufacturing, 1849-1899," *Business History Review*, Spring 1971, pp. 79-84. The census data were converted according to the *1963 Census of Manufactures, Industry Description,* U. S. Bureau of the Census. [Lists which convert census manufacturing data to the SIC categories are presented in the Appendix, Part I.]

2. The analysis here is concerned with the following census regions: New England, Middle Atlantic, East North Central, West North Central, South Atlantic, East South Central, and West South Central. Due to data limitations for most states in the Mountain and Pacific regions in 1860, no attempt is made to include the Far West in the analysis.

State and Regional Patterns
in
American Manufacturing

1

Regional Patterns of Manufacturing Development During 1860-1900

The most comprehensive treatment of manufacturing development in the American economy is that of Victor Clark. For years his study has served as the standard reference for scholars of American industrial history.[1] Clark provides a comprehensive analysis of many facets of American manufacturing development, focusing on an individual industry appraisal of developments in productive capacity, technology, organizational structure, employment, wages, profits, and related factors. However, as a result of the exhaustive nature of Clark's study and the absence of any central theme, it is very difficult for the reader to grasp the broad outlines of nineteenth century industrial development. It is also difficult to interpret the significance of many of Clark's assertions due to the scant use of the available empirical evidence in the census and, in numerous instances, the inappropriate use of census data. With respect to the latter point, Clark and other scholars have used the census figures on the gross value of output to gauge regional industrial developments.[2] The appropriate accounting concept for the estimation of final product is value added, defined as the gross value of output minus the intermediate production expenses.[3] Utilization of the gross value of output to approximate final product results in a relative overstatement of production in industries, such as milling, that consume large amounts of resources and other inputs. As suggested in the Preface, the scant use of existing census data results from defects in the data collection procedures followed in the census.

This study is much less ambitious than Clark's and focuses on an analysis, by state and census region, of the structural composition of American manufacturing during the late nineteenth century. The attempt here is to refine the available census data in order to provide careful estimates of manufacturing value added by two-digit industry for states and regions. These estimates can be used to analyze state and regional patterns of industrial growth during the crucial period 1860-1900. In addition to the state, regional, and national trends in output which are surveyed in this work, the appendix tables provide state and regional estimates, by two-digit industry, of employment, labor costs, capital invested, output-labor ratios, capital-output ratios, and capital-labor ratios. The appendix data can be used as the basis for analyzing other aspects of America's industrial history. In their present form the data are conducive to the study of relative efficiency between states and regions within particular industries and the study of state and regional variation in factor utilization and production techniques.

At present, the scholar of American industrial history has a very limited stock of empirical information concerning the structural composition of industrial growth during the late nineteenth century, although numerous qualitative remarks and judgments on the patterns of industrial growth have been offered in the literature. At the national level, it is generally argued that, on the eve of the Civil War, American manufacturing consisted primarily of light manufacturing industries such as cotton and woolen textiles, apparel, boots, shoes, and other leather products and resource-oriented manufacturing industries such as lumber, flour and meal, and iron.[4] It is argued that most of this light manufacturing was concentrated in the northeastern states, particularly southern New England, and that Pennsylvania had become the major center of the iron industry and New York had achieved dominance as a center for apparel production.[5] Antebellum manufacturing outside the Northeast is traditionally regarded as highly resource-oriented.[6] According to Taylor, in 1860 the West led all regions in the production of lumber, flour and meal, liquor, packing house products, and agricultural machinery; at the same time, the leading southern manufactures were lumber, tobacco, and flour and meal.[7] North has suggested that in addition to the West's concentration on resource-oriented manufacturing industries, there was some development aimed toward satisfying local consumer demand in the following industries: small machines and tools, printing and publishing, glass and stone products, leather goods, wood products, and metal fabrication.[8] Taylor claims that by 1860 some small beginnings in the South had been made in the manufacture of cotton goods, machinery, and iron.

It is commonly accepted that the late nineteenth century witnessed a relative decline in the light industries such as textiles, apparel, and boots and shoes and a relative advance in the heavy industries such as iron and steel and machinery. This movement toward the production of durable goods is evident in the Shaw and Burns work on production trends during the late nineteenth and early twentieth centuries.[9] With respect to the regional distribution of manufacturing activity, it is generally argued that there was a shift of manufacturing out of the Northeast toward the West and South, although the Northeast remained a very important industrial center. The major developments in the West that are cited include expansion in the iron and steel, transportation equipment, and agricultural machinery industries, and continued expansion in meat packing and flour milling.[10] Southern manufacturing development during the late nineteenth century is viewed as concentrating on textile development along with increased production of lumber and iron and steel. The shift of textiles from New England to the South is pointed to in most surveys of industrial movement in America; this shift is generally attributed to the South's access to cheap labor and raw material supplies.[11] Within the southern iron and steel industry, it is generally recognized that Alabama became a major iron and steel center during the late nineteenth century and Tennessee showed some development in this area.[12]

The broad trends noted above have largely been distilled by the authors from the existing census data which in themselves, as previously mentioned, have several deficiencies in their present form. Specifically, many of Clark's assertions with respect to industry trends are based on the gross value of output and there is no adjustment to exclude nonmanufacturing activity. These same conceptual problems color much of the secondary treatment of manufacturing included in the standard textbooks. As a result, it is difficult to determine the appropriateness of the above conclusions. By correcting for the deficiencies in the collected census data and classifying the data according to the SIC coding system, this study provides a check on the accuracy of the traditional views on the broad trends in late nineteenth century American industrialization and also extends the analysis to a more rigidly defined industrial and spatial base.

Table 1 provides estimates of value added, by two-digit industry, for the United States as a whole in 1860 and 1900.[13] The figures support the traditional view and indicate that much antebellum manufacturing development occurred in the resource processing industries, particularly food and lumber and wood products, and in the light manufacturing industries, especially textiles, apparel, and leather products. However, as a group, the primary metals industries and the related fabricated metals, machinery, and transportation equipment industries accounted for almost one-fourth of total value added in 1860. During the period 1860-1900, both textiles and leather products suffered a significant relative decline, and, as is generally acknowledged, the aggregate weight of all light industries declined relative to

TABLE 1

CURRENT DOLLAR UNITED STATES MANUFACTURING VALUE

ADDED AND PERCENTAGE DISTRIBUTION, 1860 and 1900[a]

SIC Code Number and Industry	1860 Current Dollar Value Added ($000)	1860 Percentage Distribution	1900 Current Dollar Value Added ($000)	1900 Percentage Distribution
20 Food	$ 89,868.2	12.1	$ 727,379.2	14.9
21 Tobacco	14,252.1	1.9	174,804.7	3.6
22 Textiles	106,984.6	14.3	416,595.3	8.5
23 Apparel	58,169.5	7.8	454,117.1	9.3
24 Lumber and Wood Products	72,013.9	9.7	342,293.5	7.0
25 Furniture	17,856.8	2.4	102,800.8	2.1
26 Paper	10,933.6	1.5	95,220.2	2.0
27 Printing and Publishing	21,697.8	2.9	282,514.7	5.8
28 Chemicals	20,303.6	2.7	174,566.4	3.6
29 Petroleum and Coal Products	11,413.2	1.5	89,015.3	1.8
30 Rubber	3,154.1	0.4	40,425.0	0.8
31 Leather	25,765.8	3.5	47,742.1	1.0
Leather Products	58,707.5	7.9	158,416.4	3.2
32 Stone, Clay and Glass	27,544.7	3.7	290,210.4	5.9
33 Primary Metals	55,547.8	7.5	366,289.7	7.5
34 Fabricated Metals	35,245.8	4.7	228,767.1	4.7
35 Non-electrical Machinery	47,631.5	6.4	434,929.8	8.9
36 Electrical Machinery	- -	- -	- -[a]	- -
37 Transportation Equipment	37,896.3	5.1	242,477.4	5.0
38 Instruments	3,131.2	0.4	28,752.0	0.6
39 Miscellaneous	27,799.8	3.7	189,874.9	3.8
Total	745,917.8		4,887,192.0	

[a]In all cases the United States total represents the total for the seven census regions being considered in this study.

Source: See text.

total manufacturing. The food and lumber industries retained their high antebellum ranking, and the percentage share of total value added accounted for by the resource processing industries showed no perceptible change. The heavy industries, SIC 33-37, showed only a slight relative advance, with an increase from 23.7 percent of total value added in 1860 to 26.1 percent in 1900. It appears that the traditional view underemphasizes the relative importance of heavy industry in the mid-nineteenth century and overemphasizes the relative expansion in this area during the last decades of the century. On balance, structural shifts within manufacturing resulted in a more diversified manufacturing sector at the end of the period.

There were substantial regional differences in the aggregate weight of manufacturing as a sector and in the industrial composition within manufacturing.[14] Table 2 provides estimates of the percentage distribution of manufacturing value added within the various census regions in 1860. (See the Appendix, Part II, for regional estimates of current dollar value added.) The figures support the commonly accepted notion of northeastern concentration on light industries, especially textiles and leather products in New England and apparel in the Middle Atlantic states. However, heavy industry was also important to the Middle Atlantic region, and, as a group, the metals, machinery, and equipment industries were as important to the region as the light industries. Manufacturing outside of the Northeast appears to have been highly concentrated on resource processing industries, especially food and lumber, coupled with a heavy emphasis on tobacco manufacture in the South Atlantic region. Light manufactures in general were unimportant in the West and South, but there is evidence of relative concentration on textile production in the South Atlantic region. With regard to the metals, machinery, and equipment industries (SIC 33-37), a striking degree of regional similarity in manufacturing structure is shown, with each region deriving 20 to 25 percent of aggregate manufacturing value added from these industries. Both

TABLE 2

PERCENTAGE DISTRIBUTION OF MANUFACTURING VALUE ADDED ACROSS

TWO DIGIT INDUSTRIES, BY REGION, 1860

SIC Code Number and Industry	New England	Middle Atlantic	East North Central	West North Central	South Atlantic	East South Central	West South Central
20 Food	3.3	11.8	24.6	26.2	12.9	16.9	14.7
21 Tobacco	0.4	1.3	0.9	4.4	16.0	4.5	1.3
22 Textiles	32.4	9.5	1.8	2.9	9.1	6.7	2.6
23 Apparel	6.3	10.9	6.0	2.6	1.1	2.7	8.4
24 Lumber and Wood Products	4.6	6.8	17.8	22.5	16.2	19.6	29.8
25 Furniture	1.8	2.4	4.3	2.0	1.5	1.8	0.9
26 Paper	2.3	1.4	0.9	0.1	1.1	0.3	0.0
27 Printing and Publishing	1.5	4.4	2.3	1.5	1.0	2.1	1.4
28 Chemicals	1.4	3.5	1.9	1.5	7.8	1.8	1.6
29 Petroleum and Coal Products	1.0	2.0	1.0	1.8	1.2	1.9	0.4
30 Rubber	0.6	0.6	0.0	–	–	–	–
31 Leather	2.9	4.6	1.9	1.2	2.8	4.3	1.3
Leather Products	14.1	5.3	5.9	5.5	3.6	6.0	9.0
32 Stone, Clay and Glass	2.1	4.7	3.6	5.4	3.5	2.7	4.7
33 Primary Metals	4.5	10.1	6.4	7.6	6.7	6.8	0.7
34 Fabricated Metals	5.8	4.3	4.5	4.4	2.6	4.8	6.0
35 Non-electrical Machinery	5.4	6.0	9.4	5.1	5.0	8.0	9.7
36 Electrical Machinery	–	–	–	–	–	–	–
37 Transportation Equipment	4.1	5.2	5.1	3.9	7.5	7.8	6.7
38 Instruments	0.6	0.6	0.1	0.0[a]	–	0.0	–
39 Miscellaneous Manufacturing	4.7	4.6	1.9	1.4	0.3	1.2	0.8

[a] In this and all succeeding tables, 0.0 signifies values of less than .05.

Source: See text.

North and Taylor indicate that during the antebellum period there was some movement in the West and South from resource processing industries toward production aimed at satisfying local demands. The data in Table 2 support this notion of diversification away from resource-oriented manufacturing.

The broad structure of the regional distribution of industrial production in 1900 remained much as it had been on the eve of the Civil War (see Table 3). (See the Appendix, Part IV, for the current dollar figures.) Light manufactures still provided a large share of value added in the northeastern regions, although, in nearly all cases, the individual industries suffered rather sharp relative declines. The metals, machinery, and equipment industries made a slight relative advance in New England and the Middle Atlantic regions, with most of this increase occurring as a result of the marked rise in the machinery industry. Western manufacturing remained highly concentrated on resource processing industries, especially food products; of the light industries, only apparel contributed a substantial share to value added. The work of Hunter and Clark suggests that the late nineteenth century witnessed a significant advance of the iron and steel, transportation equipment, and agricultural machinery industries in the West. The figures in Table 3 add clear support to this view. By the end of the century, the East North Central region was more heavily concentrated on the fabricated metals and machinery industries than any other region of the United States and the metals, machinery, and equipment group as a whole accounted for almost one-third of the region's total industrial production. This degree of specialization was not approached in any other region.

Southern manufacturing at the end of the nineteenth century was characterized by a high degree of emphasis on resource-oriented activity, with food, lumber, and tobacco providing between 40 percent (South Atlantic) and 60 percent (West South Central) of regional output. Heavy industry (SIC 33-37) as a group declined as a share of aggregate value added in each of the southern regions, although the rise of the iron and steel

TABLE 3

PERCENTAGE DISTRIBUTION OF MANUFACTURING VALUE ADDED ACROSS TWO DIGIT INDUSTRIES, BY REGION, 1900

SIC Code Number and Industry	New England	Middle Atlantic	East North Central	West North Central	South Atlantic	East South Central	West South Central
20 Food	6.9	11.6	21.0	27.5	9.4	18.4	28.2
21 Tobacco	0.7	3.4	2.5	6.7	14.0	9.0	2.0
22 Textiles	24.5	8.0	1.1	0.7	17.4	5.1	1.3
23 Apparel	5.9	13.5	7.4	7.1	2.6	5.0	5.1
24 Lumber and Wood Products	3.8	3.3	8.5	9.9	19.3	21.2	29.8
25 Furniture	1.7	1.8	3.2	1.9	1.2	1.3	1.1
26 Paper	4.0	2.1	1.5	0.4	0.7	0.1	0.2
27 Printing and Publishing	4.5	6.4	5.5	8.2	3.0	4.3	6.7
28 Chemicals	2.0	4.2	3.0	2.9	8.7	4.4	1.6
29 Petroleum and Coal Products	1.1	2.4	1.7	1.9	0.9	1.2	1.3
30 Rubber	3.2	0.4	0.4	0.2	-	0.0	-
31 Leather	1.0	1.3	0.7	0.2	1.1	1.2	0.0
Leather Products	8.3	2.1	2.3	3.4	1.3	1.7	2.9
32 Stone, Clay and Glass	4.6	6.9	5.8	6.2	3.8	3.9	4.0
33 Primary Metals	3.1	10.3	7.7	3.1	6.0	8.7	0.9
34 Fabricated Metals	5.0	3.8	7.2	3.9	1.2	2.1	1.9
35 Non-electrical Machinery	9.5	9.3	10.7	5.1	3.0	5.3	3.6
36 Electrical Machinery[a]	-	-	-	-	-	-	-
37 Transportation Equipment	2.6	4.2	6.2	7.8	5.9	6.0	8.3
38 Instruments	0.8	0.8	0.4	0.4	0.0	0.1	0.2
39 Miscellaneous	6.6	4.2	3.2	2.5	0.4	1.0	0.9

[a] Included in SIC 35.

Source: See text.

industry in Alabama did show up in the East South Central region. The often cited shift of textiles from New England to the South, which began during the last year of the century, is reflected in the rise of SIC 22 in the South Atlantic region. By 1900 this area began to approach New England's degree of specialization in textiles.

For each region, the significance of the structural shifts within manufacturing during 1860-1900 can be determined by utilizing a chi-square test to calculate the degree of independence of the 1900 percentage distribution from that which existed in 1860.[15] For each region it was hypothesized that there had been no significant change during 1860-1900 in the two-digit industry weights. The following values for the chi-square statistic were calculated: New England, 11.88; Middle Atlantic, 7.84 (P $\geq$ .975); East North Central, 10.97; West North Central, 19.50; South Atlantic, 15.49; East South Central, 11.27; West South Central, 19.17; and United States, 8.54 (P $\geq$ .975).[16] Only in the nation as a whole and in the Middle Atlantic region could the hypothesis that there had been no significant change in industrial structure be accepted; in all other regions, it was impossible to accept the notion of dependence between the 1860 and 1900 industrial distributions.

A supplementary procedure that casts further light on the degree of intraregional structural change during the late nineteenth century is to use rank correlation techniques to determine the independence of the two-digit industry rank ordering in 1900 from that in 1860.[17] For each region, the percentage distribution of manufacturing value added across the two-digit industries for both 1860 and 1900 were ranked. The hypothesis of dependence between the 1860 and 1900 rank orderings was specified as follows: within regions, there was a significant positive relationship between the rank ordering of industries in 1860 and 1900. Spearman's rank correlation coefficient (r_s) was calculated and yielded the following results: New England, r_s = .791 (P $\leq$ .001); Middle Atlantic, r_s = .806 (P < .001); East North Central, r_s = .915 (P $\leq$ .001); West North Central, r_s = .523

(P $\leq$ .05); South Atlantic, r_s = .859 (P $\leq$ .001); East South Central, r_s = .798 (P $\leq$ .001); West South Central, r_s = .810 (P $\leq$ .001); and United States, r_s = .876 (P $\leq$ .001).[18] In every region, a significant relationship was found between the 1860 and 1900 industrial rankings and the hypothesis was accepted in each case. However, these results are not inconsistent with those achieved through the use of the chi-square test. The joint results from both statistical tests indicate that there were a number of significant shifts in individual industry weights during the late nineteenth century, but the broad outlines of manufacturing structure, as reflected in the rank ordering of industries, did not change substantially during this period.

Another way to view comparative changes in manufacturing structure during the late nineteenth century is to examine the regional industry shares of national value added. (See Tables 4 and 5.) Table 4 clearly demonstrates the dominant position of the northeastern regions relative to the rest of the nation on the eve of the Civil War. Only in the resource processing industries of food, tobacco, and lumber was the Northeast's contribution less than 65 percent of the national output. On the other hand, the western region's most significant contribution to national value added occurred in food and lumber and wood products. The South's most significant industry impact came in the resource processing industries of tobacco and tobacco products, lumber and wood products, and chemicals.[19] In looking at the percentage distribution of manufacturing value added within particular regions, it was concluded that there were some elements of structural similarity between the Northeast, West, and South, especially in the share of manufacturing value added produced by the metals, machinery, and equipment industries. Viewing the relative shares of national output in Table 4 places the issue of regional manufacturing development in an entirely different setting, and, with the exception of the East North Central region and tobacco and turpentine production in the South Atlantic region, the quantitative impact of the West and South on antebellum national industrial production was

TABLE 4

REGIONAL CONTRIBUTIONS TO NATIONAL INDUSTRY VALUE ADDED, 1860

(Percentages)

SIC Code Number and Industry	New England	Middle Atlantic	East North Central	West North Central	South Atlantic	East South Central	West South Central
20 Food	7.6	43.0	29.1	7.4	5.0	5.6	2.1
21 Tobacco	6.2	29.5	6.4	7.9	39.5	9.4	1.2
22 Textiles	63.3	29.1	1.8	0.7	3.0	1.9	0.3
23 Apparel	22.6	61.5	10.9	1.1	0.6	1.4	1.9
24 Lumber and Wood Products	13.4	30.9	26.2	8.0	7.9	8.2	5.4
25 Furniture	20.7	43.9	25.8	2.9	3.0	2.9	0.7
26 Paper	44.9	41.9	8.9	0.2	3.5	0.7	0.0
27 Printing and Publishing	14.5	66.9	11.5	1.8	1.7	2.9	0.8
28 Chemicals	14.6	56.6	9.7	1.9	13.5	2.7	1.0
29 Petroleum and Coal Products	19.1	57.9	9.7	4.1	3.6	5.0	0.5
30 Rubber	40.0	60.0	0.0	-	-	-	-
31 Leather	23.7	58.0	7.5	1.1	3.8	5.1	0.7
Leather Products	50.2	29.5	10.7	2.4	2.1	3.0	2.0
32 Stone, Clay and Glass	15.9	55.5	13.9	5.0	4.5	2.9	2.2
33 Primary Metals	16.9	59.3	12.2	3.5	4.3	3.6	0.2
34 Fabricated Metals	34.2	40.3	13.5	3.2	2.6	4.1	2.2
35 Non-electrical Machinery	23.7	41.2	20.9	2.7	3.7	5.0	2.7
36 Electrical Machinery	-	-	-	-	-	-	-
37 Transportation Equipment	22.7	45.0	14.2	2.6	7.0	6.2	2.3
38 Instruments	40.1	57.5	1.9	0.4	-	0.0	-
39 Miscellaneous Manufacturing	35.5	54.0	7.1	1.3	0.4	1.3	0.4
Total	28.0	43.9	14.3	3.4	4.7	4.0	1.8

REGIONAL CONTRIBUTIONS TO NATIONAL INDUSTRY VALUE ADDED, 1900

(Percentages)

SIC Code Number and Industry	New England	Middle Atlantic	East North Central	West North Central	South Atlantic	East South Central	West South Central
20 Food	7.6	32.0	36.5	13.5	2.7	3.9	3.5
21 Tobacco	3.0	39.5	18.0	13.8	16.7	8.0	1.1
22 Textiles	47.0	38.3	3.2	0.6	8.7	1.9	0.3
23 Apparel	10.3	59.5	20.6	5.6	1.2	1.7	1.1
24 Lumber and Wood Products	9.0	19.2	31.6	10.4	11.8	9.6	8.5
25 Furniture	13.5	34.8	39.7	6.5	2.5	2.0	1.0
26 Paper	33.2	43.8	19.5	1.7	1.5	0.1	0.2
27 Printing and Publishing	12.7	45.6	24.5	10.4	2.2	2.3	2.3
28 Chemicals	9.3	47.7	21.8	5.9	10.4	3.9	0.9
29 Petroleum and Coal Products	9.6	53.0	23.9	7.8	2.2	2.1	1.4
30 Rubber	64.1	21.9	12.1	1.9	–	0.1	–
31 Leather	16.2	54.3	19.3	1.4	4.9	3.9	0.1
Leather Products	42.1	26.7	18.4	7.8	1.7	1.7	1.8
32 Stone, Clay and Glass	12.7	47.9	25.5	7.7	2.7	2.1	1.4
33 Primary Metals	6.9	56.3	26.4	3.1	3.4	3.7	0.3
34 Fabriacted Metals	17.6	32.9	40.0	6.2	1.1	1.4	0.8
35 Non-electrical Machinery	17.5	42.9	31.2	4.3	1.5	1.9	0.8
36 Electrical Machinery	–	–	–	–	–	–	–
37 Transportation Equipment	8.7	34.9	32.6	11.6	5.0	3.9	3.3
38 Instruments	22.1	53.4	17.3	5.4	0.3	0.7	0.8
39 Miscellaneous	28.0	45.6	20.7	4.2	0.4	0.8	0.4
Total	16.3	41.0	25.9	7.3	4.3	3.2	2.0

Source: See text.

generally rather minor.

A comparison of Tables 4 and 5, which exhibit the regional industry shares in 1860 and 1900, respectively, shows the degree of change in relative industrial production during the late nineteenth century. New England's share of national value added declined in every industry except food and rubber, but the region continued to produce important shares of national output in many industries. Of particular note is New England's dominant position in the textile industry at the end of the century. Most scholars document the rise of southern textiles in the 1880s, but it does not appear from Table 5 that New England had lost much of its relative position in the industry by the end of the century. The Middle Atlantic region remained a dominant force in American manufacturing and accounted for 40 percent of national output in the majority of industries. The region's share of aggregate output declined very slightly, with the most significant declines occurring in rubber and printing and publishing.

The East North Central region made the greatest relative gains in manufacturing, increasing its share of total value added from 14.3 percent to 25.9 percent and achieving significant relative increases in every industry. By the turn of the century, the region presented a picture of broadly based industrial development. The westward drift of heavy industry is clearly documented by the region's high share of national production in the primary and fabricated metals, machinery, and transportation equipment industries. Industry contributions in the other regions were generally of minor significance, and regional shares exceeding 10 percent were almost exclusively found in the resource processing industries. Manufacturing in the West North Central region expanded at a relatively rapid pace, and the area increased its share of national value added in almost every industry. Southern manufacturing expansion during 1860-1900 lagged behind the national pace, and, as a result, there was a general decline in production shares in most industries. The most often noted areas of industrial expansion in the South of

the late nineteenth century, textiles and primary metals, do not
appear to have had much impact on national production at the
end of the century. In fact, the South contributed a slightly
greater share of the nation's output of primary metals in 1860
than in 1900 and only in the South Atlantic region was there
any relative rise in textile production.

The significance of intraregional changes in the percentage
shares of national value added were also subjected to empirical
test by calculating the chi-square statistic and Spearman's rank
correlation coefficient. By using the chi-square test, for each
region it was hypothesized that the 1860 and 1900 industry
shares were not significantly different. The calculated values of
the chi-square statistic were as follows: New England, 27.27;
Middle Atlantic, 25.24; East North Central, 72.65; West North
Central, 11.17; South Atlantic, 13.99; East South Central, 5.48
($P \geq .995$); and West South Central, 5.41 ($P \geq .995$). Only in the
East and West South Central regions were the industry shares
sufficiently similar to accept the hypothesis. In calculating
Spearman's rank correlation coefficient, for each region the hypothesis was specified as follows: there was a significant positive
relationship between the industry shares in 1860 and 1900. The
calculated values of r_s were as follows: New England, $r_s = .834$
($P \leq .001$); Middle Atlantic, $r_s = .575$ ($P \leq .02$); East North
Central, $r_s = .917$ ($P \leq .001$); West North Central, $r_s = .682$
($P \leq .01$); South Atlantic, $r_s = .801$ ($P \leq .001$); East South Central, $r_s = .765$ ($P \leq .01$); and West South Central, $r_s = .662$
($P \leq .01$). The joint results from the chi-square and rank correlation tests suggest that the many significant industry shifts that
did take place during this period were not so marked as to change
the entire complexion of American manufacturing.

An excellent example of the different information conveyed by
the chi-square and rank correlation analysis is provided by the
results in the East North Central region. As reflected in the very
high chi-square statistic, no area of the country underwent a more
far reaching restructuring of its manufacturing sector during the
late nineteenth century than the East North Central region. How-

ever, the rank correlation coefficient calculated between industry shares in 1860 and 1900 for the East North Central region
was higher than that for any other region. As a result, one can
argue, by referring to the actual percentage shares of national
value added, that the relative industrial composition of the region's manufacturing underwent significant change during 1860-
1900. At the same time, one can contend that the broad industry outlines of the region's manufacturing shares, as reflected by
the rank order, underwent no significant change during this
period. With this in mind, the reader is advised to approach the
chi-square and rank correlation results with caution and to be
careful in interpreting their significance.

A more analytical appraisal of industry concentration patterns
and the geographic dispersion of American manufacturing can
be obtained by utilizing a coefficient of industrial localization
constructed as follows:

$$C_{R_i} = \sum_{r=1}^{k} (VA_i^r/VA_i^n - PI^r/PI^n)$$

where VA = value added, PI = personal income, r and n desig-
nate region and nation respectively, i represents the ith industry,
and k is defined to include all positive values for each industry.[20]
The assumption is that personal income shares, since they reflect
the size of the population and the income received, adequately
represent consumer market potential. Differences in the regional
distribution of consumer markets and production will be com-
pensated for by trade. If production is localized in accordance
with consumer markets, the coefficient will approach zero; if
production is concentrated away from consumer markets, the
coefficient will approach unity. The simple measure of localization being used carries the implicit assumption of no international export of manufactured goods. It also carries such assumptions as no regional variation in income distribution and
no regional variation in consumer taste; these would be required
to insure that the structure of consumption did not vary

regionally.[21] As a result of these simplifying assumptions, caution should be used in interpreting the size of the coefficient. The numerical value of the coefficient represents the percentage of total value added that would have to enter interregional trade in order to yield a distribution of production in accordance with existing consumer markets.

By using the value added series provided here and Richard Easterlin's personal income series for the seven census regions, it is possible to construct the coefficient of localization for each of the two-digit manufacturing industries.[22] Table 6 indicates that on the eve of the Civil War production was most localized in lumber and wood products, transportation equipment, and machinery. The size of the coefficient suggests that less than 20 percent of output in these industries had to be shipped across regions to consumer markets. The machinery and transportation equipment industries, in particular, present several clear examples of local production aimed at fulfilling local demands. For example, if one studies the factors behind the two-digit aggregation of antebellum southern machine output, one finds that the three southern regions produced 90.3 percent of the nation's output of cotton gins. The East South Central region, which was the center of the American cotton industry in 1860, produced 51.1 percent of the nation's cotton gins.[23] In 1860, the two western regions produced 48.4 percent of all implements and machinery geared to agriculture. Machinery concerned with textile and apparel production was completely dominated by the Northeast. New England and the Middle Atlantic states produced 99.1 percent of all textile machinery and 94.5 percent of all sewing machines and related products; New England's shares of national output in these industries were 76.0 percent and 61.8 percent, respectively.

Slightly less localized production was characteristic of food, furniture, chemicals, petroleum and coal, stone, clay, and glass, and primary and fabricated metals. In each of these industries, approximately 20 to 25 percent of the nation's total manu-

TABLE 6

REGIONAL COEFFICIENT OF LOCALIZATION OF MANUFACTURING INDUSTRY, 1860 AND 1900

SIC Code Number and Industry	1860 Coefficient	1900 Coefficient
20 Food	.222	.143
21 Tobacco	.338	.215
22 Textiles	.487	.469
23 Apparel	.320	.298
24 Lumber and Wood Products	.144	.176
25 Furniture	.227	.233
26 Paper	.347	.368
27 Printing and Publishing	.294	.181
28 Chemicals	.232	.215
29 Petroleum and Coal Products	.250	.233
30 Rubber	.479	.536
31 Leather	.296	.303
Leather Products	.356	.316
32 Stone, Clay and Glass	.201	.214
33 Primary Metals	.241	.285
34 Fabricated Metals	.224	.258
35 Non-electrical Machinery	.181	.269
36 Electrical Machinery	- -	- -
37 Transportation Equipment	.156	.133
38 Instruments	.455	.353
39 Miscellaneous Manufacturing	.374	.334

Source: See text.

facturing value added would have had to enter interregional trade in order to find suitable markets. Production was more concentrated away from markets in printing and publishing, leather and leather products, tobacco, apparel, paper, and miscellaneous manufacturing; for each of these industries the coefficient indicated that 30 to 40 percent of value added would have had to be distributed across regions to consumer markets. The most concentrated production was found in textiles, rubber, and instruments where slightly less than 50 percent of total manufacturing output was produced apart from consumer markets.

The industry pattern of location coefficients in 1900 was very similar to that in 1860. Production was still highly concentrated in textiles and rubber and highly localized in lumber and wood products and transportation equipment. On balance, the changes that did take place during the late nineteenth century led to a slight decline in the degree of regional manufacturing concentration, as shown by a decline in the coefficient for aggregate manufacturing from .277 in 1860 to .252 in 1900.[24]

The coefficient of localization for each industry can be disaggregated to determine the regional composition of the export surplus. The following ratio for regions with an export surplus provides an index of approximate regional shares of interregional trade:

$$\frac{(VA_i^r / VA_i^n - PI^r / PI^n)}{C_{R_i}}$$

This ratio has been calculated for 1860 and 1900; the figures appear in Tables 7 and 8.[25] The results bear testimony to the heavy concentration of antebellum manufacturing in the Northeast. The only significant nonresource-oriented manufacturing export potential outside of the Northeast was shown by the East North Central region in machinery and furniture. The westward

TABLE 7

PERCENTAGE SHARES OF MANUFACTURING VALUE ADDED INVOLVED IN INTERREGIONAL TRADE, 1860

SIC Code Number and Industry	New England	Middle Atlantic	East North Central	West North Central	South Atlantic	East South Central	West South Central
20 Food	– –	24.8	60.8	14.4	– –	– –	– –
21 Tobacco	– –	– –	– –	10.9	89.1	– –	– –
22 Textiles	100.0	– –	– –	– –	– –	– –	– –
23 Apparel	25.0	75.0	– –	– –	– –	– –	– –
24 Lumber and Wood Products	– –	– –	73.6	26.4	– –	– –	– –
25 Furniture	26.9	28.2	44.9	– –	– –	– –	– –
26 Paper	87.3	12.7	– –	– –	– –	– –	– –
27 Printing and Publishing	– –	100.0	– –	– –	– –	– –	– –
28 Chemicals	– –	82.3	– –	– –	17.7	– –	– –
29 Petroleum and Coal Products	18.0	82.0	– –	– –	– –	– –	– –
30 Rubber	53.0	47.0	– –	– –	– –	– –	– –
31 Leather	30.7	69.3	– –	– –	– –	– –	– –
Leather Products	100.0	– –	– –	– –	– –	– –	– –
32 Stone, Clay and Glass	6.5	89.6	– –	3.9	– –	– –	– –
33 Primary Metals	9.5	90.5	– –	– –	– –	– –	– –
34 Fabricated Metals	87.5	12.5	– –	– –	– –	– –	– –
35 Non-electrical Machinery	50.3	20.4	29.3	– –	– –	– –	– –
36 Electrical Machinery	– –	– –	– –	– –	– –	– –	– –
37 Transportation Equipment	51.9	48.1	– –	– –	– –	– –	– –
38 Instruments	56.0	44.0	– –	– –	– –	– –	– –
39 Miscellaneous	55.9	44.1	– –	– –	– –	– –	– –

Source: See text.

TABLE 8

PERCENTAGE SHARES OF MANUFACTURING VALUE ADDED INVOLVED IN INTERREGIONAL TRADE, 1900

SIC Code Number and Industry	New England	Middle Atlantic	East North Central	West North Central	South Atlantic	East South Central	West South Central
20 Food	–	16.1	83.9	–	–	–	–
21 Tobacco	–	45.6	–	–	45.6	8.8	–
22 Textiles	77.8	18.4	–	–	3.8	–	–
23 Apparel	–	100.0	–	–	–	–	–
24 Lumber and Wood Products	–	–	40.4	–	27.8	19.9	11.9
25 Furniture	12.9	21.9	65.2	–	–	–	–
26 Paper	61.7	38.3	–	–	–	–	–
27 Printing and Publishing	12.2	87.8	–	–	–	–	–
28 Chemicals	–	83.7	–	–	16.3	–	–
29 Petroleum and Coal Products	–	100.0	–	–	–	–	–
30 Rubber	100.0	–	–	–	–	–	–
31 Leather	18.8	81.2	–	–	–	–	–
Leather Products	100.0	–	–	–	–	–	–
32 Stone, Clay and Glass	10.3	85.0	4.7	–	–	–	–
33 Primary Metals	–	93.3	6.7	–	–	–	–
34 Fabricated Metals	27.5	12.4	60.1	–	–	–	–
35 Non-electrical Machinery	26.0	49.1	24.9	–	–	–	–
36 Electrical Machinery	–	–	–	–	–	–	–
37 Transportation Equipment	–	39.1	60.9	–	–	–	–
38 Instruments	32.9	67.1	–	–	–	–	–
39 Miscellaneous	52.4	47.6	–	–	–	–	–

Source: See text.

drift of manufacturing into the East North Central region and the rise of a diversified sector in that region are clearly evident from a comparison of the manufacturing export base coefficients in Tables 7 and 8. The remaining areas in the West and South made only minor contributions to interregional trade in manufactured goods. The southern manufacturing development in textiles and primary metals does not appear to have proceeded to the point where the region could generate exportable surpluses.

NOTES

1. Victor S. Clark, *History of Manufactures in the United States*, 3 vols. (New York: McGraw-Hill for the Carnegie Institution, 1929); especially see Vol. 1, Ch. 18, and Vol. 2.

Another standard reference is the work of Albert S. Bolles, *Industrial History of the United States* (Norwich, Conn.: The Henry Bill Publishing Co., 1881). Bolles provides a survey of individual industries, manufacturing and nonmanufacturing, which covers the period from colonial days through the Civil War era.

J. Leander Bishop, *A History of American Manufactures* (Philadelphia: Edward Young and Co., 1864), provides a chronological approach to American manufacturing development from 1608 to 1860. Of particular interest for readers of this study is Ch. 7, in Vol. 2, which provides a detailed statement, in many cases by individual establishment, of the leading manufactures on the eve of the Civil War.

2. This use of the gross value of output is apparent in Ch. 16, Vol. 2, of Clark's work, which deals with the regional distribution of manufacturing during the late nineteenth century. Also see Gilbert C. Fite and Jim E. Reese, *An Economic History of the United States* (Boston: Houghton Mifflin Co., 1973), Ch. 12, and Bishop, *A History of American Manufactures*, Vol. 2, Ch. 7.

3. In the standard textbook treatment of national income and product accounts, value added at any stage of production is defined as the gross value of output (sales receipts) minus the cost of materials and intermediate products not produced in that stage but bought from other firms for use in production; for example, see Paul A. Samuelson, *Economics*, 9th ed. (New York: McGraw-Hill Book Co., 1973), pp. 183-186.

4. See the following: George R. Taylor, *The Transportation Revolution, 1815-1860* (New York: Holt, Rinehart and Winston, 1951), Ch. 11;

Douglass C. North, *Growth and Welfare in the American Past* (Englewood Cliffs, N. J.: Prentice-Hall, Inc., 1966), Ch. 6; Lance E. Davis, et al., *American Economic Growth* (New York: Harper & Row, Publishers, 1972), Ch. 12; Ross Robertson, *History of the American Economy*, 3d ed. (New York: Harcourt Brace Jovanovich, Inc., 1973), Ch. 8; and Barry W. Poulson, "Estimates of the Value of Manufacturing Output in the Early Nineteenth Century," *Journal of Economic History*, September 1969, pp. 521-525.

5. An analysis of development in the light manufacturing industries is provided by Samuel Rezneck, "Light Manufactures," in *Growth of the American Economy*, Harold F. Williamson, ed. (New York: Prentice-Hall, Inc., 1951).

6. See Taylor, *Transportation Revolution*, Ch. 11; Fite and Reese, *Economic History*, Ch. 12; Robertson, *American Economy*, Ch. 8; Clark, *History of Manufactures*, Vol. 2, Ch. 16, and Douglass C. North, *The Economic Growth of the United States, 1790-1860* (Englewood Cliffs, N. J.: Prentice-Hall, Inc., 1961), Chs. 10-12.

7. See Taylor, *Transportation Revolution*, Ch. 11.

8. See North, *Economic Growth*, Ch. 11.

9. See Arthur F. Burns, *Production Trends in the United States Since 1870* (New York: National Bureau of Economic Research, 1934) and William H. Shaw, *Value of Commodity Output Since 1869* (New York: National Bureau of Economic Research, 1947). The rank ordering of the leading manufacturing industries provided by Davis, et al., *American Economic Growth*, Ch. 12, and Poulson, "Estimates of Value," also support this notion of a shift toward heavy industry.

10. The rise of heavy industry in the West is cited by Louis C. Hunter, "The Heavy Industries," in *Growth of the American Economy*, Harold F. Williamson, ed. (New York: Prentice-Hall, Inc., 1951). Clark cites the rise of heavy industry as well as the continued emphasis on the milling industries. John M. Peterson and Ralph Gray, *Economic Development of the United States* (Homewood, Ill.: Richard D. Irwin, Inc., 1969), Ch. 9, point to late nineteenth century western development in farm machinery, milling, and meat packing.

11. See Peterson and Gray, *Economic Development*, Ch. 9; Fite and Reese, *Economic History*, Ch. 12; and, Clark, *History of Manufactures*, Vol. 2, Ch. 16. See Davis et al. *American Economic Growth*, Ch. 12, for some interesting qualifications of these standard location arguments.

12. See Clark, *History of Manufactures*, Vol. 2, Ch. 16, and Hunter, "The Heavy Industries."

13. Throughout this study, the United States represents the sum of the seven census regions referred to in note 2 in the Preface.

14. Estimates of manufacturing value added were provided for the

following regions of states: New England (Maine, New Hampshire, Vermont, Massachusetts, Rhode Island, and Connecticut); Middle Atlantic (New York, New Jersey, Pennsylvania, Delaware, and Maryland); East North Central (Ohio, Indiana, Illinois, Michigan, and Wisconsin); West North Central (Minnesota, Iowa, Missouri, Kansas, Nebraska, North Dakota, and South Dakota); South Atlantic (Virginia, West Virginia, North Carolina, South Carolina, Georgia, and Florida); East South Central (Kentucky, Tennessee, Alabama, and Mississippi); and West South Central (Arkansas, Louisiana, Oklahoma, and Texas). These are the traditional geographic divisions of the United States as defined by the Bureau of the Census, with the exception that Delaware and Maryland are included in the Middle Atlantic states rather than in the South Atlantic, and the District of Columbia is excluded from the South Atlantic.

All state and regional comparisons with national performance are made against the sum of the states in these seven regions.

15. See any standard statistics textbook, such as John Neter and William Wasserman, *Fundamental Statistics for Business and Economics* (Boston: Allyn and Bacon, Inc., 1966), Ch. 14, for an explanation of the chi-square test of independence.

16. P repesents the probability that statistical dependence exists between the 1860 and 1900 industry distributions. Values of P are shown only in those cases in which the probability of accepting a correct hypothesis is greater than or equal to .95.

17. Since the rank test only captures the ordinal position of industries rather than the actual frequency (percentage), it is a much less severe test of the degree of structural change. Significant industry shifts can take place that do not show up in the rank correlation analysis. For example, during 1860-1900 the share of textiles in New England's manufacturing value added declined from 32.4 percent to 24.5 percent, yet there was no change in rank and textiles remained the region's leading industry.

18. For a description of rank correlation techniques, see William L. Hays and Robert L. Winkler, *Statistics: Probability, Inference, and Decision,* Vol. 2 (New York: Holt, Rinehart and Winston, Inc., 1970), pp. 243-252. Also see Sidney Siegel, *Nonparametric Statistics* (New York: McGraw-Hill Book Co., 1956), p. 219.

The significance of the rank correlation coefficients is shown by P, where P represents the probability of error of obtaining the calculated r_s.

19. Almost all of the chemical production in the South consisted of crude and distilled turpentine.

20. This is a rather common type of construct used in regional economic analysis. For a description and application of a similar coefficient of localization, see Hugh O. Nourse, *Regional Economics* (New York: McGraw-Hill Book Co., 1968), pp. 64-68.

21. For a discussion of some of the issues involved in regional variation in the equality of income distribution, see Robert E. Gallman, "Trends in the Size Distribution of Wealth in the Nineteenth Century: Some Speculations," *Six Papers on the Size Distribution of Wealth and Income*, Conference on Research in Income and Wealth, Studies in Income and Wealth, Vol. 33 (New York: Columbia University Press, 1969). A number of pertinent comments on regional variation in income distribution recently appeared in the special volume of *Agricultural History*, Vol. 44, January 1970, *The Structure of the Cotton Economy of the Antebellum South*, William N. Parker, ed. Of particular interest are the following papers: Gavin Wright, "Economic Democracy and the Concentration of Agricultural Wealth in the Cotton South, 1850-1860"; William Parker, "Slavery and Southern Economic Development: An Hypothesis and Some Evidence"; and Stanley L. Engerman, "The Antebellum South: What Probably Was and What Should Have Been."

22. The personal income ratios were adapted from Richard A. Easterlin, "Regional Income Trends, 1840-1950," in *American Economic History*, Seymour Harris, ed. (New York: McGraw-Hill Book Co., 1961), p. 535. The 1860 regional shares in personal income were computed as follows: New England, 14.6 percent; Middle Atlantic, 37.5 percent; East North Central, 15.6 percent; West North Central, 4.2 percent; South Atlantic, 9.4 percent; East South Central, 9.4 percent; and West South Central, 8.3 percent. The 1900 regional shares were as follows: New England, 10.5 percent; Middle Atlantic, 29.7 percent; East North Central, 24.5 percent; West North Central, 15.9 percent; South Atlantic, 6.9 percent; East South Central, 6.1 percent; and West South Central, 6.4 percent.

23. See any standard textbook treatment of locational patterns in the American cotton industry; for example, Charles Hession and Hyman Sardy, *Ascent to Affluence* (Boston: Allyn and Bacon, Inc., 1969), p. 347.

24. The weighted coefficient for total manufacturing was calculated as follows:

$$\sum_{r=1}^{k} (VA_i^r/VA_i^n - PI^r/PI^n) \cdot \frac{VA_i^n}{VA_T^n}$$

where all symbols are as before and T represents total manufacturing. The significance of the slight decline in the coefficient during 1860-1900 is difficult to measure. However, for the purposes here it is enough to say that the data clearly support the thesis that, on average, there was no tendency toward increased regional concentration in manufacturing during the late nineteenth century.

25. The calculations of the coefficient of localization and the resulting estimates of the manufacturing export base are not intended to be exact. Rather, they provide an index of the broad outlines of the regional manufacturing export potential.

2

State Patterns
of Manufacturing Development
During 1860-1900

This chapter reviews the manufacturing structure and industry contributions of the individual states. Available statistics indicate that within the broad regional groupings, Northeast, West, and South, and within each census region, there was a great degree of structural diversity between states. The two-digit percentage distribution figures for the antebellum period shown in Table 9 lend support to many of the traditionally accepted notions concerning the spatial distribution of manufacturing. The most often cited features in New England's mid-nineteenth century manufacturing structure are the heavy concentration on textiles throughout the region, the concentration of the boot and shoe industry in Massachusetts, and the development of light metals industries in Connecticut.[1] The data in Table 9 are in agreement with these traditional views. In the case of Connecticut, textiles and the related apparel industry accounted for a far greater portion of the state's manufacturing output than the fabricated metals industries, although no other state

TABLE 9

PERCENTAGE DISTRIBUTION OF MANUFACTURING VALUE ADDED ACROSS TWO DIGIT

INDUSTRIES, BY STATE, 1860

SIC Code Number and Industry	Maine	New Hampshire	Vermont	Massachu- setts	Rhode Island	Connect- icut	New York	New Jersey
20 Food	3.9	2.4	4.5	3.5	5.1	1.8	13.2	8.1
21 Tobacco	0.1	0.2	0.3	0.3	0.6	0.8	1.4	1.2
22 Textiles	26.8	50.8	25.6	29.4	56.8	23.6	6.7	12.3
23 Apparel	5.6	4.3	2.2	5.9	3.3	10.7	12.5	13.0
24 Lumber and Wood Products	20.7	7.5	12.5	3.0	1.8	2.2	7.0	4.9
25 Furniture	1.1	1.3	3.2	2.4	0.6	0.8	3.2	0.7
26 Paper	2.8	2.0	1.3	2.7	0.1	2.7	1.5	2.0
27 Printing and Publishing	1.4	1.2	1.0	1.8	0.8	1.3	5.5	0.8
28 Chemicals	1.1	0.7	0.3	1.3	0.6	2.7	3.4	3.4
29 Petroleum and Coal Products	2.8	0.3	0.2	1.2	0.7	0.4	2.8	0.1
30 Rubber	--	--	--	0.2	0.7	2.2	0.8	2.1
31 Leather	4.8	3.2	4.8	3.7	0.1	1.0	4.5	3.2
Leather Products	7.1	10.0	4.1	21.7	1.5	4.8	5.0	8.2
32 Stone, Clay and Glass	3.3	1.3	9.2	2.3	0.7	1.0	4.0	5.7
33 Primary Metals	3.5	2.4	4.1	5.0	2.9	5.3	6.5	9.7
34 Fabricated Metals	3.3	2.5	4.5	3.7	6.7	13.9	4.6	5.8
35 Non-electrical Machinery	4.4	3.7	13.8	4.6	7.2	6.7	6.7	5.0
36 Electrical Machinery	--	--	--	--	--	--	--	--
37 Transportation Equipment	6.4	5.6	6.4	2.6	1.2	8.0	4.2	9.8
38 Instruments	0.0	--	0.1	0.4	0.1	2.1	0.6	--
39 Miscellaneous Manufacturing	0.9	0.6	1.9	4.3	8.5	8.0	5.9	4.0

TABLE 9
(continued)

SIC Code Number and Industry	Pennsylvania	Delaware	Maryland	Ohio	Indiana	Illinois	Michigan
20 Food	10.1	9.0	19.5	18.7	29.1	39.6	16.1
21 Tobacco	0.9	1.6	3.2	1.2	0.7	0.6	0.3
22 Textiles	12.1	12.1	11.2	2.2	3.2	0.6	1.0
23 Apparel	8.6	2.4	10.6	9.7	2.6	2.3	2.1
24 Lumber and Wood Products	7.2	5.8	5.4	10.6	25.1	12.3	36.7
25 Furniture	1.8	0.9	2.5	5.4	4.7	3.0	3.1
26 Paper	1.1	2.6	1.4	1.4	0.6	0.2	0.5
27 Printing and Publishing	4.5	1.6	1.9	2.7	1.3	2.9	1.8
28 Chemicals	3.8	7.3	1.3	2.5	0.5	2.1	0.9
29 Petroleum and Coal Products	1.6	0.6	1.7	1.5	0.2	1.3	0.2
30 Rubber	0.0	–	–	–	–	0.0	–
31 Leather	4.3	8.8	4.7	2.5	–	0.8	2.9
Leather Products	5.5	4.2	6.3	6.1	6.4	5.2	6.1
32 Stone, Clay and Glass	5.3	3.0	4.4	3.8	2.6	4.3	3.6
33 Primary Metals	15.1	4.3	9.7	9.6	1.8	4.1	5.6
34 Fabricated Metals	3.7	3.5	3.3	3.8	3.7	3.5	7.7
35 Non-electrical Machinery	5.4	6.6	6.0	10.7	10.6	10.9	5.2
36 Electrical Machinery	–	–	–	–	–	–	–
37 Transportation Equipment	4.7	25.2	4.9	4.7	6.5	5.3	5.0
38 Instruments	0.7	–	0.2	0.1	–	0.0	0.1
39 Miscellaneous Manufacturing	3.6	0.5	1.8	2.8	0.4	1.0	1.1

TABLE 9
(continued)

SIC Code Number and Industry	Wisconsin	Minnesota	Iowa	Missouri	Kansas	Nebraska	Virginia
20 Food	26.6	27.2	39.3	23.6	12.4	15.8	14.7
21 Tobacco	0.6	0.3	0.5	6.4	–	–	28.7
22 Textiles	1.0	0.2	1.4	4.0	–	–	6.0
23 Apparel	4.6	0.4	1.4	3.4	–	1.3	1.5
24 Lumber and Wood Products	30.0	48.5	24.0	15.0	66.7	60.7	9.3
25 Furniture	2.7	4.3	3.8	1.5	0.6	1.3	1.2
26 Paper	0.9	–	0.2	0.0	–	–	0.8
27 Printing and Publishing	1.8	1.7	2.3	1.3	0.2	5.4	0.5
28 Chemicals	1.6	–	0.1	2.2	0.1	–	0.5
29 Petroleum and Coal Products	0.7	–	0.9	2.5	–	–	1.7
30 Rubber	–	–	–	1.1	–	–	–
31 Leather	1.8	0.4	1.9	1.1	0.0	–	3.0
Leather Products	5.9	7.2	6.3	5.6	1.0	5.4	3.7
32 Stone, Clay and Glass	2.9	0.4	1.8	6.2	14.4	1.2	3.9
33 Primary Metals	3.4	1.7	1.7	10.7	–	–	11.0
34 Fabricated Metals	6.7	5.1	5.5	4.3	0.6	3.5	3.7
35 Non-electrical Machinery	3.3	0.0	5.7	5.8	1.3	–	3.7
36 Electrical Machinery	–	–	–	–	–	–	–
37 Transportation Equipment	4.5	2.0	2.9	4.5	2.4	1.4	5.7
38 Instruments	0.0	–	–	0.1	–	–	–
39 Miscellaneous Manufacturing	1.0	0.6	0.3	1.8	0.3	4.0	0.4

TABLE 9
(continued)

SIC Code Number and Industry	North Carolina	South Carolina	Georgia	Florida	Kentucky	Tennessee	Alabama
20 Food	10.6	11.4	14.0	0.7	23.3	16.0	7.5
21 Tobacco	7.5	–	0.5	–	6.1	5.9	0.1
22 Textiles	9.5	9.2	18.3	1.2	7.3	5.1	11.3
23 Apparel	0.2	0.9	1.0	0.2	4.2	1.3	0.6
24 Lumber and Wood Products	13.7	26.0	21.9	69.7	12.6	19.7	28.1
25 Furniture	0.8	0.5	4.1	–	2.1	1.5	1.4
26 Paper	1.9	1.3	1.5	–	0.4	0.2	–
27 Printing and Publishing	1.0	0.4	0.2	0.1	1.6	3.9	1.1
28 Chemicals	34.4	12.3	1.8	3.3	1.6	0.3	6.2
29 Petroleum and Coal Products	0.7	–	1.1	–	3.2	0.9	0.8
30 Rubber	–	–	–	–	–	–	–
31 Leather	3.1	1.9	3.3	–	3.6	6.9	3.6
Leather Products	2.3	4.2	4.7	1.0	5.7	6.2	4.9
32 Stone, Clay and Glass	1.3	3.7	2.9	11.5	2.6	1.1	4.9
33 Primary Metals	1.7	0.8	3.3	3.9	7.7	10.0	1.5
34 Fabricated Metals	1.6	1.4	1.5	1.7	5.2	4.3	4.1
35 Non-electrical Machinery	1.4	10.0	10.7	1.6	4.4	6.3	15.9
36 Electrical Machinery	–	–	–	–	–	–	–
37 Transportation Equipment	7.9	15.7	9.1	5.1	6.3	10.2	7.9
38 Instruments	–	–	–	–	0.0	–	–
39 Miscellaneous Manufacturing	0.1	0.3	0.2	–	2.1	0.2	0.1

TABLE 9
(continued)

SIC Code Number and Industry	Mississippi	Louisiana	Arkansas	Texas
20 Food	3.8	11.2	14.5	25.0
21 Tobacco	0.2	1.8	0.8	—
22 Textiles	4.4	3.4	1.3	1.1
23 Apparel	2.2	12.4	1.5	0.2
24 Lumber and Wood Products	37.7	20.4	56.3	43.3
25 Furniture	1.5	0.6	0.8	1.9
26 Paper	—	0.0	—	—
27 Printing and Publishing	1.8	0.7	0.9	3.8
28 Chemicals	0.0	2.3	—	0.3
29 Petroleum and Coal Products	0.5	0.6	—	—
30 Rubber	—	—	—	—
31 Leather	3.2	0.3	5.9	2.2
Leather Products	7.8	11.1	3.7	5.3
32 Stone, Clay and Glass	3.6	6.4	0.9	1.7
33 Primary Metals	2.4	1.1	0.1	—
34 Fabricated Metals	5.0	6.4	3.6	6.1
35 Non-electrical Machinery	16.3	12.6	4.5	3.8
36 Electrical Machinery	—	—	—	—
37 Transportation Equipment	9.0	7.9	5.0	4.3
38 Instruments	—	—	—	—
39 Miscellaneous Manufacturing	0.7	0.8	0.1	1.0

Source: See text.

in the union came close to Connecticut's degree of concentration on metal fabrication.

The typical view of manufacturing in the Middle Atlantic states focuses on the importance of the apparel industry in all states, especially in New York, and the iron industry in Pennsylvania. Table 9 supports these views and also indicates a rather heavy degree of specialization in textiles and food processing in most states in the region and concentration on primary metals in Maryland and New Jersey. As would be expected, the Western states, excluding Ohio, were heavily committed to resource processing manufacturing. In addition, there was rather significant development in the machinery industry in Ohio, Indiana, and Illinois and in primary metals in Ohio.[2] Antebellum southern manufacturing was rather heavily concentrated on the resource processing industries, but a number of exceptions can be cited. The antebellum development of the iron industry in the Richmond area that was cited by Clark is reflected in Virginia's concentration on primary metals. Machinery production, especially cotton gins, agricultural machinery, and steam engines, accounted for a significant portion of manufacturing in Alabama, Georgia, Mississippi, South Carolina, and Louisiana. The transportation equipment industry, especially production of railroad cars and related equipment, was significant to the economies of most southern states. Other notable industrial developments included textiles in Alabama, Georgia, and the Carolinas, chemical production (turpentine) in the Carolinas, and primary metals in Tennessee.

Table 10 shows the two-digit industrial distribution within manufacturing for the individual states in 1900. The results in Chapter 1 indicated that the late nineteenth century witnessed a rather sharp decline in light industry, except in the case of South Atlantic textiles, a decline in resource-oriented manufacturing in the West and a rise in the South, and a slight decline in heavy industry outside the Northeast and East North Central regions. It is clear from a comparison of Tables 9 and 10 that, in the majority of cases, state changes in the composition of

TABLE 10

PERCENTAGE DISTRIBUTION OF MANUFACTURING VALUE ADDED ACROSS TWO DIGIT INDUSTRIES, BY STATE, 1900

SIC Code Number and Industry	Maine	New Hampshire	Vermont	Massachusetts	Rhode Island	Connecticut	New York	New Jersey	Pennsylvania
20 Food	9.6	6.5	8.3	7.5	5.2	5.0	13.3	10.8	9.1
21 Tobacco	0.3	0.7	0.2	0.8	0.2	0.7	3.7	3.0	2.9
22 Textiles	25.4	33.8	10.1	24.2	43.7	14.3	5.1	16.2	9.5
23 Apparel	4.2	3.2	4.4	6.4	2.6	7.7	21.2	6.0	5.6
24 Lumber and Wood Products	13.3	12.9	15.5	2.4	1.1	1.4	3.1	1.9	3.9
25 Furniture	1.0	1.1	3.2	2.2	0.5	1.2	2.5	0.7	1.2
26 Paper	11.5	7.0	7.3	3.6	0.8	2.4	2.8	1.4	1.4
27 Printing and Publishing	3.9	1.4	2.4	6.3	2.2	2.2	9.5	2.0	4.2
28 Chemicals	1.0	0.7	6.7	2.4	1.4	1.4	4.2	5.8	3.4
29 Petroleum and Coal Products	0.6	0.7	1.7	1.2	1.0	0.9	2.3	3.0	2.2
30 Rubber	- -	- -	- -	3.1	6.2	4.8	0.2	2.5	0.1
31 Leather	0.9	1.2	0.3	1.4	0.1	0.1	0.6	1.8	1.8
Leather Products	8.6	15.3	1.7	11.9	0.7	1.1	2.5	2.6	1.5
32 Stone, Clay and Glass	8.1	4.0	10.5	4.1	3.0	3.4	6.5	8.3	7.2
33 Primary Metals	0.6	0.3	0.3	2.1	1.1	9.5	1.1	8.3	23.7
34 Fabricated Metals	1.3	1.7	2.3	3.3	2.7	14.1	3.9	2.8	3.8
35 Non-electrical Machinery	3.4	4.3	6.0	9.9	11.5	11.8	7.9	12.4	10.4
36 Electrical Machinery	- -	- -	- -	- -	- -	- -	- -	- -	- -
37 Transportation Equipment	5.1	2.8	7.8	1.9	2.0	3.3	2.7	3.9	5.7
38 Instruments	0.2	0.2	0.8	0.5	0.4	2.2	0.9	1.0	0.5
39 Miscellaneous	1.0	2.2	1.5	4.8	13.7	12.5	6.0	5.6	1.9

TABLE 10
(continued)

SIC Code Number and Industry	Delaware	Maryland	Ohio	Indiana	Illinois	Michigan	Wisconsin	Minnesota	Iowa
20 Food	11.5	16.3	14.0	24.2	27.7	10.6	23.2	24.8	30.1
21 Tobacco	0.5	7.1	3.6	1.1	1.6	4.3	2.3	2.0	3.4
22 Textiles	5.3	4.8	0.8	2.0	0.6	1.2	2.1	0.7	0.6
23 Apparel	3.0	17.3	6.2	4.5	10.4	5.7	4.8	6.4	7.3
24 Lumber and Wood Products	2.6	4.5	5.1	9.3	3.3	22.5	20.2	25.7	9.8
25 Furniture	0.6	2.6	2.1	4.0	2.6	6.4	4.3	2.3	1.7
26 Paper	4.6	1.4	1.7	1.4	0.8	1.4	3.2	0.2	0.5
27 Printing and Publishing	1.6	4.5	4.9	4.5	7.1	4.5	3.4	8.4	9.0
28 Chemicals	3.9	5.5	3.7	2.2	2.4	6.4	0.8	1.2	2.7
29 Petroleum and Coal Products	1.3	2.2	2.0	1.3	1.8	1.3	1.0	1.4	1.6
30 Rubber	0.6	0.2	0.7	0.1	0.4	0.0	0.2	-	0.0
31 Leather	13.5	0.4	0.4	0.3	0.4	0.9	2.9	0.0	0.1
Leather Products	1.1	1.8	3.1	1.4	2.1	1.7	2.6	3.7	1.1
32 Stone, Clay and Glass	3.8	6.0	7.2	11.6	5.0	3.1	2.2	6.1	7.4
33 Primary Metals	10.6	3.7	14.8	5.2	6.1	2.4	3.1	0.2	1.0
34 Fabricated Metals	1.9	4.4	6.7	6.8	8.3	6.4	6.3	4.4	5.3
35 Non-electrical Machinery	10.5	6.2	14.5	7.2	9.9	9.5	9.4	4.5	4.8
36 Electrical Machinery	-	-	-	-	-	-	-	-	-
37 Transportation Equipment	22.1	6.0	5.6	10.7	4.8	8.9	5.4	5.6	11.1
38 Instruments	0.4	0.4	0.1	0.2	0.8	0.2	0.2	0.3	0.2
39 Miscellaneous	0.6	4.7	2.8	2.0	3.9	2.6	2.4	2.1	2.3

TABLE 10
(continued)

SIC Code Number and Industry	Missouri	Kansas	Nebraska	North Dakota	South Dakota	Virginia	West Virginia	North Carolina
20 Food	20.7	42.2	40.1	36.4	33.1	10.7	10.1	7.9
21 Tobacco	12.6	1.4	4.1	1.6	3.6	23.5	5.7	23.6
22 Textiles	0.5	0.6	1.7	1.3	0.2	5.0	1.9	28.9
23 Apparel	8.5	4.4	5.8	7.6	5.8	3.2	3.7	1.9
24 Lumber and Wood Products	6.0	2.0	1.6	1.3	6.6	15.2	20.5	20.6
25 Furniture	2.3	0.9	0.6	0.2	0.4	0.7	1.1	2.2
26 Paper	0.5	0.7	0.6	1.6	–	1.6	1.0	0.0
27 Printing and Publishing	8.0	6.3	7.6	20.9	16.6	3.8	2.7	1.9
28 Chemicals	4.2	1.6	3.1	0.4	0.2	3.6	1.1	2.1
29 Petroleum and Coal Products	2.4	2.3	1.4	1.5	1.5	1.1	1.3	0.4
30 Rubber	0.5	–	–	–	–	–	–	–
31 Leather	0.2	0.1	0.7	–	0.8	2.1	2.2	0.9
Leather Products	4.3	2.8	2.7	8.5	5.9	2.2	1.2	0.6
32 Stone, Clay and Glass	6.6	4.9	4.9	5.6	6.0	3.3	9.7	2.1
33 Primary Metals	2.3	9.6	8.7	–	9.6	7.9	26.5	1.1
34 Fabricated Metals	4.0	2.3	2.4	5.7	3.1	1.7	1.9	0.5
35 Non-electrical Machinery	6.7	4.8	1.9	2.2	1.0	4.4	2.7	1.8
36 Electrical Machinery	–	–	–	–	–	–	–	–
37 Transportation Equipment	7.4	11.4	6.6	3.8	4.1	9.5	6.4	3.0
38 Instruments	0.6	0.4	0.5	–	0.5	0.0	0.1	0.0
39 Miscellaneous	1.7	1.3	5.0	1.4	1.0	0.5	0.2	0.5

TABLE 10
(continued)

SIC Code Number and Industry	South Carolina	Georgia	Florida	Kentucky	Tennessee	Alabama	Mississippi
20 Food	7.9	12.2	3.7	23.3	18.9	8.4	16.6
21 Tobacco	0.1	0.0	29.9	18.6	3.6	0.8	–
22 Textiles	54.9	19.3	0.1	2.6	4.2	10.7	5.3
23 Apparel	2.2	2.9	0.9	6.9	5.3	2.1	2.2
24 Lumber and Wood Products	13.4	21.1	27.9	12.9	24.0	20.0	49.5
25 Furniture	0.4	2.0	0.2	1.6	1.9	0.4	0.4
26 Paper	0.3	0.6	–	0.1	0.2	–	–
27 Printing and Publishing	2.6	4.0	2.2	3.9	6.4	2.6	3.7
28 Chemicals	9.1	16.9	26.8	1.9	4.8	6.8	8.0
29 Petroleum and Coal Products	0.6	1.3	0.7	1.6	1.3	0.7	0.4
30 Rubber	–	–	–	–	0.1	–	–
31 Leather	0.0	0.6	–	1.3	1.5	1.0	0.0
Leather Products	0.5	1.7	0.3	2.3	2.0	0.6	0.6
32 Stone, Clay and Glass	2.8	3.9	0.9	4.0	4.5	3.3	3.3
33 Primary Metals	0.1	0.5	–	4.2	5.6	25.1	–
34 Fabricated Metals	0.8	1.4	0.3	3.0	2.1	0.8	0.7
35 Non-electrical Machinery	1.2	4.6	1.1	4.1	5.9	8.2	1.9
36 Electrical Machinery	–	–	–	–	–	–	–
37 Transportation Equipment	2.7	6.2	4.8	6.1	6.3	8.3	7.2
38 Instruments	–	0.2	–	0.3	0.0	0.0	–
39 Miscellaneous	0.4	0.6	0.2	1.3	1.4	0.2	0.2

TABLE 10
(continued)

SIC Code Number and Industry	Louisiana	Arkansas	Texas	Oklahoma
20 Food	35.2	13.1	28.1	48.7
21 Tobacco	4.4	0.2	0.8	1.3
22 Textiles	1.2	0.5	1.9	- -
23 Apparel	6.6	2.6	5.0	5.1
24 Lumber and Wood Products	26.1	62.0	19.4	2.2
25 Furniture	1.1	1.2	1.1	0.4
26 Paper	0.1	0.1	0.3	- -
27 Printing and Publishing	4.9	4.1	9.1	17.4
28 Chemicals	3.1	0.5	0.9	1.4
29 Petroleum and Coal Products	1.5	0.7	1.4	0.2
30 Rubber	- -	- -	- -	- -
31 Leather	0.0	0.0	0.1	- -
Leather Products	2.1	1.0	4.3	6.0
32 Stone, Clay and Glass	1.6	2.6	6.5	11.1
33 Primary Metals	0.1	0.0	2.1	- -
34 Fabricated Metals	2.0	0.6	2.3	2.5
35 Non-electrical Machinery	4.5	1.5	3.9	1.3
36 Electrical Machinery	- -	- -	- -	- -
37 Transportation Equipment	4.0	8.9	12.0	2.1
38 Instruments	0.3	0.1	0.2	- -
39 Miscellaneous	1.2	0.3	0.6	0.3

Source: See text.

manufacturing output paralleled those in their respective regions.

In each New England state, the percentage share of light industries in aggregate manufacturing value added declined. However, textile production continued to dominate the manufacturing of New England, and, in every state except Vermont, the industry was the most important in terms of aggregate production. During the late nineteenth century, the machinery industry became intensified in the southern New England states and the primary and fabricated metals industries showed significant development in Connecticut. Miscellaneous manufacturing, which largely consisted of jewelry, musical instruments, and ordnance, markedly expanded in Rhode Island and Connecticut.

Pennsylvania became much more entrenched in the primary metals industries, and, by 1900, the industry accounted for almost one-fourth of the state's industrial production. New York became much more concentrated on the apparel industry, and, by the turn of the century, the industry accounted for over one-fifth of the state's industrial production. Expansion of machinery production was especially marked in New Jersey, Pennsylvania, and Delaware, and textile development was significant in New Jersey.

The overall trends in industrial production in the East North Central region were a marked advance in heavy industry, a significant shift away from resource processing industries, and a decline in the light manufacturing industries. Much of the decline in resource processing manufacturing took place in lumber and wood products; food processing remained the most important industry in most states in the region. Most of the advance in heavy industry took place in Ohio and the bulk of this was concentrated on primary metals and machinery. The machinery industry advanced in Michigan and Wisconsin, and the transportation equipment industry made gains in Indiana and Michigan. Industrial trends in the West North Central states resembled those in the East North Central states. Heavy industry increased in importance in each state except Missouri and the resource processing industries, especially lumber and wood products, declined sharply. One notable exception was the increased emphasis on food processing in Kansas and Nebraska.

Late nineteenth century shifts in industrial concentration patterns in the southern states were varied; it is, therefore, difficult to generalize across the region as a whole. The rise of textiles then occurring in the South appears to have been concentrated in the Carolinas and Georgia. By the turn of the century, South Carolina exhibited a greater degree of specialization in textile production than any state in the Union, and only Rhode Island and New Hampshire exceeded North Carolina's degree of specialization. Within the East South Central states, the rise of primary metals in Alabama is clearly documented, but Tennessee appears to have suffered a relative decline in this industry.[3] By 1900, Alabama and West Virginia were more heavily concentrated on primary metals production than any other states in the South. Another notable feature of manufacturing development in the South was the increased emphasis on food manufacture, mostly sugar refining, in Louisiana.

The significance of structural shifts within the individual states has been analyzed by calculating the chi-square statistic and Spearman's rank correlation coefficient. Based on the calculation of the chi-square statistic, in no state was it possible to accept the hypothesis of a significant positive relationship between the 1860 and 1900 industrial distribution. (See Table 11.) The structural composition of manufacturing had changed significantly in every state and the notion of rigidity in state industrial structure during the late nineteenth century can be rejected. On the other hand, the rank correlation coefficients in Table 11 suggest that in the majority of states there was a significant positive relationship between the rank ordering of industries in 1860 and 1900. As a result, one must conclude that the many significant intrastate structural changes that did occur during the late nineteenth century did not significantly alter the rank position of industries in most states.

A view of relative state manufacturing development, as seen through the percentage shares of national value added, is pro-

TABLE 11

CALCULATION OF THE CHI-SQUARE STATISTIC AND SPEARMAN'S RANK CORRELATION

COEFFICIENT FOR HYPOTHESIS OF NO CHANGE IN THE INDUSTRIAL DISTRIBUTION

OF VALUE ADDED WITHIN STATES, 1860-1900

State	Chi-Square Statistic	Γ_s
Maine	20.49[a]	.757**[b]
New Hampshire	17.42	.724**
Vermont	33.21	.614*
Massachusetts	15.48	.683**
Rhode Island	14.94	.750**
Connecticut	16.27	.729**
New York	15.84	.631**
New Jersey	21.48	.648**
Pennsylvania	11.16	.860***
Delaware	14.87	.876***
Maryland	20.62	.381
Ohio	14.46	.739**
Indiana	27.42	.683**
Illinois	22.07	.734**
Michigan	25.34	.653**
Wisconsin	11.65	.841***
Minnesota	36.76	.418
Iowa	36.66	.508*
Missouri	24.91	.512*
Kansas	118.83	.420
Nebraska	99.65	.172
Kentucky	15.93	.728**
Tennessee	20.09	.665**
Alabama	34.81	.617**
Virginia	11.54	.814***
North Carolina	58.13	.562*
South Carolina	62.70	.745**
Georgia	26.98	.653**
Florida	86.72	.364
Mississippi	45.38	.324
Louisiana	38.68	.690**
Arkansas	17.70	.711**
Texas	31.72	.633**

[a]The chi-square statistic was not significant at $P \geq .95$ in any case.

[b]The significance level of Γ_s is shown with a * where * = ($P \leq .05$), ** = ($P \leq .01$), and *** = ($P \leq .001$).

Source: See text.

vided in Tables 12 and 13. New York, Pennsylvania, and Massachusetts are generally singled out as the leading industrial states during the antebellum period; the figures in Table 12 provide strong empirical support for this view.[4] As would be expected, Massachusetts' industry shares were greatest in leather products and textiles. Pennsylvania's industrialization was most concentrated on primary metals, but the estimates indicate a much more diversified manufacturing sector than is generally recognized.[5] New York's economy was characterized by a high degree of diversification and its industry shares were considerable in most industries.[6] The production of manufactured goods outside of the northeastern and East North Central states, excluding Virginia, Missouri, and Kentucky, was relatively minor, and, in most instances, production shares were less than 1 percent.

Table 13 exhibits state industry shares at the end of the nineteenth century. The figures clearly depict the westward drift of manufacturing activity, with especially heavy losses for the southern New England states and heavy gains for Ohio and Illinois. The only significant relative industry advance for Massachusetts occurred in rubber production; in most of the other two-digit industries the declines were substantial. Connecticut also experienced a general relative decline in manufacturing. Of particular interest are the state's sharp declines in fabricated metals, transportation equipment, and instruments.

The westward movement of industrialization is particularly apparent in Ohio and Illinois, where substantial relative gains were made in most industries. Marked gains were made in the metals, machinery, and transportation equipment industries, and, by 1900, Illinois and Ohio ranked first and third, respectively, in terms of the aggregate production of fabricated metals, fourth and third in machinery, third and second in primary metals, third and fourth in transportation equipment, and third and fifth in total manufacturing.

The structural pattern of industrialization in Pennsylvania and New York was much less diversified at the end of the cen-

TABLE 12

STATE CONTRIBUTIONS TO NATIONAL INDUSTRY VALUE ADDED, 1860
(Percentages)

SIC Code Number and Industry	Maine	New Hampshire	Vermont	Massachusetts	Rhode Island	Connecticut	New York	New Jersey
20 Food	0.7	0.4	0.3	4.3	1.1	0.8	23.2	2.9
21 Tobacco	0.1	0.3	0.1	2.7	0.8	2.3	15.2	2.6
22 Textiles	3.8	8.0	1.4	30.8	10.7	8.6	9.9	3.7
23 Apparel	1.4	1.2	0.2	11.4	1.2	7.1	33.8	7.2
24 Lumber and Wood Products	4.3	1.7	1.0	4.7	0.5	1.2	15.4	2.2
25 Furniture	0.9	1.2	1.0	15.2	0.7	1.7	28.1	1.3
26 Paper	3.8	3.0	0.7	27.6	0.3	9.5	21.3	5.9
27 Printing and Publishing	1.0	1.0	0.3	9.2	0.8	2.4	39.8	1.2
28 Chemicals	0.8	0.5	0.1	7.4	0.7	5.1	26.7	5.4
29 Petroleum and Coal Products	3.7	0.5	0.1	12.0	1.2	1.5	38.2	0.4
30 Rubber	–	–	–	8.6	4.5	26.9	38.6	21.1
31 Leather	2.8	2.1	1.1	16.2	0.1	1.5	27.7	4.0
Leather Products	1.8	2.9	0.4	41.4	0.5	3.2	13.2	4.5
32 Stone, Clay and Glass	1.8	0.8	2.0	9.3	0.5	1.5	23.1	6.7
33 Primary Metals	0.9	0.7	0.4	10.1	1.1	3.7	18.6	5.7
34 Fabricated Metals	1.4	1.2	0.7	11.7	3.8	15.4	20.7	5.3
35 Non-electrical Machinery	1.4	1.3	1.7	10.8	3.0	5.5	22.0	3.4
36 Electrical Machinery	–	–	–	–	–	–	–	–
37 Transportation Equipment	2.5	2.5	1.0	7.8	0.7	8.2	17.5	8.3
38 Instruments	0.0	–	0.1	12.7	0.7	26.5	28.7	–
39 Miscellaneous Manufacturing	0.4	0.4	0.4	17.1	6.1	11.1	33.4	4.6
Total	2.0	2.2	0.8	15.1	2.7	5.2	21.1	4.3

TABLE 12
(Continued)

SIC Code Number and Industry	Pennsylvania	Delaware	Maryland	Ohio	Indiana	Illinois	Michigan
20 Food	13.3	0.4	3.3	10.2	4.7	9.0	2.1
21 Tobacco	7.8	0.4	3.4	4.2	0.7	0.8	0.2
22 Textiles	13.4	0.4	1.6	1.0	0.4	0.1	0.1
23 Apparel	17.5	0.2	2.7	8.2	0.6	0.8	0.4
24 Lumber and Wood Products	11.8	0.3	1.1	7.2	5.1	3.5	6.1
25 Furniture	12.3	0.2	2.1	14.9	3.8	3.4	2.1
26 Paper	11.9	0.9	1.9	6.3	0.8	0.3	0.6
27 Printing and Publishing	24.3	0.3	1.3	6.1	0.8	2.7	1.0
28 Chemicals	22.2	1.3	1.0	5.9	0.4	2.1	0.5
29 Petroleum and Coal Products	17.0	0.2	2.2	6.3	0.2	2.3	0.2
30 Rubber	0.2	-	-	-	-	0.0	-
31 Leather	19.7	1.3	2.7	4.8	-	0.6	1.4
Leather Products	11.1	0.3	1.6	5.0	1.6	1.8	1.2
32 Stone, Clay and Glass	22.9	0.4	2.4	6.7	1.4	3.2	1.5
33 Primary Metals	32.1	0.3	2.6	8.4	0.5	1.5	1.2
34 Fabricated Metals	12.5	0.4	1.4	5.3	1.5	2.1	2.6
35 Non-electrical Machinery	13.4	0.5	1.9	11.0	3.3	4.7	1.3
36 Electrical Machinery	-	-	-	-	-	-	-
37 Transportation Equipment	14.7	2.5	2.0	6.1	2.5	2.9	1.6
38 Instruments	27.9	-	0.9	1.4	-	0.2	0.4
39 Miscellaneous Manufacturing	15.0	0.1	1.0	5.1	0.3	0.8	0.5
Total	15.9	0.5	2.0	6.6	2.0	2.7	1.6

TABLE 12
(Continued)

SIC Code Number and Industry	Wisconsin	Minnesota	Iowa	Missouri	Kansas	Nebraska	Virginia
20 Food	3.1	0.4	2.3	4.5	0.2	0.1	2.9
21 Tobacco	0.5	0.0	0.2	7.7	-	-	36.1
22 Textiles	0.1	0.0	0.1	0.6	-	-	1.0
23 Apparel	0.8	0.0	0.1	1.0	-	0.0	0.5
24 Lumber and Wood Products	4.4	1.0	1.7	3.6	1.4	0.3	2.3
25 Furniture	1.6	0.3	1.1	1.4	0.0	0.0	1.2
26 Paper	0.9	-	0.1	0.1	-	-	1.3
27 Printing and Publishing	0.8	0.1	0.5	1.0	0.0	0.1	0.4
28 Chemicals	0.8	-	0.0	1.8	0.0	-	0.5
29 Petroleum and Coal Products	0.7	-	0.4	3.8	-	-	2.6
30 Rubber	-	-	-	-	-	-	-
31 Leather	0.7	0.0	0.4	0.7	0.0	-	2.1
Leather Products	1.1	0.2	0.6	1.6	0.0	0.0	1.1
32 Stone, Clay and Glass	1.1	0.0	0.3	3.8	0.8	0.0	2.5
33 Primary Metals	0.6	0.0	0.2	3.3	-	-	3.6
34 Fabricated Metals	2.0	0.2	0.8	2.1	0.0	0.0	1.9
35 Non-electrical Machinery	0.7	0.0	0.6	2.1	0.0	-	1.4
36 Electrical Machinery	-	-	-	-	-	-	-
37 Transportation Equipment	1.3	0.1	0.4	2.0	0.1	0.0	2.7
38 Instruments	0.1	-	-	0.4	-	-	-
39 Miscellaneous Manufacturing	0.3	0.0	0.0	1.1	0.0	0.1	0.3
Total	1.4	0.2	0.7	2.3	0.2	0.1	2.4

TABLE 12
(Continued)

SIC Code Number and Industry	North Carolina	South Carolina	Georgia	Florida	Kentucky	Tennessee	Alabama
20 Food	0.7	0.4	1.0	0.0	3.7	1.4	0.4
21 Tobacco	3.2	-	0.2	-	6.2	3.2	0.0
22 Textiles	0.5	0.3	1.0	0.0	1.0	0.4	0.5
23 Apparel	0.0	0.1	0.1	0.0	1.0	0.2	0.1
24 Lumber and Wood Products	1.2	1.2	1.9	1.3	2.5	2.1	1.9
25 Furniture	0.3	0.1	1.4	-	1.7	0.6	0.4
26 Paper	1.0	0.4	0.8	-	0.5	0.2	-
27 Printing and Publishing	0.3	0.1	0.9	0.0	1.1	1.4	0.2
28 Chemicals	10.3	2.0	0.6	0.2	1.1	0.1	1.5
29 Petroleum and Coal Products	0.4	-	0.6	-	4.0	0.6	0.4
30 Rubber	-	-	-	-	-	-	-
31 Leather	0.7	0.2	0.8	-	2.0	2.0	0.7
Leather Products	0.2	0.2	0.5	0.0	1.4	0.8	0.4
32 Stone, Clay and Glass	0.3	0.4	0.6	0.6	1.3	0.3	0.9
33 Primary Metals	0.2	0.0	0.4	0.1	2.0	1.4	0.1
34 Fabricated Metals	0.3	0.1	0.3	0.1	2.1	0.9	0.6
35 Non-electrical Machinery	0.2	0.7	1.4	0.0	1.3	1.0	1.6
36 Electrical Machinery	-	-	-	-	-	-	-
37 Transportation Equipment	1.3	1.4	1.5	0.2	2.4	2.0	1.0
38 Instruments	-	-	-	-	0.1	-	-
39 Miscellaneous Manufacturing	0.0	0.0	0.0	-	1.2	0.1	0.0
Total	0.8	0.4	0.8	0.2	1.9	1.0	0.6

TABLE 12
(Continued)

SIC Code Number and Industry	Mississippi	Louisiana	Arkansas	Texas
20 Food	0.1	1.1	0.3	0.8
21 Tobacco	0.0	1.1	0.1	-
22 Textiles	0.1	0.3	0.0	0.0
23 Apparel	0.1	1.8	0.0	0.0
24 Lumber and Wood Products	1.7	2.4	1.2	1.7
25 Furniture	0.3	0.3	0.1	0.3
26 Paper	-	0.0	-	-
27 Printing and Publishing	0.3	0.3	0.1	0.5
28 Chemicals	0.0	1.0	-	0.0
29 Petroleum and Coal Products	0.1	0.5	-	-
30 Rubber	-	-	-	-
31 Leather	0.4	0.1	0.4	0.3
Leather Products	0.4	1.6	0.1	0.3
32 Stone, Clay and Glass	0.4	2.0	0.1	0.2
33 Primary Metals	0.1	0.2	0.0	-
34 Fabricated Metals	0.5	1.6	0.2	0.5
35 Non-electrical Machinery	1.1	2.3	0.1	0.2
36 Electrical Machinery	-	-	-	-
37 Transportation Equipment	0.8	1.8	0.2	0.3
38 Instruments	-	-	-	-
39 Miscellaneous Manufacturing	0.1	0.3	0.0	0.1
Total	0.4	1.2	0.2	0.4

TABLE 13

STATE CONTRIBUTIONS TO NATIONAL INDUSTRY VALUE ADDED, 1900

(Percentages)

SIC Code Number and Industry	Maine	New Hampshire	Vermont	Massachusetts	Rhode Island	Connecticut	New York	New Jersey
20 Food	0.7	0.4	0.3	4.5	0.6	1.1	17.2	3.4
21 Tobacco	0.1	0.2	0.0	1.9	0.1	0.6	19.9	4.0
22 Textiles	3.3	4.0	0.6	25.1	8.6	5.3	11.6	9.0
23 Apparel	0.5	0.3	0.2	6.1	0.5	2.6	44.1	3.1
24 Lumber and Wood Products	2.1	1.8	1.2	3.0	0.3	0.6	8.5	1.3
25 Furniture	0.5	0.5	0.8	9.4	0.4	1.8	22.7	1.5
26 Paper	6.5	3.6	2.0	16.5	0.7	3.9	27.5	3.5
27 Printing and Publishing	0.7	0.2	0.2	9.6	0.6	1.2	31.7	1.7
28 Chemicals	0.3	0.2	1.0	5.9	0.7	1.3	22.5	7.7
29 Petroleum and Coal Products	0.4	0.4	0.5	5.9	1.0	1.5	24.6	7.9
30 Rubber	-	-	-	33.0	12.6	18.5	5.7	14.4
31 Leather	1.1	1.3	0.1	13.1	0.2	0.4	12.1	8.8
Leather Products	2.9	4.7	0.3	32.6	0.4	1.1	15.0	3.8
32 Stone, Clay and Glass	1.5	0.7	1.7	6.2	0.9	1.8	21.1	6.6
33 Primary Metals	0.1	0.0	0.0	2.5	0.2	4.0	2.7	5.3
34 Fabricated Metals	0.3	0.4	0.2	6.2	1.0	9.5	16.2	2.8
35 Non-electrical Machinery	0.4	0.5	0.4	9.9	2.2	4.2	17.1	6.6
36 Electrical Machinery	-	-	-	-	-	-	-	-
37 Transportation Equipment	1.1	0.6	0.8	3.4	0.7	2.1	10.2	3.7
38 Instruments	0.4	0.3	0.7	7.8	1.1	11.8	30.0	8.3
39 Miscellaneous	0.3	0.5	0.2	11.0	5.9	10.1	29.2	6.7
Total	1.1	1.0	0.5	8.9	1.6	3.2	19.3	4.7

TABLE 13
(Continued)

SIC Code Number and Industry	Pennsyl- vania	Delaware	Maryland	Ohio	Indiana	Illinois	Michigan	Wisconsin
20 Food	9.1	0.3	2.1	6.8	5.0	18.2	2.1	4.5
21 Tobacco	11.9	0.0	3.7	7.3	1.0	4.4	3.5	1.8
22 Textiles	16.4	0.2	1.0	0.7	0.7	0.7	0.4	0.7
23 Apparel	8.9	0.1	3.5	4.8	1.5	11.0	1.8	1.5
24 Lumber and Wood Products	8.2	0.1	1.2	5.2	4.1	4.6	9.4	8.3
25 Furniture	8.1	0.1	2.3	7.1	5.9	12.0	8.8	5.9
26 Paper	10.6	0.9	1.4	6.3	2.3	4.1	2.1	4.7
27 Printing and Publishing	10.7	0.1	1.5	6.2	2.4	12.0	2.3	1.7
28 Chemicals	14.2	0.4	2.9	7.4	1.9	6.7	5.3	0.6
29 Petroleum and Coal Products	18.1	0.3	2.2	7.9	2.3	9.9	2.1	1.6
30 Rubber	1.1	0.3	0.5	6.4	0.5	4.6	0.1	0.6
31 Leather	27.7	5.0	0.7	3.0	0.8	4.3	2.8	8.4
Leather Products	6.7	0.1	1.1	6.9	1.3	6.3	1.6	2.3
32 Stone, Clay and Glass	18.1	0.2	1.9	8.7	6.0	8.2	1.5	1.0
33 Primary Metals	46.9	0.5	0.9	14.2	2.1	7.9	1.0	1.2
34 Fabricated Metals	12.0	0.1	1.8	10.3	4.5	17.3	4.0	3.9
35 Non-electrical Machinery	17.3	0.4	1.3	11.7	2.5	10.9	3.1	3.0
36 Electrical Machinery	-	-	-	-	-	-	-	-
37 Transportation Equipment	17.1	1.6	2.2	8.1	6.6	9.4	5.2	3.1
38 Instruments	13.3	0.2	1.4	1.5	1.2	12.7	1.1	0.9
39 Miscellaneous	7.5	0.1	2.2	5.4	1.6	10.0	1.9	1.9
Total	14.8	0.4	1.9	7.2	3.1	9.8	2.9	2.9

TABLE 13
(Continued)

SIC Code Number and Industry	Minnesota	Iowa	Missouri	Kansas	Nebraska	North Dakota	South Dakota	Virginia	West Virginia
20 Food	2.6	2.2	4.2	2.1	2.1	0.1	0.2	0.7	0.4
21 Tobacco	0.9	1.0	10.7	0.3	0.9	0.0	0.1	6.6	1.0
22 Textiles	0.1	0.1	0.2	0.1	0.2	0.0	0.0	0.6	0.1
23 Apparel	1.1	0.8	2.8	0.4	0.5	0.0	0.0	0.3	0.2
24 Lumber and Wood Products	5.8	1.5	2.6	0.2	0.2	0.0	0.1	2.2	1.8
25 Furniture	1.8	0.9	3.3	0.3	0.2	0.0	0.0	0.4	0.3
26 Paper	0.2	0.3	0.7	0.3	0.2	0.0	–	0.8	0.3
27 Printing and Publishing	2.3	1.7	4.2	0.8	1.0	0.2	0.2	0.7	0.3
28 Chemicals	0.5	0.8	3.5	0.3	0.7	0.0	0.0	1.0	0.2
29 Petroleum and Coal Products	1.2	1.0	4.0	1.0	0.6	0.0	0.1	0.6	0.4
30 Rubber	–	0.0	1.9	–	–	–	–	–	–
31 Leather	0.0	0.1	0.5	0.1	0.6	–	0.1	2.1	1.4
Leather Products	1.8	0.4	4.1	0.7	0.7	0.1	0.1	0.7	0.2
32 Stone, Clay and Glass	1.6	1.3	3.4	0.6	0.6	0.1	0.1	0.6	1.0
33 Primary Metals	0.0	0.1	0.9	1.0	0.9	–	0.1	1.1	2.2
34 Fabricated Metals	1.5	1.2	2.6	0.4	0.4	0.1	0.0	0.4	0.3
35 Non-electrical Machinery	0.8	0.6	2.3	0.4	0.2	0.0	0.0	0.5	0.2
36 Electrical Machinery	–	–	–	–	–	–	–	–	–
37 Transportation Equipment	1.8	2.4	4.5	1.7	1.0	0.0	0.1	1.9	0.8
38 Instruments	0.7	0.3	3.2	0.6	0.6	–	0.1	0.0	0.1
39 Miscellaneous	0.9	0.7	1.3	0.3	1.0	0.0	0.0	0.1	0.0
Total	1.6	1.1	3.0	0.8	0.8	0.1	0.1	1.0	0.6

TABLE 13
(Continued)

SIC Code Number and Industry	North Carolina	South Carolina	Georgia	Florida	Kentucky	Tennessee	Alabama
20 Food	0.4	0.2	0.8	0.1	2.1	1.1	0.4
21 Tobacco	5.5	0.0	0.0	3.5	7.0	0.8	0.2
22 Textiles	2.9	3.1	2.1	0.0	0.4	0.4	0.9
23 Apparel	0.2	0.1	0.3	0.0	1.0	0.5	0.2
24 Lumber and Wood Products	2.5	0.9	2.8	1.7	2.5	2.8	2.0
25 Furniture	0.9	0.1	0.9	0.0	1.1	0.8	0.1
26 Paper	0.0	0.1	0.3	–	0.1	0.1	–
27 Printing and Publishing	0.3	0.2	0.6	0.2	0.9	0.9	0.3
28 Chemicals	0.5	1.2	4.4	3.1	0.7	1.1	1.3
29 Petroleum and Coal Products	0.2	0.2	0.7	0.2	1.2	0.6	0.3
30 Rubber	–	–	–	–	–	0.1	–
31 Leather	0.8	0.0	0.5	–	1.8	1.3	0.7
Leather Products	0.1	0.1	0.5	0.0	1.0	0.5	0.1
32 Stone, Clay and Glass	0.3	0.2	0.6	0.1	0.9	0.6	0.4
33 Primary Metals	0.1	0.0	0.1	–	0.8	0.6	2.3
34 Fabricated Metals	0.1	0.1	0.3	0.0	0.9	0.4	0.1
35 Non-electrical Machinery	0.2	0.1	0.5	0.1	0.6	0.6	0.6
36 Electrical Machinery	–	–	–	–	–	–	–
37 Transportation Equipment	0.5	0.3	1.2	0.4	1.6	1.1	1.2
38 Instruments	0.0	–	0.3	–	0.6	0.0	0.1
39 Miscellaneous	0.1	0.0	0.1	0.0	0.4	0.3	0.0
Total	0.8	0.5	0.9	0.4	1.3	0.8	0.7

TABLE 13
(Continued)

SIC Code Number and Industry	Mississippi	Louisiana	Arkansas	Texas	Oklahoma
20 Food	0.4	1.7	0.3	1.6	0.1
21 Tobacco	-	0.9	0.0	0.2	0.0
22 Textiles	0.2	0.1	0.0	0.2	-
23 Apparel	0.1	0.5	0.1	0.4	0.0
24 Lumber and Wood Products	2.3	2.7	3.5	2.3	0.0
25 Furniture	0.1	0.4	0.2	0.4	0.0
26 Paper	-	0.0	0.0	0.1	-
27 Printing and Publishing	0.2	0.6	0.3	1.3	0.1
28 Chemicals	0.7	0.6	0.1	0.2	0.0
29 Petroleum and Coal Products	0.1	0.6	0.1	0.7	0.0
30 Rubber	-	-	-	-	-
31 Leather	0.0	0.0	0.0	0.1	-
Leather Products	0.1	0.5	0.1	1.1	0.1
32 Stone, Clay and Glass	0.2	0.2	0.2	0.9	0.0
33 Primary Metals	-	0.0	0.0	0.2	-
34 Fabricated Metals	0.0	0.3	0.1	0.4	0.0
35 Non-electrical Machinery	0.1	0.4	0.1	0.4	0.0
36 Electrical Machinery	-	-	-	-	-
37 Transportation Equipment	0.5	0.6	0.7	2.0	0.0
38 Instruments	-	0.4	0.1	0.3	-
39 Miscellaneous	0.0	0.2	0.0	0.2	0.0
Total	0.3	0.7	0.4	0.8	0.0

tury than it had been during the antebellum period. Pennsylvania was much more specialized in the primary metals industries and New York in apparel production.

Production outside of the Northeast and East North Central states increased slightly during 1860-1900. The share of aggregate manufacturing production of all states in the West North Central, South Atlantic, East South Central, and West South Central regions only advanced from 13.6 percent to 16.7 percent. Earlier in this chapter, a significant advance in textile production relative to manufacturing as a whole was cited in the Carolinas. This increased emphasis on textiles is placed in a different perspective when the states' shares of national textile production are viewed. Similarly, the dominant position of primary metals in Alabama's economy appears to have had little significant impact on national production in that industry.

The significance of changes in state shares of national industry value added was examined by chi-square and rank correlation techniques. (See Table 14.) The chi-square analysis indicates that the hypothesis of no significant difference between the 1860 and 1900 percentage contributions to national industry value added can be accepted in the majority of states. In view of the data in Tables 12 and 13, one might anticipate that the hypothesis of dependence would be accepted in the states in the West North Central, South Atlantic, East South Central, and West South Central regions. Production shares in these states in most industries were very small, generally less than 1 percent, in both sample years. In the larger industrial states, the hypothesis of no change cannot be accepted and there appears to have been marked deviation between the 1860 and 1900 industry patterns. Since the rank correlation analysis does not capture the quantitative industry weights, the results are unaffected by degree of industrialization, and, in the majority of states, the hypothesis of a significant relationship between the 1860 and 1900 rankings of industry shares can be accepted.

The state industry shares of national value added can be used in conjunction with census population figures to construct

TABLE 14

CALCULATION OF THE CHI-SQUARE STATISTIC AND SPEARMAN'S RANK CORRELATION

COEFFICIENT FOR HYPOTHESIS OF NO CHANGE IN THE INDUSTRY SHARES OF

NATIONAL VALUE ADDED, 1860-1900

State	Chi-Square Statistic	r_s
Maine	7.24$^{\prime a}$	.735**[b]
New Hampshire	4.76$^{\prime\prime\prime}$	.669**
Vermont	4.60$^{\prime\prime\prime}$	.475
Massachusetts	29.58	.669**
Rhode Island	8.01$^{\prime}$	.529*
Connecticut	13.05	.847***
New York	44.67	.607**
New Jersey	26.90	.278
Pennsylvania	25.99	.536*
Delaware	4.30$^{\prime\prime\prime}$	.706**
Maryland	4.91$^{\prime\prime\prime}$	.282
Ohio	16.18	.411
Indiana	9.03$^{\prime}$	.703**
Illinois	15.71	.377
Michigan	7.19$^{\prime\prime}$	.475*
Wisconsin	5.75$^{\prime\prime}$	.697**
Minnesota	1.75$^{\prime\prime\prime}$	.710**
Iowa	4.54$^{\prime\prime\prime}$	.539*
Missouri	10.18	.590*
Kansas	8.65$^{\prime}$	.291
Nebraska	4.04$^{\prime\prime\prime}$	.238
Virginia	8.63$^{\prime}$	.579*
North Carolina	13.24	.608*
South Carolina	4.37$^{\prime\prime}$	.636*
Georgia	4.94$^{\prime\prime}$	.708**
Florida	4.85	.623*
Kentucky	3.23$^{\prime\prime\prime}$	.763**
Tennessee	3.65$^{\prime\prime\prime}$	.561*
Alabama	3.89$^{\prime\prime\prime}$	.540*
Mississippi	2.82$^{\prime\prime\prime}$	.010
Louisiana	4.86$^{\prime\prime}$	.431
Arkansas	1.48$^{\prime\prime\prime}$	.635*
Texas	2.52$^{\prime\prime\prime}$	.738**

[a]The significance of the chi-square statistic is shown by a $^{\prime}$ where $^{\prime}$ = P $\geq$ .95, $^{\prime\prime}$ = P $\geq$ .99, and $^{\prime\prime\prime}$ = P $\geq$ .999.

[b]See note b to Table 11.

Source: See text.

a coefficient of localization similar to that outlined in Chapter 1.
Using population shares, rather than income shares, to represent
consumer markets, the coefficient can be constructed as follows:[7]

$$C_{S_i} = \sum_{r=1}^{k} (VA_i^s / VA_i^n - P^s / P^n)$$

where P = population, s designates state, and all other symbols are
as before. This measure, which appears in Table 15, represents
the percentage of value added that would have to enter interstate
trade in order to distribute production equally across consumer
markets. The industry measures are similar in rank to those in
Table 6. However, since this coefficient reflects the volume of
trade across state rather than regional boundaries, in all cases the
numerical value of the coefficient is larger. In both periods production was highly concentrated in textiles, apparel, paper, rubber, instruments, and miscellaneous manufacturing, and was
localized in food, lumber and wood products, and transportation
equipment. The weighted measure for total manufacturing
showed a slight decline during 1860-1900 in the degree of spatial
concentration of manufacturing production.

The value added and population shares can also be used to
indicate areas of export surplus, assuming that industry value
added shares in excess of population shares are indicative of
export potential. However, the reader should be cautioned that
the above calculations of the state coefficients of localization and
the manufacturing export base coefficients of the individual states
are only to be taken as crude approximations. The following
calculation yields an index of each state's percentage share of the
total interstate export:

$$\frac{(VA_i^s / VA_i^n - P^s / P^n)}{C_{S_i}}$$

TABLE 15

STATE COEFFICIENT OF LOCALIZATION OF MANUFACTURING INDUSTRY,

1860 and 1900

SIC Code Number and Industry	1860 Coefficient	1900 Coefficient
20 Food	.248	.258
21 Tobacco	.425	.381
22 Textiles	.586	.562
23 Apparel	.491	.443
24 Lumber and Wood Products	.177	.225
25 Furniture	.373	.372
26 Paper	.507	.486
27 Printing and Publishing	.484	.350
28 Chemicals	.452	.340
29 Petroleum and Coal Products	.438	.376
30 Rubber	.788	.707
31 Leather	.427	.475
Leather Products	.455	.420
32 Stone, Clay and Glass	.355	.366
33 Primary Metals	.422	.543
34 Fabricated Metals	.394	.384
35 Non-electrical Machinery	.322	.405
36 Electrical Machinery	- -	- -
37 Transportation Equipment	.309	.233
38 Instruments	.684	.513
39 Miscellaneous	.570	.482
Total	.406	.388

Source: See text.

The calculations of the above ratio for 1860 and 1900, which appear in Tables 16 and 17, respectively, suggest that a small group of states dominated the interstate export of manufactured goods in 1860. The six states of Massachusetts, Rhode Island, Connecticut, New York, New Jersey, and Pennsylvania generated 75 percent or more of the interregional export of manufactured goods in all industries except food, tobacco, and lumber and wood products. Massachusetts alone accounted for 20 percent or more of the interstate export in textiles, furniture, paper, leather, leather products, fabricated metals, machinery, and miscellaneous manufacturing. Connecticut's most significant share of the export occurred in rubber (32.2 percent), fabricated metals (35.3 percent), and instruments (36.5 percent). New York contributed 30 percent or more of the interstate export total in food, apparel, furniture, printing and publishing, chemicals, petroleum and coal products, rubber, leather, stone, clay, and glass, non-electrical machinery, and miscellaneous machinery. Pennsylvania produced approximately 30 percent or more of the interstate export total in printing and publishing, chemicals, stone, clay, and glass, primary metals, and instruments.

The remaining states were characterized by much less diversification, as reflected in rather limited contributions to antebellum interstate trade. The only marked evidence of any export surplus in the northern New England states in 1860 occurred in Maine (lumber and wood products) and New Hampshire (textiles). Ohio produced shares of total interstate export exceeding 10 percent in food, lumber and wood products, and non-electrical machinery. In the other western states, the only sizeable export shares were found in Illinois (food) and Michigan and Wisconsin (lumber and wood products). The only significant shares of manufacturing export in the South were shown in Virginia (tobacco) and North Carolina (chemicals).

Table 17 clearly shows the more localized nature of manufacturing at the end of the nineteenth century. Most of the conclusions reached earlier with respect to changes in relative concentration are borne out in the figures. An analysis of state by state

TABLE 16

STATE PERCENTAGE SHARES OF INTERSTATE TRADE IN MANUFACTURING VALUE ADDED, 1860[a]

SIC Code Number and Industry	Maine	New Hampshire	Vermont	Massachusetts	Rhode Island	Connecticut	New York	New Jersey	Pennsylvania
20 Food	–	–	–	1.2	2.0	–	42.7	2.8	15.7
21 Tobacco	–	–	–	–	0.5	1.9	6.1	0.9	–
22 Textiles	3.1	11.8	0.7	45.7	17.2	12.1	–	2.6	6.8
23 Apparel	–	0.2	–	15.1	1.2	11.4	43.2	10.2	16.5
24 Lumber and Wood Products	13.0	3.4	–	4.0	–	–	15.8	–	13.6
25 Furniture	–	0.3	–	30.0	0.3	0.5	41.6	–	7.8
26 Paper	3.6	3.7	–	46.5	–	15.8	17.2	7.3	4.9
27 Printing and Publishing	–	–	–	10.7	0.4	1.9	56.2	–	30.8
28 Chemicals	–	–	–	7.5	0.2	8.0	31.2	7.1	28.3
29 Petroleum and Coal Products	3.9	–	–	18.3	1.4	–	58.4	–	17.4
30 Rubber	–	–	–	5.8	4.9	32.2	33.0	24.0	–
31 Leather	1.9	2.3	0.2	28.6	–	–	35.4	4.2	24.1
Leather Products	–	4.0	–	82.2	–	3.7	1.3	5.1	3.7
32 Stone, Clay and Glass	–	–	2.8	14.9	–	–	29.6	12.7	38.0
33 Primary Metals	–	–	–	14.5	1.2	5.2	14.2	8.3	53.8
34 Fabricated Metals	–	0.3	–	19.5	8.1	35.3	20.6	7.9	7.9
35 Non-electrical Machinery	–	0.6	2.2	21.1	7.5	12.4	29.2	3.7	12.4
36 Electrical Machinery	–	–	–	–	–	–	–	–	–
37 Transportation Equipment	1.6	4.5	–	12.3	0.3	21.7	15.9	19.7	17.2
38 Instruments	–	–	–	12.7	0.1	36.5	23.5	–	27.0
39 Miscellaneous	–	–	–	23.0	9.6	16.8	36.5	4.2	9.8

TABLE 16
(Continued)

SIC Code Number and Industry	Delaware	Maryland	Ohio	Indiana	Illinois	Michigan	Wisconsin	Minnesota
20 Food	–	4.4	10.5	1.2	13.7	–	2.4	–
21 Tobacco	–	2.8	–	–	–	–	–	–
22 Textiles	–	–	–	–	–	–	–	–
23 Apparel	–	1.0	1.2	–	–	–	–	–
24 Lumber and Wood Products	–	–	–	4.0	–	20.9	10.7	2.3
25 Furniture	1.0	–	19.6	–	–	–	–	–
26 Paper	–	–	–	–	–	–	–	–
27 Printing and Publishing	–	–	–	–	–	–	–	–
28 Chemicals	2.0	–	–	–	–	–	–	–
29 Petroleum and Coal Products	–	–	–	–	–	–	–	–
30 Rubber	–	–	–	–	–	–	–	–
31 Leather	2.1	1.2	–	–	–	–	–	–
Leather Products	–	–	–	–	–	–	–	–
32 Stone, Clay and Glass	–	–	–	–	–	–	–	–
33 Primary Metals	–	0.6	1.9	–	–	–	–	–
34 Fabricated Metals	–	0.9	–	–	–	0.5	–	–
35 Non-electrical Machinery	0.3	–	10.6	–	–	–	–	–
36 Electrical Machinery	–	–	–	–	–	–	–	–
37 Transportation Equipment	6.8	–	–	–	–	–	–	–
38 Instruments	–	–	–	–	–	–	–	–
39 Miscellaneous	–	–	–	–	–	–	–	–

TABLE 16
(Continued)

SIC Code Number and Industry	Iowa	Missouri	Kansas	Nebraska	Kentucky	Virginia	North Carolina	Florida	Louisiana
20 Food	0.4	2.8	0.4	–	–	–	–	–	–
21 Tobacco	–	9.2	–	–	5.9	72.7	–	–	–
22 Textiles	–	–	–	–	–	–	–	–	–
23 Apparel	–	–	–	–	–	–	–	–	–
24 Lumber and Wood Products	–	–	6.2	1.1	–	–	–	4.5	0.6
25 Furniture	–	–	–	–	–	–	–	–	–
26 Paper	–	–	–	–	–	–	–	–	–
27 Printing and Publishing	–	–	–	–	–	–	–	–	–
28 Chemicals	–	–	–	–	–	–	15.7	–	–
29 Petroleum and Coal Products	–	–	–	–	0.7	–	–	–	–
30 Rubber	–	–	–	–	–	–	–	–	–
31 Leather	–	–	–	–	–	–	–	–	–
Leather Products	–	–	–	–	–	–	–	–	–
32 Stone, Clay and Glass	–	–	1.4	–	–	–	–	0.3	–
33 Primary Metals	–	–	–	–	–	–	–	–	–
34 Fabricated Metals	–	–	–	–	–	–	–	–	–
35 Non-electrical Machinery	–	–	–	–	–	–	–	–	–
36 Electrical Machinery	–	–	–	–	–	–	–	–	–
37 Transportation Equipment	–	–	–	–	–	–	–	–	–
38 Instruments	–	–	–	–	–	–	–	–	–
39 Miscellaneous	–	–	–	–	–	–	–	–	–

[a]Those states in which it appeared that no exportable surplus was available in any industry are not shown in the table.

TABLE 17

STATE PERCENTAGE SHARES OF INTERSTATE TRADE IN MANUFACTURING VALUE ADDED, 1900[a]

SIC Code Number and Industry	Maine	New Hampshire	Vermont	Massachusetts	Rhode Island	Connecticut	New York	New Jersey	Pennsylvania
20 Food	- -	- -	- -	2.2	- -	- -	27.3	3.2	1.3
21 Tobacco	- -	- -	- -	- -	- -	- -	25.6	3.7	8.2
22 Textiles	4.1	6.1	0.2	37.8	14.3	7.2	2.7	11.3	13.6
23 Apparel	- -	- -	- -	5.0	- -	3.1	76.7	1.0	0.3
24 Lumber and Wood Products	5.2	5.5	3.1	- -	- -	1.6	- -	- -	- -
25 Furniture	- -	- -	0.8	14.8	- -	1.6	33.8	- -	- -
26 Paper	11.4	6.3	3.1	26.0	0.2	5.5	35.8	1.8	3.8
27 Printing and Publishing	- -	- -	- -	16.4	0.1	- -	61.7	- -	5.5
28 Chemicals	- -	- -	1.5	5.8	0.1	0.1	36.5	14.9	16.0
29 Petroleum and Coal Products	- -	- -	- -	5.3	1.1	0.6	38.5	14.0	24.6
30 Rubber	- -	- -	- -	41.1	17.0	24.3	- -	16.7	- -
31 Leather	0.2	1.5	- -	19.4	- -	- -	4.2	13.0	39.9
Leather Products	4.6	9.8	- -	68.3	- -	- -	11.6	2.7	- -
32 Stone, Clay and Glass	1.5	0.3	3.4	6.4	0.7	1.5	30.0	11.0	25.5
33 Primary Metals	- -	- -	- -	- -	- -	5.0	- -	4.9	70.2
34 Fabricated Metals	- -	- -	- -	6.0	1.0	21.5	15.9	0.5	8.4
35 Non-electrical Machinery	- -	- -	- -	14.9	3.9	7.3	17.3	9.9	21.1
36 Electrical Machinery	- -	- -	- -	- -	- -	- -	- -	- -	- -
37 Transportation Equipment	0.7	- -	1.5	- -	0.4	3.6	0.4	4.7	35.8
38 Instruments	- -	- -	0.5	7.6	0.9	20.6	38.8	11.1	8.8
39 Miscellaneous	- -	- -	- -	14.7	10.9	18.3	39.7	8.5	- -

TABLE 17
(Continued)

SIC Code Number and Industry	Delaware	Maryland	Ohio	Indiana	Illinois	Michigan	Wisconsin	Minnesota
20 Food	0.1	1.6	4.0	5.9	44.5	—	6.3	0.7
21 Tobacco	—	5.4	3.9	—	—	0.3	—	—
22 Textiles	—	—	—	—	—	—	—	—
23 Apparel	—	4.1	—	—	9.7	—	—	—
24 Lumber and Wood Products	—	—	—	2.7	—	26.8	24.1	14.9
25 Furniture	—	1.8	3.5	6.5	14.2	14.6	8.1	—
26 Paper	1.2	—	1.1	—	—	—	3.8	—
27 Printing and Publishing	—	—	1.1	—	15.2	—	—	—
28 Chemicals	0.4	3.6	4.8	—	—	5.6	—	—
29 Petroleum and Coal Products	—	1.5	5.8	—	8.6	—	—	—
30 Rubber	—	—	0.9	—	—	—	—	—
31 Leather and Leather Products	10.1	—	2.7	—	—	—	11.6	—
32 Stone, Clay and Glass	—	—	8.0	—	—	—	—	—
33 Primary Metals	0.5	0.7	15.5	6.8	4.1	—	—	—
34 Fabricated Metals	—	0.3	11.8	2.6	2.2	1.6	2.5	—
35 Non-electrical Machinery	—	—	14.7	—	27.6	—	—	—
36 Electrical Machinery	0.4	—	—	—	10.4	—	0.3	—
37 Transportation Equipment	5.8	2.5	10.0	13.3	11.6	7.9	0.9	—
38 Instruments	—	—	—	—	11.6	—	—	—
39 Miscellaneous	—	1.1	—	—	6.8	—	—	—

TABLE 17
(Continued)

SIC Code Number and Industry	Missouri	Kansas	Nebraska	Virginia	West Virginia	North Carolina	South Carolina	Georgia
20 Food	– –	0.3	2.4	– –	– –	– –	– –	– –
21 Tobacco	16.8	– –	– –	10.6	– –	7.5	– –	– –
22 Textiles	– –	– –	– –	– –	– –	0.4	2.2	– –
23 Apparel	– –	– –	– –	– –	– –	– –	– –	– –
24 Lumber and Wood Products	– –	– –	– –	– –	2.0	– –	– –	– –
25 Furniture	– –	– –	– –	– –	– –	– –	– –	– –
26 Paper	– –	– –	– –	– –	– –	– –	– –	– –
27 Printing and Publishing	– –	– –	– –	– –	– –	– –	– –	– –
28 Chemicals	– –	– –	– –	– –	– –	– –	– –	3.8
29 Petroleum and Coal Products	– –	– –	– –	– –	– –	– –	– –	– –
30 Rubber	– –	– –	– –	– –	– –	– –	– –	– –
31 Leather	– –	– –	– –	– –	0.1	– –	– –	– –
Leather Products	– –	– –	– –	– –	– –	– –	– –	– –
32 Stone, Clay and Glass	– –	– –	– –	– –	1.5	– –	– –	– –
33 Primary Metals	– –	– –	– –	– –	– –	– –	– –	– –
34 Fabricated Metals	– –	– –	– –	– –	– –	– –	– –	– –
35 Non-electrical Machinery	–	–	–	–	–	–	–	–
36 Electrical Machinery	–	–	–	–	–	–	–	–
37 Transportation Equipment	0.8	– –	– –	– –	– –	– –	– –	– –
38 Instruments	– –	– –	– –	– –	– –	– –	– –	– –
39 Miscellaneous	– –	– –	– –	– –	– –	– –	– –	– –

TABLE 17
(Continued)

SIC Code Number and Industry	Florida	Kentucky	Mississippi	Louisiana	Arkansas
20 Food	– –	– –	– –	– –	– –
21 Tobacco	7.3	10.6	– –	– –	– –
22 Textiles	– –	– –	– –	– –	– –
23 Apparel	– –	– –	– –	– –	– –
24 Lumber and Wood Products	4.2	– –	0.7	3.5	7.6
25 Furniture	– –	– –	– –	– –	– –
26 Paper	– –	– –	– –	– –	– –
27 Printing and Publishing	– –	– –	– –	– –	– –
28 Chemicals	7.0	– –	– –	– –	– –
29 Petroleum and Coal Products	– –	– –	– –	– –	– –
30 Rubber	– –	– –	– –	– –	– –
31 Leather	– –	– –	– –	– –	– –
31 Leather Products	– –	– –	– –	– –	– –
32 Stone, Clay and Glass	– –	– –	– –	– –	– –
33 Primary Metals	– –	– –	– –	– –	– –
34 Fabricated Metals	– –	– –	– –	– –	– –
35 Non-electrical Machinery	–	–	–	–	–
36 Electrical Machinery	–	–	–	–	–
37 Transportation Equipment	– –	– –	– –	– –	– –
38 Instruments	– –	– –	– –	– –	– –
39 Miscellaneous	– –	– –	– –	– –	– –

^aThose states in which it appeared that no exportable surplus was available in any industry are not shown in the table.

developments during the late nineteenth century is left for the interested reader to evaluate.

NOTES

1. See Rezneck's paper ("Light manufacture," in *Growth of the American Economy*) on light manufacturing industries.

2. This development, referred to earlier in Chapter 1, largely represented the production of agricultural machinery, farm implements, and steam engines and related equipment.

3. Clark, *History of Manufactures*, Vol. 2, Ch. 16, pointed to Alabama and Tennessee as the major center of the iron and steel industry in the late nineteenth century South. The figures in Table 10 suggest that West Virginia and Alabama experienced the heaviest concentration in this area.

4. Clark, *History of Manufactures*, Vol. 2, Ch. 16, points to this dominant position of Massachusetts in New England during the middle and late nineteenth century and this is evident in Tables 12 and 13.

5. Most sources point to Pennsylvania's specialization in the iron industry, but Rezneck indicates that the state was also involved in significant production in textiles, apparel, watches, and cameras.

6. Most accounts of New York's antebellum manufacturing structure cite the state's dominance in textiles and apparel. While this heavy commitment to apparel production is noted in Table 12, it is also evident that the state dominated many other industries, including printing and publishing, rubber, and petroleum and coal products.

7. Easterlin's personal income series (in "Regional Income Trends") is not available by state for 1860; therefore, population shares have been substituted for income in order to determine market potential. Population shares are commonly used in state and regional analysis to approximate demand; see John R. Moroney and James M. Walker, "A Regional Test of the Heckscher-Ohlin Hypothesis," *Journal of Political Economy*, December 1966, pp. 573-586, and, Edwin F. Estle, "A More Conclusive Regional Test of the Heckscher-Ohlin Hypothesis," *Journal of Political Economy*, December 1967, pp. 886-888.

3

Factors Underlying
the Locational Pattern
of Late Nineteenth Century
American Manufacturing

This chapter considers several factors which may have played a significant role in determining the state and regional locational pattern of American manufacturing during the late nineteenth century. Earlier chapters indicated that sharp differences in relative concentration and manufacturing structure existed between states and regions in the period 1860-1900. It was also suggested that during this period American manufacturing generally was dominated by the northeastern states, with the majority of exportable surpluses being generated by this area. Several possible solutions aimed at explaining these state and regional structural differences and the relative concentration of manufacturing in the Northeast can be pursued by considering the effects of factor supply conditions and local consumer demand on industry locational patterns. Advantages for the Northeast in factor supplies such as water power, iron, coal, timber, labor, and capital, and nearness to markets have been suggested as the major factors accounting for the initial concentration of manufacturing industry in the area.[1] Once this initial concentration was set in motion, economies of scale and external economies resulting from the clustering of industry in the area would tend to encourage a greater degree of spatial concentration.

The relationship between factor supply conditions and industry concentration patterns can be subjected to empirical test by use of the classical doctrine of comparative cost and the Heckscher-Ohlin hypothesis.[2] The comparative cost proposition suggests that an area will concentrate production on those industries in which real labor costs are relatively low.[3] The Heckscher-Ohlin hypothesis suggests that an area will exhibit relatively heavy concentration on those industries that maximize utilization of that area's relatively abundant factors of production. In constructing the tests of the usefulness of the classical comparative cost proposition as an explanatory tool for late nineteenth century state and regional concentration patterns in manufacturing, the concern here is with the relative supply of labor across states and regions and the resulting concentration on labor/nonlabor intensive industries. In constructing the tests of the Heckscher-Ohlin hypothesis, the concern is with state and regional supplies of labor relative to capital and the resulting concentration on relatively labor or capital intensive industries.

In order to determine the relative supply of manufacturing labor across states and regions, an examination was made of wage rates in selected industrial occupations. A cross section of industries was chosen to include occupations of varying skills and industries producing relatively homogeneous products. In 1860, wage rates in the following industries were examined: blacksmithing, boots and shoes, bread, brick, carpentering, carriages, cotton goods, flour and meal, iron castings, leather, lime, malt liquors, sawed lumber, machinery (steam engines), millinery, printing, saddlery and harness, soap and candles, tin, copper and sheet iron ware, wagons, and woolen goods. Wage rates markedly above the national average,were found in Massachusetts, Connecticut, Illinois, Minnesota, Missouri, Kansas, Florida, and Louisiana; wage rates markedly below the national average were found in New York, New Jersey, Pennsylvania, Delaware, Maryland, Ohio, Michigan, Wisconsin, Virginia, North Carolina, South Carolina, Kentucky, and Arkansas.[4] (See Appendix, Part XXVIII.) In the remaining states, despite significant differences in particular industries, on balance, wages were not significantly above or below the average for the nation.

The same procedure was used to determine relative supplies of labor across states and regions in 1900. Wage rates in the following industries were surveyed: bicycle repairing, blacksmithing, bookbinding, boots and shoes (factory), bread, brick and tile, carpentering, railroad cars (general shop construction and repairs), men's clothing (factory), cooperage, cotton goods, flouring and grist mill, foundry and machine shop, furniture (factory), manufactured ice, hosiery and knit goods, iron and steel, leather, lime and cement, distilled liquors, malt liquors, lumber and timber, lumber (planing mill products), masonry, mineral and soda waters, plumbing, printing and publishing (newspapers), saddlery and harness, slaughtering and meat packing, ship and boat building (wooden), tinsmithing, coppersmithing, etc., tobacco (cigars and cigarettes), and watch, clock, and jewelry repairing. (See Appendix, Part XXIX.) Massachusetts, Rhode Island, Connecticut, New York, New Jersey, and Illinois were characterized by relatively high wages; Vermont, Delaware, Maryland, Ohio, Indiana, Michigan, Wisconsin, Minnesota, Iowa, Kansas, Virginia, West Virginia, North Carolina, South Carolina, Georgia, Florida, Kentucky, Tennessee, Alabama, Mississippi, Arkansas, Louisiana, and Oklahoma were characterized by relatively low wages. Wages in the remaining states were not decidedly different from the national average.

States and regions with significantly above average wage rates were classified as labor scarce, and states and regions with significantly below average wage rates were classified as labor abundant. In testing the relevance of the classical comparative cost doctrine in explaining nineteenth century state and regional industrial location patterns, labor supply differences were taken into account by utilizing the concept of the output-labor ratio. It was hypothesized that states and regions with above average labor costs would specialize in nonlabor intensive industries, i.e., those industries with high output-labor ratios. Conversely, areas characterized by relatively cheap labor would specialize in labor intensive industries. (See Appendix, Parts XIV-XVII, for output-labor ratios by state and region for 1860 and 1900.)

Two measures of industrial concentration within states were used. Industry per capita relatives, calculated as the ratio of per capita value added in the particular state or region to per capita value added in the nation as a whole, served as the basis for ranking relative industry concentration in the various states and regions. It should be clear that the size of the per capita relative for any industry depends on the significance of the industry to the nation as a whole. As a result, utilization was also made of the state and regional percentage distribution of manufacturing value added across the two-digit industries.

The following two variants of the classical comparative cost doctrine were subjected to test for states and regions with manufacturing labor costs significantly above or below the national average:

Hypothesis 1: For relatively high-wage (low-wage) areas there is a positive (inverse) rank ordering between per capita relatives and output-labor ratios.

Hypothesis 2: For relatively high-wage (low-wage) areas there is a positive (inverse) rank ordering between the percentage distribution of manufacturing value added and output-labor ratios.

Spearman's rank correlation coefficient was calculated for each hypothesis for 1860 and 1900. The results from the regional tests, as shown in Table 18, are not favorable to either variant of the classical doctrine. For 1860 the correct sign was only obtained in six out of ten cases and the only significant relationship occurred in the Middle Atlantic region for Hypothesis 2. In 1900 the hypothesized sign was only obtained in five of the fourteen tests and the results were nonsignificant in each case.

The results from the state tests of the two variants of the classical comparative cost doctrine appear in Tables 19 and 20, and, again, there is no support for any significant relationship between labor availability and industrial concentration. For

TABLE 18

SPEARMAN'S RANK CORRELATION COEFFICIENTS FOR REGIONAL TESTS

OF THE CLASSICAL COMPARATIVE COST DOCTRINE

Region and Year	Hypothesized Relationship	Hypothesis 1	Hypothesis 2
1860[a]			
New England	+	-.039	-.461*[b]
Middle Atlantic	-	.374	-.469
East North Central	-	.014	-.110
West North Central	+	.300	.079
South Atlantic	-	-.152	-.382
1900			
New England	+	-.154	-.307
Middle Atlantic	+	.257	.093
East North Central	-	.167	.185
West North Central	-	.374	.196
South Atlantic	-	-.358	-.372
East South Central	-	.324	.132
West South Central	-	.200	-.023

[a] Wage rates were too similar to the national average in the East South Central and West South Central regions to specify the sign of the hypotheses.

[b] Cases in which the coefficient was significant are shown by a *, where * = (P ≤ .05), ** = (P ≤ .01), and *** = (P ≤ .001).

Source: See text.

TABLE 19

SPEARMAN'S RANK CORRELATION COEFFICIENTS FOR STATE TESTS OF THE

CLASSICAL COMPARATIVE COST DOCTRINE: 1860[a]

State	Hypothesized Relationship	Hypothesis 1	Hypothesis 2
Massachusetts	+	-.226	-.460
Connecticut	+	-.050	-.279
New York	−	.562	-.354
New Jersey	−	-.331	-.472
Pennsylvania	−	.120	-.403
Delaware	−	.096	-.194
Maryland	−	-.094	-.628**
Ohio	−	.093	-.137
Illinois	+	.307	.118
Michigan	−	-.112	-.158
Wisconsin	−	-.211	-.081
Minnesota	+	.490	.580*
Missouri	+	.412	.203
Kansas	+	.791**	.739**
Virginia	−	.026	-.260
North Carolina	−	-.124	-.331
South Carolina	−	-.215	-.296
Florida	+	.530	.462
Kentucky	−	-.110	-.491*
Arkansas	−	.534	.700
Louisiana	+	-.045	-.194

[a]See note b to Table 18.

Source: See text.

TABLE 20

SPEARMAN'S RANK CORRELATION COEFFICIENTS FOR STATE TESTS OF THE

CLASSICAL COMPARATIVE COST DOCTRINE: 1900[a]

State	Hypothesized Relationship	Hypothesis 1	Hypothesis 2
Vermont	-	.350	.391
Massachusetts	+	-.191	-.258
Rhode Island	+	.116	.010
Connecticut	+	-.116	-.211
New York	+	.251	.185
New Jersey	+	.136	-.114
Delaware	-	.441	.075
Maryland	-	.334	-.118
Ohio	-	.335	.251
Indiana	-	.233	.086
Illinois	+	.409	.337
Michigan	-	.242	.297
Wisconsin	-	-.062	-.088
Minnesota	-	.350	.235
Iowa	-	.598	.502
Kansas	-	.326	.064
Virginia	-	.085	-.125
West Virginia	-	-.041	.070
North Carolina	-	.069	-.039
South Carolina	-	-.067	-.116
Georgia	-	-.201	-.249
Florida	-	.324	.319
Kentucky	-	.109	-.093
Tennessee	-	.363	.132
Alabama	-	-.212	-.206
Mississippi	-	-.018	-.023
Arkansas	-	.136	.048
Louisiana	-	.589	.253
Oklahoma	-	.607	.521

[a]See note b to Table 18.

Source: See text.

1860 the correct sign was obtained for Hypothesis 1 in twelve out of twenty-one cases. However, only in Kansas was the relationship significantly strong to accept the hypothesis. In all but four states the correct sign was obtained for Hypothesis 2 but the degree of association was only significant in Maryland, Minnesota, Kansas, and Kentucky. The results for 1900 are even less favorable for the classical doctrine. The correct sign was obtained only in ten of twenty-nine cases for Hypothesis 1 and twelve of twenty-nine cases for Hypothesis 2, and in no instance were the results significant for either hypothesis. It appears from the state and regional tests of the two variants of the classical comparative cost doctrine that labor cost variations had little impact on concentration patterns in American manufacturing during the late nineteenth century.

Given the results in Tables 18-20, some question might arise concerning the strength of operation of the labor market during the late nineteenth century. A simple test to show to what extent the market worked can be provided by analyzing the following proposition: within given industries, did relatively labor abundant regions use relatively labor intensive production techniques and did the converse hold for labor scarce regions? An index of relative labor scarcity was constructed for each two-digit industry, calculated as the ratio of the wage rate in the ith industry in the particular state to the wage rate in the ith industry in the nation as a whole. (See Appendix, Part XXIII, for state and regional estimates of labor cost by two-digit industry.) Similarly, an index of the relative labor intensity of production was developed for each two-digit industry by taking the ratio of the output-labor ratio in the ith industry in the particular state to the output-labor ratio in the ith industry in the nation as a whole. These measures of labor scarcity and labor intensity of production were calculated for all states for 1860 and 1900, and the following hypothesis was specified and tested for each two-digit industry:

Hypothesis 3: There is a positive rank ordering between labor scarcity and output-labor ratios.

The results, as shown in Table 21, suggest that relative labor

TABLE 21

SPEARMAN'S RANK CORRELATION COEFFICIENTS BETWEEN RELATIVE COSTS

OF LABOR AND OUTPUT-LABOR RATIOS[a]

SIC Code Number and Industry	Coefficient 1860	Coefficient 1900
20 Food	.781***	.820***
21 Tobacco	.639***	.021
22 Textiles	.744***	.794***
23 Apparel	.763***	.887***
24 Lumber and Wood Products	.454**	.896***
25 Furniture	.749***	.865***
26 Paper	.296	.939***
27 Printing & Publishing	.711***	.884***
28 Chemicals	.777***	.856***
29 Petroleum and Coal Products	- -[b]	.653***
30 Rubber	- -[b]	- -[b]
31 Leather and Leather Products	.609***	.569**
32 Stone, Clay, and Glass	.705***	.913***
33 Primary Metals	.603***	.786***
34 Fabricated Metals	.549**	.640***
35 Non-electrical Machinery	.562**	.797***
36 Electrical Machinery	- -	- -
37 Transportation Equipment	.540**	.608***
38 Instruments	- -[b]	.188
39 Miscellaneous	.455*	.706***

[a] See note b to Table 18.

[b] Number of state observations insufficient to clearly test relationship.

Source: See text.

costs were significantly related to the relative use of labor in production.

In order to test the Heckscher-Ohlin hypothesis, an account has to be made of state and regional variations in capital supply relative to labor supply.[5] However, there are problems in obtaining adequate state and regional estimates of the capital stock utilized in manufacturing and an index of the spatial distribution of capital supplies across the United States. As a result of data limitations, the testing of the Heckscher-Ohlin hypothesis was restricted to the year 1900. As early as 1850, the manufacturing census included a detailed accounting of total capital invested by industry; however, no great reliability can be placed on the capital estimates prior to the 1890 census.[6] Beginning in 1890, a much more detailed accounting procedure was used to determine the amount of capital invested in the various manufacturing industries. The capital invested data for 1900 have been aggregated to the two-digit basis and have been used to construct industry capital-labor ratios for each state and region. (See Appendix, Parts XXII and XXIII; for industry capital-output ratios, see Appendix, Parts XXIV and XXV.) These industry capital-labor ratios are intended to demonstrate the relative capital intensity of production across states.

While it is generally accepted that capital was relatively abundant in the Northeast and scarce in the South and West during the late nineteenth century, the exact degree of state and regional differences in the relative availability of capital is not easily determined. The 1890 census provided a detailed examination of the American mortgage market, including state estimates of the average annual rate of interest paid on mortgage debt. These figures can be used to approximate state and regional differences in capital availability at the end of the century.[7] (See Table 22.) Comparison of labor scarcity, as reflected by wage rates, vis-à-vis capital scarcity, as reflected by mortgage rates, indicates that the following states had relatively abundant capital in 1900: Massachusetts, Rhode Island, Connecticut, New York, New Jersey, Pennsylvania, and Illinois. (Compare

TABLE 22

AVERAGE ANNUAL RATES OF INTEREST ON THE REAL ESTATE

MORTGAGE DEBT: 1890

Area	Rate of Interest
Alabama	7.98
Arkansas	9.06
Connecticut	5.64
Delaware	5.71
Florida	9.78
Georgia	8.09
Illinois	6.70
Indiana	6.84
Iowa	7.63
Kansas	8.68
Kentucky	6.25
Louisiana	7.67
Maine	6.15
Maryland	5.86
Massachusetts	5.44
Michigan	7.13
Minnesota	7.66
Mississippi	9.50
Missouri	7.68
Nebraska	8.30
New Hampshire	5.98
New Jersey	5.73
New York	5.49
North Carolina	7.72
North Dakota	9.35
Ohio	6.56
Pennsylvania	5.61
Rhode Island	5.72
South Carolina	8.37
South Dakota	9.46
Tennessee	6.00
Texas	9.60
Vermont	5.97
Virginia	6.02
West Virginia	6.06
Wisconsin	6.84
United States	6.60

Source: See text.

Appendix, Part XXIX, with Table 22.) Similarly, the following states appeared to be relatively capital scarce in 1900: Ohio, Indiana, Michigan, Wisconsin, Minnesota, Iowa, Missouri, Kansas, Nebraska, North Dakota, South Dakota, North Carolina, South Carolina, Georgia, Florida, Alabama, Mississippi, Arkansas, and Louisiana. Since it was unclear whether capital or labor was relatively more abundant in the remaining states, they were excluded from the analysis. The New England and Middle Atlantic regions were taken as relatively capital abundant, and the southern and western regions were considered relatively capital scarce.

The following two variants of the Heckscher-Ohlin hypothesis were specified for the capital abundant and capital scarce areas for 1900:

Hypothesis 4: For capital abundant (scarce) areas there is a positive (inverse) rank ordering between per capita relatives and capital-labor ratios.

Hypothesis 5: For capital abundant (scarce) areas there is a positive (inverse) rank ordering between the percentage distribution of manufacturing value added and capital-labor ratios.

The test results (see Table 23) are not favorable to either variant of the Heckscher-Ohlin hypothesis. For the regional tests, the specified sign was only obtained in six out of fourteen cases, and in no instance was the degree of association significant. The specified sign was obtained in a minority of cases for the state tests and the only significant relationship for Hypothesis 4 occurred in New Jersey.

The results obtained to this point suggest that relative industrial concentration between states and regions, and industrial concentration within a particular state or region's manufacturing sector, were not significantly related to state and regional differences in labor and capital supplies. However, within given industries, production techniques across states were highly correlated with relative labor scarcity.[8] What accounts for the apparent paradox of these results? What factors explain the spatial concentration patterns in late nineteenth century Ameri-

TABLE 23

SPEARMAN'S RANK CORRELATION COEFFICIENTS FOR STATE AND REGIONAL

TESTS OF THE HECKSCHER-OHLIN HYPOTHESIS: 1900[a]

State or Region	Hypothesized Relationship	Hypothesis 4	Hypothesis 5
New England	+	.174	-.043
Middle Atlantic	+	-.029	-.110
East North Central	-	.218	.059
West North Central	-	.085	-.035
South Atlantic	-	-.135	-.134
East South Central	-	.355	.316
West South Central	-	-.042	-.101
Massachusetts	+	.032	-.061
Rhode Island	+	.223	.324
Connecticut	+	.253	.063
New York	+	-.163	-.145
New Jersey	+	.516*	.158
Pennsylvania	+	.388	.195
Ohio	-	.325	-.162
Indiana	-	.154	.044
Illinois	+	.386	.190
Michigan	-	.251	.241
Wisconsin	-	.336	.271
Minnesota	-	.216	.090
Iowa	-	.214	.191
Missouri	-	.142	-.064
Kansas	-	.355	.123
Nebraska	-	.475	.212
North Dakota	-	.052	.100
South Dakota	-	.510	.565
North Carolina	-	.107	-.014
South Carolina	-	-.029	-.015
Georgia	-	-.173	-.213
Florida	-	.481	.458
Alabama	-	.205	.242
Mississippi	-	.004	-.008
Arkansas	-	.195	.216
Louisiana	-	.118	-.006

[a] See note b to Table 18.

Source: See text.

can manufacturing? It was demonstrated in earlier chapters that, in virtually every industry, manufacturing production at that time was highly concentrated in the Northeast. It is suggested here that this spatial concentration was largely the result of local demand and that market considerations were generally strong enough to offset variations in factor supply conditions in most industries. If we use Easterlin's state income series to represent local market potential, it is possible to determine the degree of association between industrial production and local demand by testing the following hypothesis for each two-digit industry for a cross-section of all states:[9]

Hypothesis 6: There is a positive rank ordering between income shares and value added shares.

The test results in Table 24 support the notion that locational patterns in American manufacturing during 1860-1900 were strongly tied to demand factors. These results are in no way inconsistent with a large interstate flow of goods; in fact, if there were economies of scale in any industry, one would expect production to be concentrated spatially.

The results here suggest that manufacturing-production was concentrated in the Northeast and that this included heavy production in capital intensive and labor intensive industries. Across states and regions and by type of industry, there does not appear to have been any essential difference in degree of specialization that can be explained by differences in factor (labor and capital) availability. One significant difference between states that appears to have affected industry locational patterns was the size of local markets. In addition, no explicit account of the impact of local resource conditions on manufacturing concentration patterns has been made in this study, but it is clear from earlier chapters that much of the late nineteenth century manufacturing represented processing of locally available resources. For example, in 1860 food manufacture ranked as the first or second leading manufacturing industry in the majority of states outside of the Northeast. Only in Alabama, Florida, and Mississippi was food manufacture not ranked among the five leading

TABLE 24

SPEARMAN'S RANK CORRELATION COEFFICIENTS BETWEEN INCOME

SHARES AND VALUE ADDED SHARES: 1900[a]

SIC Code Number and Industry	Coefficient
20 Food	.939***
21 Tobacco	.688***
22 Textiles	.349
23 Apparel	.846***
24 Lumber and Wood Products	.663***
25 Furniture	.816***
26 Paper	.538**
27 Printing and Publishing	.944***
28 Chemicals	.649***
29 Petroleum and Coal Products	.870***
30 Rubber	- -[b]
31 Leather and Leather Products	.710***
32 Stone, Clay and Glass	.765***
33 Primary Metals	.721***
34 Fabricated Metals	.847***
35 Non-electrical Machinery	.780***
36 Electrical Machinery	- -
37 Transportation Equipment	.887***
38 Instruments	.721***
39 Miscellaneous	.730***

[a]See note b to Table 18.

[b]Number of state observations insufficient to clearly test relationship.

Source: See text.

industries in each state in the West and South. Lumber and wood products ranked as the first or second leading industry in every state in the West or South except Ohio (third) and Virginia (fourth). Production of lumber and wood products received relatively less emphasis at the end of the nineteenth century, but, in fifteen of the twenty-three western and southern states, the industry still ranked in the top three. In 1900 food manufacture ranked no lower than fourth in any state outside the Northeast. In many states within the South there was also significant manufacture of tobacco and tobacco products, textiles, and turpentine. In addition to demand and resource factors, it was demonstrated in earlier chapters that during 1860-1900 state and regional industry concentration patterns within manufacturing were characterized by a great deal of structural rigidity. The results in this chapter are consistent with the hypothesis that locational patterns in American manufacturing during this period were determined by a combination of market conditions, resource supplies, economies of scale, and external economies.

NOTES

1. See Peterson and Gray, *Economic Development,* Ch. 9, and North, *Economic Growth,* Ch. 12.

2. For an excellent summary of the classical comparative cost doctrine and the Heckscher-Ohlin hypothesis, see Richard Caves, *Trade and Economic Structure* (Cambridge: Harvard University Press, 1960), pp. 6-57. Also see Bertil Ohlin, *Interregional and International Trade* (Cambridge: Harvard University Press, 1933) and David Ricardo, *The Principles of Political Economy and Taxation,* in *The Works and Correspondence of David Ricardo,* P. Sraffa, ed. (Cambridge: Cambridge University Press, 1951).

3. Moroney and Walker, "Heckscher Hypothesis," p. 573, indicate that real labor costs in the classical sense are appropriately measured by output-labor ratios. Capital costs were generally ignored or given secondary importance in the classical treatment.

4. States were categorized as labor abundant or labor scarce only in

those cases where there was at least a 2:1 ratio between the number of industries in which wage rates were below (above) the national average relative to the number of industries in which wage rates were above (below) the national average.

5. Several regional tests of the Heckscher-Ohlin hypothesis relating to current manufacturing developments have appeared in the recent literature. See Moroney and Walker, "Heckscher Hypothesis," and Estle, "A More Conclusive Regional Test."

6. For arguments against the reliability of the total capital invested statistics before 1890, see the *Ninth Census of the United States, Industry and Wealth,* pp. 381-382, and *Tenth Census of the United States, Manufactures of the United States,* p. 39. The greater reliability of the accounting procedure adopted in the 1890 census is indicated in the *Eleventh Census of the United States, Manufacturing Industries,* Part 1, pp. 9-11, and *Twelfth Census of the United States, Manufactures,* Part 2, p. 8.

7. See the *Eleventh Census of the United States, Report on Real Estate Mortgages,* p. 259.

8. No tests of the working of the capital market were made because data were not available in adequate detail.

9. Easterlin's state income series was made available for 1840, 1880, and 1900; therefore, I have restricted the test of the relationship between demand and production to 1900. See Richard Easterlin, "Interregional Differences in Per Capita Income, Population, and Total Income, 1840-1950," in *Trends in the American Economy in the Nineteenth Century,* Conference on Research in Income and Wealth, Studies in Income and Wealth, Volume 24 (Princeton University Press, 1960), pp. 73-140.

4

Trends in the Per Capita Spatial Distribution of Manufacturing Value Added Across States and Regions, 1860-1970

Up to this point, the analysis has been concerned with manufacturing developments during the period 1860-1900. It is clear from the earlier chapters that in the late nineteenth century most manufacturing industries were concentrated in the Northeast. More recent trends have seen a dispersion of manufacturing activity throughout the West and South. This concluding chapter traces, up to 1970, the spatial redistribution of manufacturing activity relative to population. It is demonstrated that the period 1860-1970 witnessed a significant narrowing of structural differences between states and regions as judged through the per capita weight of manufacturing in the aggregate and at the two-digit industry level. State and regional trends in per capita manufacturing value added relative to the national average during 1860-1970 are examined for aggregate manufacturing by using linear regression analysis.[1] Per capita manufacturing value added relatives, constructed at the two-digit level for 1860, 1900, and 1970, are used to examine structural convergence within manu-

facturing across the seven census regions. An entropy measure of
the spatial dispersion of manufacturing value added relative to
population is utilized to examine convergence at the two-digit
level across the various states.[2]

Initially, per capita manufacturing value added was estimated
for each state and region for each census year during 1860-1970.
It was hypothesized that those states with 1860 per capita value
added levels above (below) the national average would experience
significant relative declines (advances) during the period. For
twenty-two of the thirty-five states and for six of the seven census regions the hypothesis was accepted, with $(P \leq .05)$ or less in
each case. (See Table 25 for the results.)[3] However, Table 25
alone does not reveal an accurate picture of the degree of convergence in the per capita weight of manufacturing across states
and regions. Examination of the per capita manufacturing value
added relatives in Table 26 suggests that some states, while mov-
ing in the hypothesized direction, moved well beyond the national
average; in particular note the East North Central states. Alter-
natively, in a number of cases in which the regression analysis
suggests the absence of any significant convergence, the data in
Table 26 suggest that the states in question were much closer to
the national per capita level of output in 1970 than in the middle
of the nineteenth century. Included in this latter group of states
were the following: New Jersey, Illinois, Wisconsin, Missouri,
Kansas, Nebraska, Kentucky, and Mississippi. With the exception
of Delaware, every state with per capita value added above the
national average in 1860 suffered a relative decline during 1860-
1970. Only two states below the national average in 1860,
Maine and Maryland, fell even further during the period.

The regional per capita value added trends shown in Table 26
also support the notion of general convergence in the per capita
weight of manufacturing. As before, the trends in the East North
Central region indicate that a rapid rise above the national
average had occurred by the end of the nineteenth century, but
convergence toward the national average appeared in the relatives
for the past two decades. In all other regions the trends were

TABLE 25

LINEAR TRENDS IN PER CAPITA VALUE ADDED RELATIVES, 1860-1970

State or Region	Hypothesized Sign of $\hat{b}$	Regression Equation $(y = \hat{a} + \hat{b}x)$	$\hat{\sigma}_b$	r^2
New England	$-$[a]	$y = 282.583 - 16.586x$	1.2404	.9470
Middle Atlantic	$-$	$y = 183.536 - 6.104x$	.9059	.8195
East North Central	$+$	$y = 80.238 + 7.488x$	1.1950	.7969
West North Central	$+$	$y = 46.390 + 1.546x$	.8126	.2657
South Atlantic	$+$	$y = 19.818 + 4.594x$	.4422	.9152
East South Central	$+$	$y = 16.818 + 4.089x$	.8517	.6974
West South Central	$+$	$y = 13.205 + 3.470x$	.7677	.6714
Maine	0	$y = 117.983 + 3.500x$	.9195	.5917
New Hampshire	$-$	$y = 219.656 - 12.277x$	1.2086	.9117
Vermont	$+$	$y = 99.199 - 1.821x$	.8966	.2920
Massachusetts	$-$	$y = 358.130 - 25.690x$	2.1534	.9344
Rhode Island	$-$	$y = 438.821 - 34.010x$	2.7691	.9378
Connecticut	$-$	$y = 336.494 - 18.455x$	2.0007	.8948
New York	$-$	$y = 201.989 - 8.443x$	1.6451	.7248
New Jersey	$-$	$y = 190.187 - 3.592x$	1.5335	.3542
Pennsylvania	$-$	$y = 179.350 - 5.845x$	.5736	.9122
Delaware	$-$	$y = 136.600 - 1.005x$	1.4981	.0430
Maryland	$+$	$y = 102.917 - .936x$	1.2487	.9532
Ohio	$+$	$y = 98.908 + 6.376x$	1.2108	.7349
Indiana	$+$	$y = 44.947 + 10.604x$	.8888	.9343
Illinois	$+$	$y = 88.610 + 6.127x$	2.1166	.4559
Michigan	$+$	$y = 74.727 + 9.600x$	2.0668	.6833
Wisconsin	$+$	$y = 74.971 + 3.117x$	2.7553	.1135
Minnesota	$+$	$y = 46.677 + 2.572x$	.7267	.5562
Iowa	$+$	$y = 23.347 + 4.176x$	.6197	.8196
Missouri	$+$	$y = 70.114 + 1.494x$	1.1649	.1413
Kansas	$+$	$y = 31.495 + 2.107x$	1.0374	.2920
Nebraska	$+$	$y = 40.142 + .129x$	1.0141	.0016
Dakotas	$+$	$y = 10.823 + .328x$	.2175	.2019
Virginia	$+$	$y = 28.209 + 4.460x$	.5349	.8837
West Virginia	$+$	$y = 32.995 + 4.557x$	.6751	.8351
North Carolina	$+$	$y = 6.541 + 8.449x$	.9282	.8923
South Carolina	$+$	$y = 3.690 + 6.491x$	.8097	.8654
Georgia	$+$	$y = 14.419 + 4.633x$	.5396	.8805
Florida	$+$	$y = 38.960 + .086x$	1.1475	.0006
Kentucky	$+$	$y = 37.971 + 1.977x$	1.2989	.1880
Tennessee	$+$	$y = 13.021 + 5.795x$	.8523	.8221
Alabama	$+$	$y = 6.196 + 5.469x$	.6323	.8821
Mississippi	$+$	$y = 5.927 + 2.759x$	.7497	.5752
Arkansas	$+$	$y = 4.109 + 3.656x$	.9038	.6207
Louisiana	$+$	$y = 32.269 + 1.578x$	1.2405	.1393
Texas	$+$	$y = 4.559 + 4.970x$	.7550	.8125

[a]The hypothesis of a significant negative trend is indicated by a $-$, a significant positive trend is indicated by a $+$, and the absence of any trend is indicated by a 0.

Source: See text.

TABLE 26

PER CAPITA MANUFACTURING VALUE ADDED RELATIVES, AGGREGATE MANUFACTURING
(U.S. = 100.0)

State or Region	1860	1870	1880	1890	1900	1910
New England	274.1	263.1	287.2	227.5	209.4	194.9
Middle Atlantic	163.0	166.7	179.6	176.3	174.6	160.3
East North Central	63.4	76.5	91.0	113.3	116.0	127.6
West North Central	48.6	66.9	43.2	52.2	50.9	42.5
South Atlantic	32.1	21.8	22.3	26.7	34.9	45.1
East South Central	30.5	23.7	21.7	29.5	30.1	37.4
West South Central	30.9	19.9	13.9	17.5	21.8	29.6
Maine	98.4	108.9	115.5	117.9	114.2	113.7
New Hampshire	211.1	192.3	228.3	173.3	174.3	165.0
Vermont	77.0	103.6	100.8	97.0	108.5	100.6
Massachusetts	374.9	341.0	351.9	262.7	226.7	209.6
Rhode Island	475.3	396.9	430.2	285.9	280.8	240.7
Connecticut	347.7	317.3	350.5	248.2	249.3	223.5
New York	167.1	171.9	198.4	206.0	189.9	177.3
New Jersey	197.9	158.8	201.6	155.0	179.9	179.4
Pennsylvania	167.9	182.5	169.3	160.0	168.5	145.7
Delaware	136.6	118.5	134.8	165.5	139.0	115.8
Maryland	90.1	84.9	104.9	117.9	112.2	96.3
Ohio	86.0	93.3	105.2	128.9	124.2	137.5
Indiana	44.4	59.0	60.6	69.5	87.8	96.9
Illinois	49.0	67.9	101.4	142.6	145.5	143.9
Michigan	65.4	91.6	88.0	92.4	86.4	119.7
Wisconsin	55.6	65.9	81.5	91.0	99.7	111.8
Minnesota	34.6	44.1	62.5	65.3	64.5	65.9
Iowa	31.3	32.4	32.6	35.1	34.8	42.6
Missouri	59.3	107.0	60.9	78.5	69.6	71.3
Kansas	58.8	28.8	21.2	36.5	37.0	47.5
Nebraska	52.7	45.8	20.9	40.8	52.2	43.0
Dakotas	- -	12.0	14.4	10.2	12.5	10.9
Virginia	- -	25.7	31.3	36.9	38.9	48.9
West Virginia	- -	42.9	36.4	29.7	45.6	60.5
North Carolina	25.1	12.9	12.8	17.7	31.7	46.0
South Carolina	19.3	12.5	16.8	17.5	25.5	33.0
Georgia	24.7	22.8	20.1	27.3	29.9	35.2
Florida	40.7	25.4	23.9	37.5	56.5	66.4
Kentucky	51.4	41.5	42.4	51.0	44.7	52.3
Tennessee	28.4	24.9	20.9	28.1	29.5	37.3
Alabama	20.6	11.5	10.1	22.9	27.1	31.2
Mississippi	16.9	9.4	6.3	9.8	14.8	26.0
Arkansas	14.8	8.6	6.8	13.9	21.3	27.2
Louisiana	49.8	35.5	24.2	31.5	38.0	57.5
Texas	19.8	12.9	11.4	17.1	19.5	26.0

TABLE 26
(Continued)

State or Region	1920	1930	1940	1950	1960	1970
New England	180.1	148.2	148.0	127.3	123.5	113.0
Middle Atlantic	152.0	141.7	136.0	123.0	119.0	107.4
East North Central	136.7	147.3	150.4	156.8	140.3	137.8
West North Central	45.8	52.5	51.9	58.4	69.0	76.8
South Atlantic	49.0	53.3	58.4	59.5	65.9	72.0
East South Central	30.7	34.9	39.6	48.0	62.8	82.8
West South Central	29.3	29.2	32.5	42.4	55.2	65.3
Maine	108.5	81.7	92.5	79.6	75.2	78.7
New Hampshire	156.2	118.2	110.1	106.1	103.8	86.9
Vermont	84.3	80.3	74.4	87.2	76.9	79.6
Massachusetts	187.6	150.4	141.6	124.8	123.6	107.2
Rhode Island	226.3	176.2	171.8	124.2	113.8	99.1
Connecticut	210.9	187.5	208.3	169.2	156.8	150.7
New York	155.5	147.6	127.5	113.3	112.9	99.2
New Jersey	183.2	163.8	188.5	161.0	148.5	127.6
Pennsylvania	146.8	133.1	129.3	123.8	119.9	119.6
Delaware	147.6	108.4	106.5	144.6	121.7	133.9
Maryland	91.9	96.7	120.0	99.3	91.0	68.0
Ohio	156.7	162.5	158.3	160.4	150.0	144.7
Indiana	101.9	131.1	145.6	155.8	141.2	145.4
Illinois	123.1	143.5	143.4	145.6	132.0	129.8
Michigan	174.2	159.5	176.0	185.6	146.1	145.4
Wisconsin	112.5	120.8	112.6	125.1	124.6	116.9
Minnesota	56.8	59.0	57.2	64.4	72.8	82.8
Iowa	38.1	49.0	49.6	56.5	69.7	84.1
Missouri	65.0	80.0	79.9	81.9	94.4	92.2
Kansas	37.8	40.8	34.0	51.5	59.4	69.7
Nebraska	36.0	32.5	27.0	32.6	45.9	60.8
Dakotas	9.4	10.4	12.4	12.4	14.7	17.8
Virginia	48.6	58.6	72.9	63.9	63.9	66.0
West Virginia	56.4	54.4	58.1	70.4	75.6	83.6
North Carolina	66.9	81.7	78.7	73.2	86.8	102.6
South Carolina	37.4	34.2	46.0	64.6	75.6	90.3
Georgia	35.9	37.9	46.7	57.0	66.2	75.1
Florida	51.3	34.5	32.0	25.4	38.3	41.3
Kentucky	27.1	33.7	33.9	52.0	68.2	87.9
Tennessee	37.2	46.1	56.5	57.0	75.7	97.1
Alabama	33.6	36.4	44.9	54.0	63.2	79.8
Mississippi	23.3	20.0	17.3	20.6	33.9	54.9
Arkansas	22.9	19.0	17.8	26.9	44.3	67.1
Louisiana	56.1	43.8	43.5	54.6	50.5	56.9
Texas	26.2	29.5	36.3	47.1	63.4	73.5

Source: See text.

toward the national average and they were significant in every region except the West South Central.

Regional per capita value added relatives at the two-digit level are presented in Table 27. The data indicate that a general convergence toward the national average per capita output level was characteristic of most industries during the past century and that most of the convergence occurred after 1900. A convenient means of analyzing the trends in Table 27 is provided by summing the differences from the national average as follows:

$$\sum_{r=1}^{n} d_r^i$$

where d refers to the absolute value of the difference between the national average (100.0) and the regional per capita relative, r designates the n regions, 1, . . ., n, and i refers to the ith industry. Regional convergence is indicated by a decline in the sum of the differences; as the sum of the differences approaches zero, perfect convergence is indicated. Calculation of the sum of differences, given in Table 28, indicates a sharp narrowing of regional per capita output differences in all industries except lumber and wood products and petroleum and coal products.[4] The figures also reveal that there was very little change in the per capita spatial distribution of manufacturing during 1860-1900 and that regional convergence was marked during 1900-1970. Industry comparisons of per capita spatial concentration are also permitted on the basis of the data in Table 28. For example, it is apparent that in 1970 the greatest regional differences existed in textiles, petroleum and coal products, and instruments.

An examination of two-digit industry movements in the spatial concentration of production relative to population can be provided for the individual states by use of the entropy concept. Entropy is a measure used in communication and the physical sciences to determine the degree of disorder or randomness.[5] For example, if there are i possible events (i = 1, . . ., n) that can occur and the probability of the ith event is denoted

TABLE 27

PER CAPITA MANUFACTURING VALUE ADDED RELATIVES, TWO DIGIT INDUSTRIES

(U.S. = 100.0)

1860

SIC Code Number and Industry	New England	Middle Atlantic	East North Central	West North Central	South Atlantic	East South Central	West South Central
20 Food	75.9	162.1	131.0	106.9	34.5	44.8	37.9
21 Tobacco	60.0	100.0	20.0	100.0	260.0	60.0	20.0
22 Textiles	617.1	108.6	8.6	8.6	20.0	14.3	5.7
23 Apparel	221.1	226.3	47.4	15.8	5.3	10.5	31.6
24 Lumber and Wood Products	134.8	117.4	117.4	117.4	56.5	65.2	95.7
25 Furniture	200.0	166.7	116.7	33.3	16.7	16.7	16.7
26 Paper	400.0	150.0	25.0	2.0	25.0	2.5	0.0
27 Printing and Publishing	142.9	257.1	57.1	28.6	14.3	28.6	14.3
28 Chemicals	128.6	200.0	42.9	28.6	85.7	14.3	14.3
29 Petroleum and Coal Products	175.0	200.0	50.0	50.0	25.0	25.0	7.5
30 Rubber	400.0	200.0	-	-	-	-	-
31 Leather and Leather Products	418.5	144.4	44.4	29.6	18.5	29.6	29.6
32 Stone, Clay and Glass	155.6	211.1	66.7	66.7	33.3	22.2	44.4
33 Primary Metals	166.7	222.2	55.6	50.0	27.8	27.8	5.6
34 Fabricated Metals	345.5	154.5	63.6	45.5	18.2	36.4	36.4
35 Non-electrical Machinery	240.0	160.0	93.3	40.0	26.7	40.0	46.7
36 Electrical Machinery	-	-	-	-	-	-	-
37 Transportation Equipment	225.0	175.0	66.7	41.7	50.0	50.0	41.7
38 Instruments	400.0	200.0	10.0	5.0	-	0.0	-
39 Miscellaneous	344.4	200.0	33.3	22.2	2.2	11.1	11.1
Total	274.1	163.0	63.4	48.6	32.1	30.5	30.9

TABLE 27
(Continued)

1900

SIC Code Number and Industry	New England	Middle Atlantic	East North Central	West North Central	South Atlantic	East South Central	West South Central
20 Food	96.1	135.3	162.7	93.1	21.6	37.3	41.2
21 Tobacco	37.5	170.8	83.3	95.8	137.8	75.0	12.5
22 Textiles	603.4	163.8	13.8	3.4	70.7	17.2	3.4
23 Apparel	133.3	255.6	92.1	39.7	9.5	15.9	12.7
24 Lumber and Wood Products	114.6	81.3	141.7	70.8	95.8	89.6	93.8
25 Furniture	178.6	150.0	185.7	42.9	21.4	21.4	14.3
26 Paper	438.5	192.3	92.3	15.4	15.4	2.0	2.0
27 Printing and Publishing	164.1	197.4	110.3	71.8	17.9	23.1	25.6
28 Chemicals	120.8	208.3	100.0	41.7	87.5	37.5	8.3
29 Petroleum and Coal Products	125.0	233.3	108.3	58.3	16.7	16.7	16.7
30 Rubber	766.7	83.3	50.0	16.7	-	1.0	-
31 Leather and Leather Products	458.6	141.4	82.8	44.8	20.7	20.7	13.8
32 Stone, Clay and Glass	161.0	202.4	112.2	53.7	22.0	19.5	14.6
33 Primary Metals	88.2	241.2	119.6	21.6	27.5	35.3	2.0
34 Fabricated Metals	225.0	140.6	178.1	43.8	9.4	12.5	9.4
35 Non-electrical Machinery	223.0	182.0	139.3	29.5	11.5	18.0	8.2
36 Electrical Machinery	-	-	-	-	-	-	-
37 Transportation Equipment	111.8	147.1	144.1	79.4	41.2	35.3	35.3
38 Instruments	275.0	225.0	75.0	25.0	3.0	8.0	8.8
39 Miscellaneous	351.9	188.9	92.6	29.6	3.7	7.4	3.7
Total	209.4	174.6	116.0	50.9	34.9	30.1	21.8

TABLE 27
(Continued)

1970

SIC Code Number and Industry	New England	Middle Atlantic	East North Central	West North Central	South Atlantic	East South Central	West South Central
20 Food	62.5	97.5	122.7	146.9	68.0	89.2	82.6
21 Tobacco	- -[a]	- -	- -	- -	- -	- -	- -
22 Textiles	132.7	70.8	14.8	5.0	391.1	108.9	11.9
23 Apparel	82.7	200.6	40.3	41.7	97.8	132.3	49.1
24 Lumber and Wood Products	106.5	48.4	80.0	64.7	147.0	219.1	127.0
25 Furniture	81.1	80.8	114.0	51.3	170.6	121.1	52.1
26 Paper	163.3	90.2	110.7	62.9	108.3	114.7	69.9
27 Printing and Publishing	104.3	159.4	116.9	92.8	42.9	49.7	44.6
28 Chemicals	61.0	122.9	93.3	57.7	95.1	129.0	120.9
29 Petroleum and Coal Products	13.1	59.6	89.0	78.4	16.7	39.7	426.6
30 Rubber	162.1	83.1	172.5	72.7	45.2	99.6	42.9
31 Leather and Leather Products	- -[a]	- -	- -	- -	- -	- -	- -
32 Stone, Clay and Glass	75.3	109.1	126.0	85.7	89.0	81.5	73.0
33 Primary Metals	69.6	126.2	188.1	29.3	28.3	87.5	41.9
34 Fabricated Metals	116.0	91.2	191.8	63.1	37.5	63.6	50.6
35 Non-electrical Machinery	144.8[b]	102.4	173.9	82.4	35.3	63.2	38.3
36 Electrical Machinery	- -	- -	- -	- -	- -	- -	- -
37 Transportation Equipment	95.0	67.9	200.9	87.6	36.8	39.4	65.1
38 Instruments	230.1	202.9	80.6	52.2	21.8	21.1	26.0
39 Miscellaneous	284.1	149.8	92.6	61.8	40.6	58.3	30.4
Total	113.0	107.4	137.8	76.8	72.0	82.8	65.3

[a] As a result of disclosure problems, it was impossible to calculate per capita relatives for SIC 21 and 31 in 1970.

[b] In order to facilitate comparisons with the nineteenth century, all machinery production is included in SIC 35.

TABLE 28

SUM OF THE ABSOLUTE VALUE OF THE RELATIVE REGIONAL DIFFERENCES

FROM NATIONAL PER CAPITA VALUE ADDED

SIC Code Number and Industry	1860	1900	1970
20 Food	306.9	308.7	169.8
21 Tobacco	420.0	304.2	- -[a]
22 Textiles	968.5	958.7	630.2
23 Apparel	636.8	519.0	321.3
24 Lumber and Wood Products	169.6	125.0	306.5
25 Furniture	500.0	514.3	240.4
26 Paper	795.5	803.7	174.0
27 Printing and Publishing	557.1	433.4	250.6
28 Chemicals	442.8	354.1	165.7
29 Petroleum and Coal Products	517.5	458.2	630.1
30 Rubber	900.0	1115.7	291.1
31 Leather and Leather Products	719.2	717.2	- -[a]
32 Stone, Clay and Glass	433.4	465.8	130.6
33 Primary Metals	522.1	486.2	357.7
34 Fabricated Metals	599.9	568.6	301.8
35 Non-electrical Machinery	453.3	577.1	301.9
36 Electrical Machinery	- -	- -	- -[a]
37 Transportation Equipment	449.9	311.8	309.1
38 Instruments	885.0	680.2	531.3
39 Miscellaneous	764.5	703.8	450.2
Total	531.6	462.3	161.3

[a]See notes to Table 27 (1970).

Source: See text.

by p_i, the entropy of the system (H) is denoted as follows:

$$H = \sum_{i=1}^{n} p_i \log \frac{1}{p_i}$$

In comparing the distribution of production relative to population across states, use of the entropy concept can be made by substituting value added shares for the p_i as follows:

$$H(y) = \sum_{i=1}^{n} y_i \log \frac{1}{y_i}$$

where y = value added shares, $\sum y_i = 1.00$, $y_i \geq 0$, and i refers to the i states = 1, . . ., n. If one state's share of value added is equal to one, then all others equal zero and H(y) equals zero, which is the minimum entropy value and the maximum degree of spatial concentration. If all states' value added shares are equal $(1/n)$, then H(y) equals log n, which is the maximum entropy value and the minimum degree of spatial concentration. In other words, entropy is an inverse measure of concentration in that the greater the entropy the lower the degree of concentration and vice versa.

The computation of H(y) alone is not that interesting for the purposes of this chapter since it yields a positive number, which in itself carries no information on the spatial distribution of value added relative to population. Therefore, population entropy has also been calculated:

$$H(P) = \sum_{i=1}^{n} P_i \log \frac{1}{P_i}$$

where P refers to population shares and all other symbols are as before. Then the entropy of production relative to population is calculated as R = H(y)/H(P). (See Table 29.) The conclusions suggested by Table 29 are the same as those reached earlier for the census regions. Sharp convergence in the spatial distribution of production relative to population occurred across the United States in virtually all manufacturing industries during the period

TABLE 29

STATE MANUFACTURING VALUE ADDED ENTROPY RELATIVE TO

POPULATION ENTROPY

SIC Code Number and Industry	1860	1900	1970
20 Food	.854	.858	.977[a]
21 Tobacco	.710	.814	- -[a]
22 Textiles	.720	.739	.755
23 Apparel	.679	.659	.837
24 Lumber and Wood Products	.975	.967	1.008
25 Furniture	.759	.793	.920
26 Paper	.707	.738	.971
27 Printing and Publishing	.645	.761	.847
28 Chemicals	.740	.825	.934
29 Petroleum and Coal Products	.674	.776	- -[a]
30 Rubber	.444	.582	- -[a]
31 Leather and Leather Products	.739	.773	- -[a]
32 Stone, Clay and Glass	.799	.803	.948
33 Primary Metals	.720	.611	.816
34 Fabricated Metals	.833	.782	.889
35 Non-electrical Machinery	.850	.784	.904
36 Electrical Machinery	- -	- -	- -[b]
37 Transportation Equipment	.906	.906	.824
38 Instruments	.485	.688	.699
39 Miscellaneous	.643	.724	.876
Total	.848	.855	.956

[a]Disclosure problems do not permit calculations for SIC 21, 29, 30, and 31 for 1970.

[b]See note b to Table 27 (1970).

Source: See text.

1860-1970, with most of this movement occurring in the twentieth century. The only industries in which divergence occurred were textiles and transportation equipment. In 1860 there were only five industries (20, 24, 34, 35, and 37) in which production entropy reached 80 percent of population entropy; in 1970 production entropy was in excess of 80 percent of population entropy in all industries except textiles and instruments.

This chapter has utilized several conceptually different measures to examine the spatial distribution of manufacturing industry vis-à-vis population during the period 1860-1970. In all cases, the results point to a rather sharp convergence of state and regional industrial structure. It is perhaps not surprising to most readers to find that, relative to population, aggregate manufacturing became less spatially concentrated during this period. The West and the South had certain resource advantages over the northeastern states and much of the early manufacturing was indeed centered on resource processing industries.[6] However, this chapter has demonstrated that the relative advance of manufacturing in the West and South during the past century was not only concerned with utilizing particular resource advantages of the regions but was broadly based across the two-digit industries as well. The net result of the spatial redistribution of manufacturing across the United States was a sharp movement toward more localized manufacturing in virtually all industries rather than concentrated state and regional patterns of specialization.

NOTES

1. The census manufacturing surveys included some nonmanufacturing throughout the period 1860-1920. It was mentioned earlier that the 1860 census included, as manufacturing, much construction, mining, forestry, and hand trades such as blacksmithing, carpentering, and plumbing. There was a progression to more accurate accounting procedures, and, by 1920,

the only significant nonmanufacturing item included in the census was automobile repairing. The value added series for each census year has been adjusted to net out nonmanufacturing activity.

As before, the national average referred to is the average for the seven census regions.

2. The use of entropy to measure the spatial concentration of manufacturing industry is developed later in this chapter. See note 5 for sources dealing with the concept of entropy and its application in measuring industrial concentration.

3. The regression analysis for Virginia, West Virginia, and the Dakotas is for the period 1870-1970.

4. It would be an enormous statistical task to use linear regression analysis to examine two-digit industry state and regional trends since the manufacturing data were not aggregated and presented at the two-digit level for states and regions until the *1947 Census of Manufactures.*

5. See Claude E. Shannon and Warren Weaver, *The Mathematical Theory of Communication* (Urbana: The University of Illinois Press, 1964), pp. 8-22 and 36-50. For application of the entropy concept to the measurement of industrial concentration, see the following: Ann and Ira Horowitz, "Entropy, Markov Processes and Competition in the Brewing Industry," *Journal of Industrial Economics,* July 1968, pp. 196-211; Ira Horowitz, "Numbers-Equivalents in U.S. Manufacturing Industries: 1954, 1958 and 1963," *Southern Economic Journal,* April 1971, pp. 396-408; and Henri Theil, *Economics and Information Theory* (Amsterdam: North Holland Publishing Co., 1967), pp. 290-293.

6. The resource-intensive nature of much nineteenth century southern and western manufacturing, evident throughout this book, was highlighted in Chapter 3.

5

Summary and Conclusions

This study has provided a careful review of state and regional industrial development in the United States during the late nineteenth century. Major emphasis was placed on an examination of manufacturing structure and spatial concentration patterns. In most cases, the major conclusions suggested by this study were related to and consistent with the traditional views on American manufacturing during this period. The traditional view of antebellum manufacturing focuses on the general concentration of manufacturing in the Northeast, especially New York, Pennsylvania, and Massachusetts, and on the resource-oriented nature of southern and western manufacturing. The data in this study contribute strong support to the argument of northeastern domination of mid-nineteenth century American manufacturing, but modify the argument on southern and western manufacturing because of the significant development in several nonprocessing industries that catered to local demand. The often cited drift of late nineteenth century manufacturing from the Northeast to the West and South was documented, and it was shown that a substantial portion of this change in spatial concentration reflected gains in Ohio and Illinois. Manufacturing in the remainder of the West and South was relatively insignificant, consisting primarily of resource processing or light industry.

In addition to analyzing changes in manufacturing structure and spatial concentration, this study also analyzed several factors which may have affected industrial location decisions during the late nineteenth century. It was concluded that neither the classical comparative cost doctrine nor the Heckscher-Ohlin hypothesis was especially useful in explaining these decisions. The analysis suggested that the mobile factors of production, labor and capital, were relatively unimportant in determining the locational pattern of manufacturing during 1860-1900. Rather, the immobile factors such as resource supplies, access to local demand, economies of scale, and external economies accounted for this pattern.

Trends in the per capita dispersion of manufacturing development during the period 1860-1970, both in the aggregate and at the two-digit level, were also examined. The analysis revealed that there has been a rather steady narrowing of state and regional structural differences, both in terms of the quantitative weight of total manufacturing and the relative degree of concentration on most of the two-digit industries. This state and regional structural convergence was evident during the late nineteenth century but its pace has quickened in recent decades.

While this study qualifies the traditional views of nineteenth century American manufacturing development, its general conclusions corroborate commonly accepted notions. What is new in this study is the careful preparation of empirical evidence that supports these views. The statistical reconstruction of the past, which has been the focal point of much of the new economic history, can provide an invaluable data base for study of the American economy. Such an approach is needed to clarify the issues and to refine our understanding of the essential features of American economic development. The value of this work to the new economic historian, then, is its synthesis of statistical information on state and regional manufacturing development in late nineteenth century America. The appendix series of two-digit estimates of current dollar value added, employment, labor costs, capital invested, output-labor ratios, capital-output ratios, and capital-labor ratios can serve as the basis for research into industry productivity trends during the late nineteenth century, state and regional comparative efficiency within particular industries, and state, regional, and industry variation in factor proportions. It is hoped that this study will promote research in these areas and stimulate new ideas concerning the industrialization of the American economy.

Appendix

The following lists present the 1860 and 1900 census manufacturing categories included in the Standard Industrial Classification two-digit categories.

20 Food and Kindred Products

Arrowroot, baking and yeast cakes and powders, pearl barley, bee-hives, bone boiling, bone dust, bottling, bread and crackers, breweries, butter, cheese, chocolate, cider, cocoa, ground coffee and spices, cordials and syrups, coffee roasting, confectionery, canned fish and oysters, flour and meal, food preparations, canned and preserved fruits and vegetables, ginseng, glucose, grease, hemlock bark extract, hides and tallow, hominy, prepared husks, ice, liquor coloring, liquors, refined lard, macaroni and vermicelli, malt, condensed milk, mineral water, slaughtering and meat packing, refined molasses, mustard, oleomargarine, cocoanut oil, cottonseed oil, fish and whale oil, lard oil, linseed oil, neatsfoot oil, animal oil, vegetable oil, prepared moss, provisions, pickles, preserves and sauces, rice cleaning and polishing, rice flour, syrups, soda water, starch, sugar refining, vinegar, vegetable extract.

21 Tobacco and Tobacco Products

Cigars, cigarettes, tobacco.

22 Textile Mill Products

Bagging, calico printing, carpets, cloth finishing, cotton thread, oil cloths, coach lace, cordage and twine, cotton batting and wadding, cotton coverlets, cotton flannel, cotton goods, cotton twine and yarn, dyeing and bleaching, dyeing and finishing textiles, felt goods, felting, dressed flax, flax and linen goods, hair cloth, hosiery, knit goods, linen goods, jute and jute goods, mats and rugs, mixed textiles, linen belting and hose, oakum, oil and enameled cloth, rigging, printing cotton and woolen goods, satinet printing, shoddy, sewing and twist silk, silk goods, thread, upholstery, webbing, wool carding, cleaning and pulling, woolen goods, woolen yarn, worsted goods.

23 Apparel and Related Products

Awnings and tents, bags other than paper, belts, cap fronts, clothing, cotton bags, collars and cuffs, corsets, cotton lamp wick, cotton mosquito netting, cotton table cloths, curtains, costumes, embroidery, fly nets, fringe and trimmings, men's furnishing goods, gloves and mittens, hats and caps, hoop skirts, hatter's trimmings, hat tips, horse covers, lace goods, millinery and dress making, nets, quilts, sails, seines, shirts, shoe strings, silk and fancy goods, skirt supporters, straw bonnet bleaching, straw goods, suspenders.

24 Lumber and Wood Products

Baskets, barrel heading, cheese, cigar, sugar, tobacco and packing boxes, box shooks, broom handles, brush handles, carving, clock case materials, grain cradles, cooperage, corks, hat and bonnet blocks, lasts and boot trees, looking glass and picture frames, lumber, mast hoops and hanks, masts and spars, oars, plough handles, wooden drain pipe, wooden pipe, shoe pegs, sash, doors and blinds, scythe rifles, shingles and lath, scythe snaths, splints, stair rods, staves, heading, hoops and shooks, trunk and carpet bag frames, wood turning, scroll sawing, vats, veneers, ratan, wooden clothes frames, wooden door knobs, wooden screws, wooden ware, wooden skewers, wood carpets, wood preserving, miscellaneous wood work.

25 Furniture and Fixtures

Furniture, cabinet ware, hammocks, house furnishing goods, n.e.c., chairs, mattresses and beds, medicine chests, paper shades, pianoforte stools, sewing machine cases, bed springs, show cases, umbrella furniture, venetian blinds, willow furniture, window blinds and shades.

26 Paper and Allied Products

Boot and shoe patterns, paper bags, paper boxes, card boards, card cutting, dress patterns, envelopes, fancy boxes, filter bags, paper ornaments, paper goods, n.e.c., wood pulp, paper, paper ruling, patterns and models, stationery, valentines.

27 Printing and Publishing

Book binding and blank books, cards, card cutting and designing, charts, daguerreotypists, engraving, lithography, map mounting and coloring, maps and atlases, music printing, paper staining, printing and publishing, photolithographing and photoengraving, show cards, stereotyping and electrotyping.

28 Chemicals and Allied Products

Acid, alcohol, pot and pearl ashes, ground bark, blueing, brimstone, barilla, benzoline, blacking, water proof composition, bone-black, camphene and burning fluid, charcoal, chemicals, ground drugs, dye woods and dye stuffs, ethereal oil, explosives, fertilizers, fireworks, flax dressing, furniture polish, glue, gum and gum cleaning, graphite, gunpowder, hemp dressing, ink, ivory black, lamp-black, lye, medicines, mucilage and paste, nitro-glycerine, patent medicines and compounds, ochre, castor oil, rosin and water oil, chemical and essential oil, paint, polishing preparations, cleaning preparations, perfumery and fancy soap, percussion caps, putty, druggists' preparations, pyrotechnics, quicksilver, rosin, red lead, safety-fuse, saleratus, saltpetre and nitrate of soda, soap, stove polish, ground sumac, sulphur, tar and turpentine, varnish, washing blue, white lead, whiting, oxide of zinc, zinc paint.

29 Petroleum and Coal Products

Gas, axle grease, kerosene, lubricating oil, coal oil, brewer's and burgundy pitch, paving materials, roofing composition, oil, n.e.c., petroleum refining, tar.

30 Rubber and Plastics Products

Gutta percha goods, india rubber goods, celluloid and celluloid goods, rubber and elastic goods, rubber belting and hose, rubber boots and shoes, vulcanized rubber.

31 Leather and Leather Products

Boots and shoes, carpet bags, fire hose, bellows, leather belting and hose, leather, riveted hose, leather-board, pocket books, portemonnaies, razor strops, saddlery and harness, shoe findings, trunks, valises and seamen's chests, whips.

32 Stone, Clay, and Glass Products

Aquariums, artificial building stone, brick, cement, crucibles, cement pipe, cisterns, chimney flues, earthenware, emery, fire-brick, foundry facings, glass, grindstones, isinglass, japanned ware, lime, looking glasses, kaolin and other earth grinding, mirrors, marble and stone work, millstones, slate and marble mantles, plaster and terra cotta ornaments, plaster, porcelain ware, pottery and stone ware, milled quartz, sand paper, school slates, tile, terra cotta ware, water lime.

33 Primary Metals Products

Brass and bell founding, anchors and chains, brass and copper tubing, babbitt metal and solder, brass and copper founding and finishing, brass and copper rolled, bronze castings, rolled brass and German silver, brass wire and cloth, bronze powders, coke, copper smelting and refining, galvanizing, cast iron, forged, rolled and wrought iron and steel, pig iron, iron blooms, iron and steel pipe, bar and sheet lead, pig lead, lead pipe, lead shot, lead smelting and refining, repaired and white metal, metal spinning, nails, smelted nickel, horse-shoe nails, spelter, steel, stoves, wire, wire cloth, wired steel, wire rope, smelted and rolled zinc.

34 Fabricated Metals Products

Miscellaneous agricultural implements, anvils and vices, bank locks, bath tubs, bells, blacksmith's tools, bolts, nuts and washers, brass and copper ware, bookbinder's tools, brass ornaments, candle moulds, carpenter's tools, confectioner's tools, cooper's tools, coppersmithing, copper work, currier's tools, cutlery, die-sinking, edge tools and axes, electroplating, files, fire-escapes, furnaces, hatter's tools, hinges, gas tanks, grates and fenders, gunlocks, handspikes, hardware, hoes, horse-shoes, hydrant cases, hydrants, iron and steel doors and shutters, jack screws, jeweler's dies and tools, metallic keys, lightning rods, wrought iron railing, metallic caps and labels, metal cocks and faucets, metal type, money drawers, mowing machine knives, oil tanks, architectural and ornamental ironwork, pipe tongs, plugs and wedges, plumber's materials, powder flasks, rakes, sad-irons, safes and vaults, metal sash, screws, sinks, saws, straw cutters, scythes, shoe and boot tips, shoemaker's tools, shovels, spades and forks, car, carriage, locomotive and other springs, sieves and bird cages, steam and gas fittings and valves, steam heaters and heating apparatus, stone-cutter's tools, tin, copper and sheet iron ware, tin and terne plate, tinfoil, tinned iron ware, vats, wire work, zinc statuary and building ornaments.

35 Non-electrical Machinery

Bookbinder's machinery, blocks and pumps, brick machinery, carpet sweepers, calcium lights, cheese presses, cultivators, churns, coffee roasters, cotton gins, chandeliers, dumb waiters, bobbin and spools, burglar and till alarms, grain drills, electro-magnetic machines, engraver's blocks, electrical apparatus and supplies, fans, foundry and machine shop products, car fare registers, gas fixtures and lamps, portable forges, portable gas works, loom harness, hoisting apparatus, harrows, mowing and reaping machinery, horse powers, jeweler's machinery, machinery (cotton and woolen, hay and cotton presses, paper, rice machines, ribbon looms, shingle machines, silk, stump, turbine water wheels, wood working, steam engines), machinist's tools, mineral water apparatus, fanning mills, newspaper directing machines, ploughs, printer's chases and rollers, printing and lithographic presses, pumps and hydraulic rams, cash registers, refrigerators and water coolers, scales and balances, seal and copying presses, sewing birds, sewing machines, sewing machine shuttles, shoe peg machines, separators, steering apparatus, sugar evaporators, sugar moulds, soda water apparatus, type-writers and supplies, tinner's tools and machines, type, threshers, vault lights, washing machines and clothes dryers, watchmaker's lathes, windlasses.

36 Electrical Machinery

The small amount of electrical machinery that appeared at the end of the nineteenth century was included in SIC category 35.

37 Transportation Equipment

Axles, car brakes, car linings, car fixtures, carriages, carriage trimmings, cars, omnibuses, fire engines, iron steamships, locomotives, spokes, hubs, felloes, shafts and bows, car wheels, ship and boat building, wheelbarrows, wagons and carts.

38 Instruments and Related Products

Artificial eyes, artificial limbs, cameras, clocks, dentists' materials, gasometers, gas machines and meters, gas retorts, instruments, optical goods, photographic apparatus, photographic materials, shoulder braces, speaking tubes, steam and water gauges, spectacles and eye glasses, surgical applicances, porcelain teeth, trusses, bandages and supporters, weather vanes, watches, watch and clock materials, watch cases, water meters.

39 Miscellaneous Manufacturing (includes Ordnance)

Ammunition, artist's materials, artificial feathers, flowers and fruits, bead work, belt clasps and slides, bicycles and tricycles, baseball goods, billiard cues, billiard and bagatelle tables, brass book clasps and badges, brooms, brush blocks, brushes, buttons, canes, candles, candle sticks, children's carriages and sleds, chalk and crayons, china and glass decorating, clock cases, coffins, comb plates, combs, curled hair, curtain fixtures, coconut dippers, croquet sets, enameling, fire-arms, fancy articles, n.e.c., fans, feathers, firebomb lances, fish hooks, fishing lines, nets and tackle, flags and banners, furs, gold and silver leaf and foil, gilding, glaziers diamonds, globes, gold and silver assaying and refining, hand stamps, hunting and fishing tackle, hair jewelry, hooks and eyes, jewelry, jewelry boxes and cases, lapidaries work, labels and tags, life preservers, matches, military goods, musical instruments, mops and dusters, needles, needle threaders, ordnance, pearl goods, pins, tobacco pipes, pencils, slate pencils, pens, penholders, percussion caps, regalias, banners and flags, ivory and wood rulers, reeds, sewing machine fixtures, silversmithing, sporting goods, stamped ware, stationery goods, n.e.c., sieve hoops, signs, silver manufactures, silver plated and Britannia ware, stencils and brands, stencil tools, stereoscopic cases, stuffed birds, teasels, tapes and binding, toy books and games, toys, ivory and bone turning, umbrellas and parasols, wax work, whalebone, wigs and hair work.

MANUFACTURING VALUE ADDED BY REGION, 1860
(Thousands of dollars)

SIC Code Number and Industry	New England	Middle Atlantic	East North Central	West North Central	South Atlantic	East South Central	West South Central
20 Food	6874.1	38624.1	26175.4	6694.0	4516.7	5069.0	1914.9
21 Tobacco	884.0	4203.1	912.9	1124.6	5622.7	1339.8	165.0
22 Textiles	67690.9	31088.6	1900.3	752.8	3191.1	2017.4	343.5
23 Apparel	13142.3	35759.0	6335.1	666.6	372.7	801.9	1091.9
24 Lumber and Wood Products	9678.5	22265.9	18886.0	5751.3	5666.9	5877.3	3888.0
25 Furniture	3699.0	7845.8	4600.9	521.8	539.6	526.4	123.3
26 Paper	4905.2	4576.4	968.6	17.6	386.3	76.0	3.5
27 Printing and Publishing	3144.4	14507.9	2486.0	386.1	358.1	633.2	182.1
28 Chemicals	2954.8	11495.6	1978.3	377.5	2743.0	551.7	202.7
29 Petroleum and Coal Products	2184.3	6613.6	1107.6	472.4	406.6	574.7	54.0
30 Rubber	1261.4	1892.5	0.2	-	-	-	-
31 Leather	6109.7	14945.5	1937.4	292.6	991.4	1311.4	177.8
Leather Products	29455.0	217331.5	9310.0	1413.2	1247.1	1781.6	1169.1
32 Stone, Clay and Glass	4381.8	15300.2	3829.0	1378.9	1234.6	804.8	615.4
33 Primary Metals	9398.4	32938.4	6795.0	1936.2	2366.2	2020.7	92.9
34 Fabricated Metals	12050.3	14193.9	4751.2	1114.9	924.2	1429.3	782.0
35 Non-electrical Machinery	11289.0	19647.6	9962.4	1306.7	1754.7	2403.2	1267.9
36 Electrical Machinery	-	-	-	-	-	-	-
37 Transportation Equipment	8600.8	17039.6	5400.2	992.5	2640.8	2343.6	878.8
38 Instruments	1254.6	1800.8	60.9	11.4	-	3.5	-
39 Miscellaneous Manufacturing	9871.5	15023.5	1971.8	350.6	105.7	367.2	109.5
Total	208830.0	327093.5	106369.2	25561.7	35068.4	29932.7	13062.3

APPENDIX, PART III

MANUFACTURING VALUE ADDED BY STATE, 1860
(Thousands of dollars)

SIC Code Number and Industry	Maine	New Hampshire	Vermont	Massachusetts	Rhode Island	Connecticut	New York	New Jersey
20 Food	588.0	398.0	266.2	3879.7	1029.4	712.8	20812.5	2627.1
21 Tobacco	10.6	39.2	17.5	383.0	112.0	321.7	2169.7	376.3
22 Textiles	4034.0	8514.5	1508.0	32979.7	11465.4	9189.3	10582.3	3988.2
23 Apparel	841.8	711.9	132.3	6635.0	672.8	4148.5	19685.8	4192.9
24 Lumber and Wood Products	3111.7	1249.6	734.8	3385.6	356.3	840.5	11109.2	1590.9
25 Furniture	165.5	210.9	186.5	2711.6	117.1	307.4	5010.3	233.0
26 Paper	414.1	328.7	75.4	3018.4	27.5	1041.1	2325.9	641.9
27 Printing and Publishing	210.8	206.4	59.1	1987.6	169.1	511.4	8631.8	253.1
28 Chemicals	165.1	110.2	20.6	1494.9	132.9	1031.1	5431.0	1095.6
29 Petroleum and Coal Products	423.7	52.9	10.4	1386.9	135.5	174.9	4361.1	40.0
30 Rubber	- -	- -	- -	270.1	141.6	849.7	1218.4	666.9
31 Leather	718.8	533.8	283.1	4166.1	22.9	385.1	7145.2	1041.8
Leather Products	1073.9	1677.7	242.7	24286.3	289.8	1884.2	7733.4	2651.7
32 Stone, Clay and Glass	502.9	223.9	542.1	2559.2	150.8	403.1	6366.7	1851.9
33 Primary Metals	525.0	393.6	241.7	5592.7	586.8	2058.6	10331.6	3145.6
34 Fabricated Metals	493.0	410.6	263.4	4115.4	1347.0	5420.9	7303.0	1872.2
35 Non-electrical Machinery	664.8	615.4	810.9	5141.1	1450.0	2606.8	10501.2	1613.5
36 Electrical Machinery	- -	- -	- -	- -	- -	- -	- -	- -
37 Transportation Equipment	961.1	944.4	379.4	2958.5	251.9	3105.5	6643.6	3151.7
38 Instruments	1.5	- -	3.2	397.5	23.0	829.4	898.6	- -
39 Miscellaneous Manufacturing	119.1	122.0	115.2	4749.1	1687.5	3078.6	9285.2	1269.3
Total	15025.4	16743.6	5892.6	112098.4	20169.6	38900.7	157546.6	32303.5

APPENDIX, PART III
(continued)

SIC Code Number and Industry	Pennsyl-vania	Delaware	Maryland	Ohio	Indiana	Illinois	Michigan
20 Food	11916.4	334.7	2933.4	9131.7	4256.7	8074.9	1919.6
21 Tobacco	1117.0	59.2	480.9	593.8	101.2	119.1	33.3
22 Textiles	14375.0	449.4	1693.7	1081.5	467.8	123.0	119.6
23 Apparel	10194.2	90.0	1596.1	4764.1	373.8	463.2	253.5
24 Lumber and Wood Products	8533.4	215.3	817.1	5179.1	3668.9	2510.9	4380.9
25 Furniture	2187.5	32.2	382.8	2655.1	684.8	612.1	367.3
26 Paper	1297.1	98.6	212.9	693.2	83.4	33.8	64.2
27 Printing and Publishing	5279.4	58.1	285.5	1317.1	184.0	584.0	216.5
28 Chemicals	4500.0	273.7	195.3	1203.5	73.5	428.1	109.3
29 Petroleum and Coal Products	1937.0	22.7	252.8	714.1	24.8	266.6	24.9
30 Rubber	72.0	-	-	-	-	0.2	-
31 Leather	5077.0	326.1	703.1	1245.7	-	155.6	350.5
Leather Products	6491.5	158.8	948.4	2961.8	930.6	1074.3	724.2
32 Stone, Clay and Glass	6307.1	112.4	661.9	1846.8	378.6	875.6	423.9
33 Primary Metals	17836.0	160.2	1465.0	4685.6	261.2	828.7	666.5
34 Fabricated Metals	4398.7	128.8	491.2	1864.6	535.7	724.0	921.3
35 Non-electrical Machinery	6376.9	245.0	911.0	5225.3	1553.6	2219.6	618.6
36 Electrical Machinery	-	-	-	-	-	-	-
37 Transportation Equipment	5562.1	939.8	742.4	2293.9	954.8	1082.9	591.3
38 Instruments	873.7	-	28.5	42.3	-	4.7	11.8
39 Miscellaneous Manufacturing	4180.0	19.3	269.7	1427.3	79.6	226.1	143.3
Total	118447.2	3724.2	15071.6	48926.6	14612.9	20409.6	11940.5

APPENDIX, PART III
(continued)

SIC Code Number and Industry	Wisconsin	Minnesota	Iowa	Missouri	Kansas	Nebraska	Virginia
20 Food	2792.5	392.3	2026.1	4027.2	190.3	58.1	2631.2
21 Tobacco	65.5	4.7	26.5	1093.4	-	-	5139.5
22 Textiles	108.4	2.6	74.3	675.9	-	-	1074.5
23 Apparel	480.5	5.7	71.4	584.7	-	4.8	265.0
24 Lumber and Wood Products	3146.2	699.3	1239.8	2563.1	1024.6	224.5	1668.2
25 Furniture	281.6	61.6	196.3	250.4	8.6	4.9	221.0
26 Paper	94.0	-	10.8	6.8	-	-	139.8
27 Printing and Publishing	184.4	24.8	118.8	218.7	3.7	20.1	84.4
28 Chemicals	163.9	-	3.2	372.1	2.2	-	92.8
29 Petroleum and Coal Products	77.2	-	44.2	428.2	-	-	296.7
30 Rubber	-	-	-	-	-	-	-
31 Leather	185.5	5.8	96.1	190.0	0.7	-	532.8
Leather Products	619.2	103.4	327.4	947.5	15.0	19.9	672.7
32 Stone, Clay and Glass	304.1	5.6	95.4	1052.5	220.9	4.5	695.0
33 Primary Metals	353.0	24.5	89.7	1822.0	-	-	1976.1
34 Fabricated Metals	705.6	72.9	283.0	737.3	8.8	12.9	665.0
35 Non-electrical Machinery	345.3	0.5	293.3	992.9	20.0	-	661.3
36 Electrical Machinery	-	-	-	-	-	-	-
37 Transportation Equipment	477.3	28.5	151.1	771.3	36.4	5.2	1017.2
38 Instruments	2.1	-	-	11.4	-	-	-
39 Miscellaneous Manufacturing	95.5	9.0	12.0	310.1	4.7	14.8	77.9
Total	10481.8	1441.0	5159.5	17055.5	1535.9	369.8	17911.1

APPENDIX, PART III
(continued)

SIC Code Number and Industry	Alabama	Georgia	Mississippi	North Carolina	South Carolina	Kentucky	Tennessee
20 Food	306.3	855.2	123.2	643.7	376.8	3356.6	1228.9
21 Tobacco	2.7	29.5	5.0	453.7	-	879.6	452.5
22 Textiles	543.9	1118.3	141.4	574.6	305.7	1047.3	386.3
23 Apparel	30.9	62.8	70.1	11.1	31.1	600.5	100.4
24 Lumber and Wood Products	1349.5	1343.1	1216.2	831.2	859.0	1808.9	1502.7
25 Furniture	65.5	253.1	46.9	50.0	15.5	303.3	110.6
26 Paper	-	91.9	-	111.1	43.5	58.2	17.8
27 Printing and Publishing	51.6	192.1	58.2	66.6	13.1	230.0	293.4
28 Chemicals	298.6	111.8	1.0	2085.4	407.9	227.7	24.4
29 Petroleum and Coal Products	39.0	64.9	14.7	45.0	-	454.7	66.3
30 Rubber	-	-	-	-	-	-	-
31 Leather	173.5	209.8	103.3	186.7	62.2	511.9	522.8
Leather Products	234.3	278.2	251.4	141.4	140.7	823.7	472.1
32 Stone, Clay and Glass	237.6	177.2	114.6	81.7	212.6	369.2	83.4
33 Primary Metals	73.1	205.0	76.5	103.9	27.2	1110.5	760.6
34 Fabricated Metals	194.7	93.0	160.3	96.4	46.1	749.6	324.7
35 Non-electrical Machinery	762.8	656.7	526.6	84.0	330.5	636.0	477.8
36 Electrical Machinery	-	-	-	-	-	-	-
37 Transportation Equipment	377.5	554.9	290.7	480.0	518.4	900.8	774.6
38 Instruments	-	-	-	-	-	3.5	-
39 Miscellaneous Manufacturing	5.1	10.9	21.7	7.2	9.7	321.9	18.5
Total	4800.6	6308.3	3221.8	6053.8	3309.0	14393.9	7618.0

APPENDIX, PART III
(continued)

SIC Code Number and Industry	Louisiana	Arkansas	Texas	Florida
20 Food	961.1	225.0	727.9	10.0
21 Tobacco	153.0	12.0	-	-
22 Textiles	292.3	20.5	30.7	16.4
23 Apparel	1062.7	23.6	5.6	2.7
24 Lumber and Wood Products	1755.2	875.1	1257.7	965.3
25 Furniture	54.2	12.6	56.5	-
26 Paper	3.5	-	-	-
27 Printing and Publishing	57.9	13.9	110.3	1.8
28 Chemicals	195.0	-	7.7	45.0
29 Petroleum and Coal Products	54.0	-	-	-
30 Rubber	-	-	-	-
31 Leather	21.6	91.4	64.7	-
Leather Products	955.9	58.3	155.0	14.0
32 Stone, Clay and Glass	551.4	14.5	49.5	159.1
33 Primary Metals	90.7	2.2	-	54.0
34 Fabricated Metals	547.9	55.7	178.4	23.7
35 Non-electrical Machinery	1087.2	69.4	111.3	22.1
36 Electrical Machinery	-	-	-	-
37 Transportation Equipment	678.1	77.0	123.7	70.5
38 Instruments	-	-	-	-
39 Miscellaneous Manufacturing	79.8	1.3	28.4	-
Total	8601.5	1553.3	2907.6	1384.5

APPENDIX, PART IV

MANUFACTURING VALUE ADDED BY REGION, 1900
(Thousands of dollars)

SIC Code Number and Industry	New England	Middle Atlantic	East North Central	West North Central	South Atlantic	East South Central	West South Central
20 Food	54,993.1	232,492.7	265,799.2	98,500.6	19,633.5	28,406.6	27,553.5
21 Tobacco	5,224.3	69,096.9	31,415.2	24,086.8	29,119.9	13,906.7	1,954.9
22 Textiles	195,519.5	159,531.7	13,419.8	2,530.0	36,394.8	7,923.3	1,276.2
23 Apparel	46,823.4	270,201.8	93,391.6	25,565.8	5,455.8	7,690.0	4,988.7
24 Lumber and Wood Products	30,735.6	65,854.6	108,012.6	35,477.1	40,381.8	32,719.8	29,112.0
25 Furniture	13,840.6	35,737.6	40,825.5	6,683.5	2,608.2	2,058.4	1,047.0
26 Paper	31,618.6	41,743.1	18,544.5	1,598.6	1,419.6	134.1	161.7
27 Printing and Publishing	35,741.7	128,737.1	69,177.2	29,330.4	6,354.1	6,588.3	6,585.9
28 Chemicals	16,196.3	83,328.1	38,123.0	10,339.5	18,189.5	6,810.1	1,579.9
29 Petroleum and Coal Products	8,540.4	47,197.8	21,254.3	6,922.3	1,972.8	1,880.9	1,246.8
30 Rubber	25,894.4	8,840.7	4,872.9	776.3	—	40.7	—
31 Leather	7,754.7	25,926.2	9,225.9	648.3	2,329.0	1,827.6	30.4
Leather Products	66,629.9	42,231.9	29,154.9	12,340.0	2,635.9	2,622.9	2,800.9
32 Stone, Clay and Glass	36,964.1	139,026.3	73,910.2	22,372.0	7,954.9	6,047.4	3,935.5
33 Primary Metals	25,114.9	206,230.7	96,773.2	11,269.1	12,506.7	13,499.1	896.0
34 Fabricated Metals	40,237.0	75,359.9	91,546.1	14,085.2	2,542.1	3,180.7	1,816.1
35 Non-electrical Machinery	76,245.3	186,394.5	135,822.4	18,463.4	6,315.1	8,164.6	3,524.5
36 Electrical Machinery	—	—	—	—	—	—	—
37 Transportation Equipment	21,110.6	84,659.9	78,945.9	28,122.3	12,240.6	9,342.6	8,055.5
38 Instruments	6,342.5	15,351.3	4,981.6	1,550.1	100.0	197.8	228.7
39 Miscellaneous	53,096.2	86,632.6	39,228.4	7,975.5	677.5	1,469.4	795.3
Total	798,623.1	2,004,575.4	1,264,424.4	358,636.8	208,831.8	154,511.0	97,589.5

APPENDIX, PART V

MANUFACTURING VALUE ADDED BY STATE, 1900
(Thousands of dollars)

SIC Code Number and Industry	Maine	New Hampshire	Vermont	Massachusetts	Rhode Island	Connecticut	New York	New Jersey
20 Food	5,177.7	3,173.7	2,120.8	32,558.6	4,268.8	7,693.5	124,809.2	24,905.0
21 Tobacco	186.2	274.1	55.5	3,387.8	200.8	1,119.9	34,754.8	6,994.0
22 Textiles	13,732.1	16,560.3	2,562.4	104,766.9	35,834.2	22,063.6	48,423.5	37,364.2
23 Apparel	2,268.7	1,576.9	1,116.8	27,838.3	2,135.3	11,887.4	199,781.2	13,885.3
24 Lumber and Wood Products	7,204.2	6,294.3	3,945.5	10,244.4	892.8	2,154.4	28,991.4	4,359.3
25 Furniture	537.7	541.5	805.0	9,682.5	385.0	1,888.9	23,366.2	1,528.8
26 Paper	6,221.8	3,448.4	1,868.0	15,692.5	672.5	3,715.4	26,204.9	3,312.0
27 Printing and Publishing	2,094.7	702.2	601.7	27,165.9	1,814.0	3,363.2	89,536.2	4,678.0
28 Chemicals	530.6	366.4	1,705.3	10,223.2	1,138.1	2,232.7	39,259.3	13,518.4
29 Petroleum and Coal Products	308.7	350.7	426.0	5,236.0	860.4	1,358.6	21,919.2	7,017.2
30 Rubber	-	-	-	13,324.9	5,098.9	7,470.6	2,306.2	5,817.3
31 Leather	508.5	611.6	64.9	6,274.0	85.6	210.1	5,784.7	4,214.6
Leather Products	4,662.5	7,501.9	421.6	51,691.7	613.8	1,738.4	23,806.6	5,956.5
32 Stone, Clay and Glass	4,400.4	1,963.7	4,966.2	17,937.3	2,475.7	5,220.8	61,406.4	19,071.9
33 Primary Metals	348.3	132.8	79.1	9,000.3	876.1	14,678.3	10,010.0	19,259.0
34 Fabricated Metals	702.2	843.7	578.6	14,185.7	2,203.3	21,723.5	37,032.2	6,431.6
35 Non-electrical Machinery	1,857.7	2,106.0	1,523.0	43,059.6	9,419.7	18,279.3	74,559.8	28,769.0
36 Electrical Machinery	-	-	-	-	-	-	-	-
37 Transportation Equipment	2,734.5	1,393.8	1,986.5	8,254.6	1,675.8	5,065.4	24,949.2	8,969.1
38 Instruments	103.6	75.8	212.3	2,247.2	306.5	3,397.1	8,652.8	2,402.4
39 Miscellaneous	549.0	1,013.0	405.5	20,831.1	11,129.7	19,167.9	55,471.4	12,713.8
Total	54,129.1	48,930.8	25,444.7	433,602.5	82,087.0	154,429.0	941,025.2	231,167.4

APPENDIX, PART V
(Continued)

SIC Code Number and Industry	Pennsylvania	Delaware	Maryland	Ohio	Indiana	Illinois	Michigan	Wisconsin
20 Food	65,918.3	2,019.9	14,840.3	49,414.5	36,376.1	132,268.1	15,162.3	32,578.2
21 Tobacco	20,859.1	83.6	6,405.4	12,610.0	1,683.2	7,739.1	6,168.2	3,214.7
22 Textiles	68,480.7	937.1	4,326.2	2,686.9	3,038.0	3,057.0	1,753.4	2,884.5
23 Apparel	40,289.7	523.6	15,722.0	21,877.9	6,759.7	49,879.3	8,162.5	6,712.2
24 Lumber and Wood Products	27,927.6	453.3	4,123.0	17,899.5	13,953.2	15,706.9	32,060.0	28,393.0
25 Furniture	8,359.3	98.9	2,384.4	7,273.0	6,075.9	12,348.9	9,069.9	6,057.8
26 Paper	10,125.8	810.6	1,289.8	6,009.1	2,157.1	3,887.9	1,999.1	4,491.3
27 Printing and Publishing	30,125.9	288.0	4,109.0	17,400.2	6,770.5	33,883.3	6,369.5	4,753.7
28 Chemicals	24,868.0	676.5	5,005.9	12,891.0	3,312.3	11,621.5	9,168.6	1,129.6
29 Petroleum and Coal Products	16,078.8	222.6	1,960.0	7,071.7	2,024.2	8,836.1	1,877.7	1,444.6
30 Rubber	429.9	104.7	182.6	2,572.9	182.6	1,552.9	20.5	244.0
31 Leather	13,211.5	2,372.8	342.6	1,407.8	402.4	2,063.4	1,318.2	4,034.1
Leather Products	10,598.2	200.0	1,670.6	10,949.8	2,062.7	9,959.6	2,490.2	3,692.6
32 Stone, Clay and Glass	52,439.1	670.6	5,438.3	25,191.7	17,528.6	23,785.8	4,373.3	3,030.8
33 Primary Metals	171,725.0	1,848.7	3,388.0	51,969.6	7,836.9	29,095.7	3,479.7	4,391.3
34 Fabricated Metals	27,530.1	329.3	4,036.7	23,632.8	10,262.7	39,665.1	9,095.9	8,889.6
35 Non-electrical Machinery	75,585.3	1,835.0	5,645.4	50,938.2	10,772.5	47,366.2	13,485.2	13,260.3
36 Electrical Machinery	– –	– –	– –	– –	– –	– –	– –	– –
37 Transportation Equipment	41,462.6	3,864.3	5,414.7	19,723.4	16,111.4	22,770.0	12,697.8	7,643.3
38 Instruments	3,836.0	65.3	394.8	422.5	351.8	3,642.2	308.3	256.8
39 Miscellaneous	14,176.0	115.3	4,156.1	10,208.3	2,948.7	18,916.1	3,627.1	3,528.2
Total	724,026.9	17,520.1	90,835.8	352,150.8	150,610.5	478,345.1	142,687.4	140,630.6

APPENDIX, PART V
(Continued)

SIC Code Number and Industry	Minnesota	Iowa	Missouri	Kansas	Nebraska	North Dakota	South Dakota
20 Food	19,076.1	15,935.9	30,481.4	15,635.6	15,243.4	959.4	1,168.8
21 Tobacco	1,517.5	1,778.4	18,564.6	506.0	1,548.7	43.4	128.2
22 Textiles	543.0	295.7	750.0	235.0	664.1	34.4	7.8
23 Apparel	4,905.8	3,845.2	12,563.4	1,635.6	2,211.1	199.4	205.3
24 Lumber and Wood Products	19,814.1	5,165.0	8,883.0	725.5	621.0	34.0	234.5
25 Furniture	1,791.3	888.7	3,401.7	343.2	237.7	6.1	14.8
26 Paper	157.1	259.9	667.9	243.5	229.3	40.9	-
27 Printing and Publishing	6,461.6	4,749.5	11,778.8	2,334.2	2,872.1	549.6	584.6
28 Chemicals	952.4	1,409.5	6,178.7	603.6	1,177.9	9.9	7.5
29 Petroleum and Coal Products	1,076.6	847.2	3,523.9	841.5	541.7	38.7	52.7
30 Rubber	-	3.0	773.3	-	-	-	-
31 Leather	9.5	36.0	259.6	45.0	270.4	-	27.8
Leather Products	2,839.3	582.7	6,410.5	1,042.8	1,032.9	224.4	207.4
32 Stone, Clay and Glass	4,689.3	3,889.7	9,748.8	1,820.2	1,865.3	148.1	210.6
33 Primary Metals	-42.0	512.7	3,418.3	3,545.5	3,312.4	-	338.2
34 Fabricated Metals	3,374.8	2,791.1	5,924.2	838.4	894.6	151.0	111.1
35 Non-electrical Machinery	3,470.7	2,548.4	9,829.5	1,785.2'	734.2	58.7	36.7
36 Electrical Machinery	-	-	-	-	-	-	-
37 Transportation Equipment	4,299.5	5,880.1	10,966.8	4,227.5	2,501.5	100.8	146.1
38 Instruments	194.9	82.2	920.3	162.2	174.6	-	15.9
39 Miscellaneous	1,750.2	1,392.2	2,407.3	485.2	1,875.7	35.3	29.6
Total	77,065.7	52,893.1	147,452.0	37,055.7	38,008.6	2,634.1	3,527.6

APPENDIX, PART V
(Continued)

SIC Code Number and Industry	Virginia	West Virginia	North Carolina	South Carolina	Georgia	Florida	Kentucky	Tennessee
20 Food	5,290.7	3,021.3	3,243.6	1,843.4	5,489.9	744.6	15,274.4	7,699.2
21 Tobacco	11,550.2	1,695.4	9,661.6	32.4	84.6	6,095.7	12,160.4	1,471.2
22 Textiles	2,445.2	565.9	11,839.0	12,830.3	8,701.1	13.3	1,733.6	1,726.3
23 Apparel	1,571.8	1,097.9	786.8	511.4	1,309.7	178.2	4,495.4	2,145.3
24 Lumber and Wood Products	7,477.3	6,096.1	8,434.4	3,141.7	9,545.0	5,687.3	8,446.6	9,737.7
25 Furniture	359.0	334.0	888.9	83.8	911.9	30.6	1,074.2	791.1
26 Paper	795.5	284.3	14.2	67.4	258.2	–	49.7	84.4
27 Printing and Publishing	1,881.1	809.2	795.6	603.7	1,816.4	448.1	2,529.4	2,589.2
28 Chemicals	1,796.3	337.0	866.0	2,123.1	7,610.5	5,456.6	1,269.5	1,964.1
29 Petroleum and Coal Products	542.3	396.5	151.7	143.7	605.2	133.4	1,053.1	529.3
30 Rubber	–	–	–	–	–	–	–	40.7
31 Leather	1,021.1	669.6	373.0	5.7	259.6	–	875.1	617.8
Leather Products	1,100.0	346.6	234.7	122.9	778.5	53.2	1,530.4	804.1
32 Stone, Clay and Glass	1,613.1	2,875.7	869.9	654.7	1,748.2	193.3	2,594.4	1,831.0
33 Primary Metals	3,894.0	7,891.9	454.0	20.0	246.8	–	2,770.6	2,268.7
34 Fabricated Metals	841.8	573.7	225.0	189.6	646.8	65.2	1,960.9	853.6
35 Non-electrical Machinery	2,187.8	806.2	737.8	281.2	2,069.2	232.9	2,669.9	2,412.7
36 Electrical Machinery	–	–	–	–	–	–	–	–
37 Transportation Equipment	4,684.7	1,902.9	1,233.4	630.4	2,812.0	977.2	3,974.3	2,560.2
38 Instruments	5.4	15.7	6.9	–	72.0	–	175.9	6.7
39 Miscellaneous	167.1	73.2	116.2	74.1	200.4	46.5	853.3	524.6
Total	49,224.4	29,793.1	40,932.7	23,359.5	45,166.0	20,356.1	65,491.1	40,657.9

APPENDIX, PART V
(Continued)

SIC Code Number and Industry	Alabama	Mississippi	Louisiana	Arkansas	Texas	Oklahoma
20 Food	2,831.4	2,601.6	12,612.8	2,499.6	11,398.2	1,042.9
21 Tobacco	275.1	-	1,562.8	40.8	322.8	28.5
22 Textiles	3,523.4	840.0	417.8	97.8	760.6	-
23 Apparel	701.5	347.8	2,372.8	491.6	2,014.9	109.4
24 Lumber and Wood Products	6,751.4	7,784.1	9,356.4	11,822.7	7,886.3	46.6
25 Furniture	135.0	58.1	378.3	225.8	435.2	7.7
26 Paper	-	-	42.8	16.2	102.7	-
27 Printing and Publishing	894.5	575.2	1,753.1	777.1	3,682.7	373.0
28 Chemicals	2,311.9	1,264.6	1,106.3	88.0	356.1	29.5
29 Petroleum and Coal Products	229.4	69.1	538.4	126.1	577.7	4.6
30 Rubber	-	-	-	-	-	-
31 Leather	333.3	1.4	3.8	2.3	24.3	-
Leather Products	187.9	100.5	759.2	182.8	1,729.4	129.5
32 Stone, Clay and Glass	1,106.4	515.6	575.6	486.5	2,636.2	237.2
33 Primary Metals	8,459.8	-	38.3	5.6	852.1	-
34 Fabricated Metals	257.4	108.8	705.9	123.4	932.8	54.0
35 Non-electrical Machinery	2,776.6	305.4	1,615.2	292.6	1,588.3	28.4
36 Electrical Machinery	-	-	-	-	-	-
37 Transportation Equipment	2,808.1	1,114.5	1,447.3	1,701.2	4,861.0	46.0
38 Instruments	15.2	-	115.1	18.5	95.1	-
39 Miscellaneous	64.8	26.7	394.6	59.5	335.4	5.8
Total	33,763.1	15,713.4	35,796.5	19,058.1	40,591.8	2,143.1

APPENDIX, PART VI

MANUFACTURING EMPLOYMENT BY REGION, 1860

SIC Code Number and Industry	New England	Middle Atlantic	East North Central	West North Central	South Atlantic	East South Central	West South Central	Total for Regions
20 Food	5892	27823	17086	3994	6068	5070	1301	67234
21 Tobacco	1379	6133	1570	1886	13030	2635	162	26795
22 Textiles	121513	60282	3570	1227	8540	4796	610	200538
23 Apparel	32801	97070	17962	1291	886	1942	1000	152952
24 Lumber and Wood Products	15959	34352	30631	6621	9272	7840	3950	108625
25 Furniture	6624	11381	7185	708	819	684	205	27606
26 Paper	6057	5645	1119	26	373	91	2	13313
27 Printing and Publishing	4164	16884	3663	517	464	678	199	26569
28 Chemicals	2062	7834	1206	357	5747	788	121	18115
29 Petroleum and Coal Products	1012	4465	846	116	296	433	6	7174
30 Rubber	1220	1582	1	- -	- -	- -	- -	2803
31 Leather	5623	13599	2315	243	1593	1747	244	25364
Leather Products	77220	39989	12391	2278	2481	3019	1680	139058
32 Stone, Clay and Glass	7530	25784	7667	2168	2594	1472	872	48087
33 Primary Metals	12477	46261	9836	1539	4202	3548	119	77982
34 Fabricated Metals	16807	19054	5858	1201	1158	1495	767	46340
35 Non-electrical Machinery	13335	24071	11394	1696	2357	2357	1026	56236
36 Electrical Machinery	- -	- -	- -	- -	- -	- -	- -	- -
37 Transportation Equipment	12944	24961	8515	1269	4487	3096	755	56027
38 Instruments	1714	1912	73	14	- -	2	- -	3715
39 Miscellaneous	11586	19060	1732	397	143	289	61	33268
Total	357919	488142	144620	27548	64510	41982	13080	1137801

APPENDIX, PART VII

MANUFACTURING EMPLOYMENT BY STATE, 1860

SIC Code Number and Industry	Maine	New Hampshire	Vermont	Massachusetts	Rhode Island	Connecticut	New York	New Jersey
20 Food	828	429	339	2978	437	881	13125	1779
21 Tobacco	22	90	37	616	164	450	3242	382
22 Textiles	8423	16028	2586	58608	20243	15625	20246	7768
23 Apparel	3302	1869	346	15927	1650	9707	50872	11358
24 Lumber and Wood Products	5663	2386	1436	4817	405	1252	17649	1891
25 Furniture	280	455	340	4977	166	406	6856	392
26 Paper	406	350	142	3648	48	1463	2886	879
27 Printing and Publishing	285	276	121	2506	223	753	9562	411
28 Chemicals	118	130	26	1021	103	664	3712	794
29 Petroleum and Coal Products	140	33	7	711	64	57	2874	15
30 Rubber	- -	- -	- -	298	113	809	757	817
31 Leather	747	472	339	3601	22	442	6496	1347
Leather Products	3124	5048	570	63486	552	4440	16648	5260
32 Stone, Clay and Glass	1181	404	619	4227	330	769	10456	3575
33 Primary Metals	745	633	356	7192	872	2679	12204	4291
34 Fabricated Metals	632	584	370	5517	1484	8220	9655	2828
35 Non-electrical Machinery	1200	858	728	5901	2105	2543	11716	1807
36 Electrical Machinery	- -	- -	- -	- -	- -	- -	- -	- -
37 Transportation Equipment	2082	1391	666	4304	334	4167	9105	4633
38 Instruments	2	- -	6	422	20	1264	888	- -
39 Miscellaneous	161	200	102	5309	2162	3652	11524	1510
Total	29341	31636	9136	198066	31497	60243	220473	51737

APPENDIX, PART VII
(Continued)

SIC Code Number and Industry	Pennsylvania	Delaware	Maryland	Ohio	Indiana	Illinois	Michigan	Wisconsin
20 Food	9441	228	3250	6181	3716	4348	1178	1663
21 Tobacco	2198	64	247	1016	176	136	60	182
22 Textiles	27793	1226	3249	2213	799	239	185	134
23 Apparel	28120	255	6465	14054	991	824	919	1174
24 Lumber and Wood Products	13144	403	1265	8255	5266	3429	8029	5652
25 Furniture	3518	62	553	4154	1022	792	704	513
26 Paper	1563	93	224	787	90	61	88	93
27 Printing and Publishing	6515	73	323	2046	296	686	317	318
28 Chemicals	2877	252	199	671	82	161	133	159
29 Petroleum and Coal Products	1323	12	241	545	24	185	23	69
30 Rubber	8	—	—	—	—	1	—	—
31 Leather	4879	420	457	1622	—	134	339	220
Leather Products	15492	369	2220	6071	1753	1892	1405	1270
32 Stone, Clay and Glass	9717	286	1750	3471	899	1654	852	791
33 Primary Metals	27513	203	2050	7523	356	780	736	441
34 Fabricated Metals	5646	223	702	2522	534	787	1061	954
35 Non-electrical Machinery	8490	366	1692	6070	1663	2646	760	255
36 Electrical Machinery	—	—	—	—	—	—	—	—
37 Transportation Equipment	8557	1604	1062	3534	1561	1682	875	863
38 Instruments	1012	—	12	56	—	7	8	2
39 Miscellaneous	5613	18	395	1131	109	217	151	124
Total	183419	6157	26356	71926	19337	20661	17823	14877

APPENDIX, PART VII
(Continued)

SIC Code Number and Industry	Minnesota	Iowa	Missouri	Kansas	Nebraska	Virginia	North Carolina	South Carolina
20 Food	274	1263	2306	96	55	2661	1821	779
21 Tobacco	10	39	1837	--	--	11481	1461	--
22 Textiles	8	145	1074	--	--	2222	2034	997
23 Apparel	8	185	1082	--	16	744	28	34
24 Lumber and Wood Products	1245	1968	2751	497	160	2925	1593	1442
25 Furniture	103	233	354	9	9	396	87	29
26 Paper	--	13	13	--	--	149	89	57
27 Printing and Publishing	37	198	253	6	23	163	84	18
28 Chemicals	--	6	348	3	--	101	3783	1427
29 Petroleum and Coal Products	--	--	85	--	--	211	50	--
30 Rubber	--	--	--	--	--	--	--	--
31 Leather	7	67	168	1	--	780	363	113
Leather Products	184	565	1471	20	38	1390	274	269
32 Stone, Clay and Glass	17	234	1862	44	11	1418	233	274
33 Primary Metals	30	115	1394	--	--	3616	188	60
34 Fabricated Metals	95	363	726	8	9	784	147	56
35 Non-electrical Machinery	1	243	1427	25	--	911	142	401
36 Electrical Machinery	--	--	--	--	--	--	--	--
37 Transportation Equipment	45	236	945	35	8	1838	843	785
38 Instruments	--	--	14	--	--	--	--	--
39 Miscellaneous	16	25	346	4	6	106	13	13
Total	2080	5929	18456	748	335	31850	13233	6754

APPENDIX, PART VII
(Continued)

SIC Code Number and Industry	Georgia	Florida	Kentucky	Tennessee	Alabama	Mississippi	Arkansas	Louisiana	Texas
20 Food	790	17	3385	1063	376	246	180	614	507
21 Tobacco	88	-	1951	672	4	8	28	134	-
22 Textiles	3222	65	1758	1036	1536	466	52	496	62
23 Apparel	74	6	1685	88	81	88	22	961	17
24 Lumber and Wood Products	2064	1248	2458	2003	1913	1466	977	1711	1262
25 Furniture	307	-	364	159	99	62	27	83	95
26 Paper	78	-	67	24	-	-	-	2	-
27 Printing and Publishing	196	3	258	311	70	39	19	70	110
28 Chemicals	309	127	108	15	661	4	-	115	6
29 Petroleum and Coal Products	35	-	374	30	22	7	-	6	-
30 Rubber	-	-	-	-	-	-	-	-	-
31 Leather	337	-	578	721	281	167	132	32	80
Leather Products	524	24	1316	842	461	400	95	1390	195
32 Stone, Clay and Glass	417	252	710	183	416	163	42	731	99
33 Primary Metals	298	40	1599	1717	125	107	7	112	-
34 Fabricated Metals	145	26	752	360	175	208	50	473	244
35 Non-electrical Machinery	848	55	664	672	546	475	41	867	118
36 Electrical Machinery	-	-	-	-	-	-	-	-	-
37 Transportation Equipment	936	85	1171	980	565	380	101	499	155
38 Instruments	-	-	2	-	-	-	-	-	-
39 Miscellaneous	11	-	242	21	7	19	2	41	18
Total	10679	1948	19442	10897	7338	4305	1775	8337	2968

APPENDIX, PART VIII

MANUFACTURING EMPLOYMENT BY REGION, 1900

SIC Code Number and Industry	New England	Middle Atlantic	East North Central	West North Central	South Atlantic	East South Central	West South Central	Total for Regions
20 Food	45520	159239	141471	73497	25521	23313	24800	493361
21 Tobacco	5455	71244	33937	12644	29054	9751	2116	164201
22 Textiles	293098	244675	21561	1808	92068	18654	2042	673906
23 Apparel	63521	334527	125629	41102	10494	13674	8757	597704
24 Lumber and Wood Products	41714	83756	137695	42064	70986	54313	43497	474025
25 Furniture	14649	41667	59416	8645	5087	3107	1590	134161
26 Paper	31211	46237	23474	1519	2315	196	101	105053
27 Printing and Publishing	28938	101949	67388	31451	8506	7163	7297	252692
28 Chemicals	7933	50114	23754	5586	45409	10047	1404	144247
29 Petroleum and Coal Products	6043	32965	15848	5181	1569	1633	730	63969
30 Rubber	19792	6741	5414	6				31953
31 Leather	9160	28754	11414	236	2734	1966	56	54320
Leather Products	100328	67051	53028	21999	5571	3756	3754	255487
32 Stone, Clay and Glass	44208	147801	95941	28866	15819	10888	6501	350024
33 Primary Metals	22609	159633	77342	5535	13504	14412	57	293092
34 Fabricated Metals	46827	84951	98216	15457	3380	3626	2372	254829
35 Non-electrical Machinery	80003	195305	146594	17968	8637	11071	3704	463282
36 Electrical Machinery								
37 Transportation Equipment	22089	108616	108930	38325	21169	18060	12294	329483
38 Instruments	7138	16059	5665	889	87	50	144	30032
39 Miscellaneous	54154	89359	45869	7428	1028	1359	784	199981
Total	944390	2070643	1298586	360206	362938	207039	122000	5365802

APPENDIX, PART IX

MANUFACTURING EMPLOYMENT BY STATE, 1900

SIC Code Number and Industry	Maine	New Hampshire	Vermont	Massachusetts	Rhode Island	Connecticut	New York	New Jersey
20 Food	9369	1851	2019	23806	2781	5694	79273	14049
21 Tobacco	251	336	77	3255	208	1328	32337	4346
22 Textiles	21551	25978	3770	157775	51317	32707	73151	51895
23 Apparel	4560	3019	1968	34788	2538	16648	225675	22180
24 Lumber and Wood Products	11060	8231	6224	12499	1130	2570	36890	5036
25 Furniture	676	798	1217	9756	381	1821	26371	1620
26 Paper	5332	2769	1320	17130	531	4129	28846	3731
27 Printing and Publishing	2082	884	801	20516	1655	3000	64565	5136
28 Chemicals	301	91	413	5642	512	974	22064	9498
29 Petroleum and Coal Products	283	342	881	2958	690	889	13345	6118
30 Rubber	–	–	–	12144	4379	3269	2375	3723
31 Leather	653	617	83	7525	81	201	6922	4526
Leather Products	7770	13552	757	75078	812	2359	35569	9372
32 Stone, Clay and Glass	5593	2637	5931	20186	3590	6271	48500	24937
33 Primary Metals	63	–	–	9441	171	12934	8769	11637
34 Fabricated Metals	849	894	708	15665	1809	26902	39760	7787
35 Non-electrical Machinery	2393	2295	1489	43159	10408	20259	75915	31257
36 Electrical Machinery	–	–	–	–	–	–	–	–
37 Transportation Equipment	2720	1757	1115	9977	1006	5514	33963	10996
38 Instruments	–	82	–	2647	145	4264	9590	2432
39 Miscellaneous	186	920	217	22044	11116	19671	53834	13467

APPENDIX, PART IX
(continued)

SIC Code Number and Industry	Pennsylvania	Delaware	Maryland	Ohio	Indiana	Illinois	Michigan	Wisconsin
20 Food	45058	2588	18271	26780	16793	67798	12139	17961
21 Tobacco	29397	134	5030	14163	2542	7856	6322	3054
22 Textiles	111312	991	7326	4463	4825	4258	3563	4452
23 Apparel	58914	966	26792	31181	12525	57392	14076	10455
24 Lumber and Wood Products	34258	1065	6507	23610	18759	21371	40884	33071
25 Furniture	10943	52	2681	9890	10315	14780	14266	10165
26 Paper	11539	679	1442	7644	2657	5059	3049	5065
27 Printing and Publishing	27504	390	4354	17573	7490	29120	7486	5719
28 Chemicals	14720	310	3522	6271	2158	6512	8021	792
29 Petroleum and Coal Products	12654	153	695	5233	1706	5809	1958	1142
30 Rubber	643	- -	- -	3840	- -	1152	27	395
31 Leather	14162	2643	501	1534	454	2373	1518	5535
Leather Products	18454	212	3444	20388	3465	13276	4026	11873
32 Stone, Clay and Glass	66192	712	7460	35318	24594	26470	5599	3960
33 Primary Metals	135358	1571	2352	40110	8182	23051	3467	2532
34 Fabricated Metals	32467	152	4785	28512	10236	40593	9365	9510
35 Non-electrical Machinery	80511	2271	5351	55398	12887	46882	16488	14939
36 Electrical Machinery	- -	- -	- -	- -	- -	- -	- -	- -
37 Transportation Equipment	52310	3582	7765	28496	22105	30902	17733	9694
38 Instruments	3922	- -	115	399	86	4701	398	81
39 Miscellaneous	17089	11	4958	12658	3670	20272	4481	4788

APPENDIX, PART IX
(continued)

SIC Code Number and Industry	Minnesota	Iowa	Missouri	Kansas	Nebraska	North Dakota	South Dakota	Virginia
20 Food	12232	13034	22074	14356	10236	602	963	7122
21 Tobacco	1999	2440	6710	700	566	61	168	12854
22 Textiles	813	518	403	30	30	— —	5	5768
23 Apparel	8870	7470	19140	2819	2127	285	391	3074
24 Lumber and Wood Products	19339	7060	13621	1047	736	19	242	14206
25 Furniture	2174	1285	4314	482	360	8	22	632
26 Paper	284	315	920	— —	— —	— —	— —	1351
27 Printing and Publishing	6315	6202	11651	3140	2795	578	770	2289
28 Chemicals	651	829	3367	457	282	— —	— —	1997
29 Petroleum and Coal Products	826	604	2706	468	565	— —	12	599
30 Rubber	— —	6	— —	— —	— —	— —	— —	— —
31 Leather	27		209	— —	— —	— —	— —	1018
Leather Products	4533	3717	10212	1518	1416	296	307	2761
32 Stone, Clay and Glass	6352	5513	11988	2554	2008	149	302	3129
33 Primary Metals	448	226	3296	1565	— —	— —	— —	4439
34 Fabricated Metals	3782	3393	6073	915	980	127	187	1169
35 Non-electrical Machinery	3916	2887	9308	1472	288	59	38	3178
36 Electrical Machinery	— —	— —	— —	— —	— —	— —	— —	— —
37 Transportation Equipment	6631	8186	14230	6118	2801	173	186	8024
38 Instruments	133	25	631	82	28	— —	— —	4
39 Miscellaneous	2007	2357	2438	330	266	— —	30	272

APPENDIX, PART IX
(continued)

SIC Code Number and Industry	West Virginia	North Carolina	South Carolina	Georgia	Florida	Kentucky	Tennessee	Alabama
20 Food	2909	5199	2768	6598	925	8916	6894	4004
21 Tobacco	1385	7658	80	189	6888	7968	1482	301
22 Textiles	412	33480	31650	20727	31	2795	4406	9271
23 Apparel	1280	1800	1033	2981	326	8128	3731	1192
24 Lumber and Wood Products	8205	17374	6741	15688	8772	13241	16642	12201
25 Furniture	492	2073	140	1693	57	1303	1444	251
26 Paper	388	44	122	410	– –	– –	196	– –
27 Printing and Publishing	1103	1195	839	2498	582	2656	2625	1144
28 Chemicals	100	1326	2994	22469	16523	590	1322	5342
29 Petroleum and Coal Products	146	164	145	440	75	1030	378	184
30 Rubber	– –	– –	– –	– –	– –	– –	– –	– –
31 Leather	739	488	15	474	– –	880	887	192
Leather Products	519	478	193	1523	97	2065	1145	377
32 Stone, Clay and Glass	4546	2612	1671	3476	385	3970	3357	2411
33 Primary Metals	7992	645	26	402	– –	2671	2576	9165
34 Fabricated Metals	309	494	312	1016	80	2020	1147	307
35 Non-electrical Machinery	721	1086	461	2929	262	3173	3677	3808
36 Electrical Machinery	– –	– –	– –	– –	– –	– –	– –	– –
37 Transportation Equipment	3206	2370	1272	4944	1353	6415	4296	5386
38 Instruments	– –	14	– –	69	– –	23	– –	27
39 Miscellaneous	– –	199	160	334	63	613	595	100

APPENDIX, PART IX
(continued)

SIC Code Number and Industry	Mississippi	Arkansas	Louisiana	Oklahoma	Texas
20 Food	3499	2449	13417	670	8264
21 Tobacco	– –	58	1585	54	419
22 Textiles	2182	48	844	– –	1150
23 Apparel	623	751	4460	192	3354
24 Lumber and Wood Products	12220	19668	13139	105	10585
25 Furniture	109	337	630	12	611
26 Paper	– –	– –	101	– –	– –
27 Printing and Publishing	738	1039	1918	545	3796
28 Chemicals	2793	62	1090	– –	252
29 Petroleum and Coal Products	41	105	322	6	297
30 Rubber	– –	– –	– –	– –	– –
31 Leather	7	6	7	– –	43
Leather Products	169	282	1172	171	2131
32 Stone, Clay and Glass	1150	928	1348	339	3886
33 Primary Metals	– –	– –	57	– –	– –
34 Fabricated Metals	152	161	929	95	1187
35 Non-electrical Machinery	413	336	1769	34	1565
36 Electrical Machinery	– –	– –	– –	– –	– –
37 Transportation Equipment	1963	2498	2357	68	7371
38 Instruments	– –	– –	115	– –	29
39 Miscellaneous	51	57	479	14	234

APPENDIX, PART X

AVERAGE COST OF MANUFACTURING EMPLOYEES BY REGION, 1860

SIC Code Number and Industry	New England	Middle Atlantic	East North Central	West North Central	South Atlantic	East South Central	West South Central	Average for Regions
20 Food	$273	$298	$314	$350	$199	$212	$342	$288
21 Tobacco	334	294	260	243	179	204	335	226
22 Textiles	218	319	254	239	149	175	279	245
23 Apparel	196	184	186	283	231	227	398	190
24 Lumber and Wood Products	310	297	287	309	232	270	319	290
25 Furniture	311	333	327	340	324	365	369	327
26 Paper	254	243	273	- -	355	295	- -	255
27 Printing and Publishing	353	327	323	443	407	429	498	338
28 Chemicals	355	314	316	310	185	226	369	274
29 Petroleum and Coal Products	434	404	376	448	306	378	- -	400
30 Rubber	340	254	- -	- -	- -	- -	- -	291
31 Leather and Leather Products	242	278	295	333	265	309	395	265
32 Stone, Clay and Glass	299	289	234	330	215	251	253	278
33 Primary Metals	366	341	354	445	306	304	443	345
34 Fabricated Metals	358	325	330	389	326	391	460	344
35 Non-electrical Machinery	411	363	380	378	340	411	523	382
36 Electrical Machinery	- -	- -	- -	- -	- -	- -	- -	- -
37 Transportation Equipment	393	384	347	365	303	386	666	378
38 Instruments	377	388	421	343	- -	- -	- -	384
39 Miscellaneous	394	342	336	335	292	384	454	360

APPENDIX, PART XI

AVERAGE COST OF MANUFACTURING EMPLOYEES BY STATE, 1860
(dollars)

SIC Code Number and Industry	Maine	New Hampshire	Vermont	Massachusetts	Rhode Island	Connecticut	New York	New Jersey
20 Food	$226	$297	$297	$291	$320	$215	$330	$300
21 Tobacco	327	272	280	321	315	376	288	280
22 Textiles	209	231	199	216	224	211	203	215
23 Apparel	135	180	211	195	195	221	187	208
24 Lumber and Wood Products	293	294	279	332	367	352	300	336
25 Furniture	365	283	290	303	377	394	340	339
26 Paper	248	287	251	243	262	277	247	254
27 Printing and Publishing	303	303	290	381	388	296	348	317
28 Chemicals	374	283	291	354	383	367	292	328
29 Petroleum and Coal Products	404	394	377	455	349	375	371	427
30 Rubber	–	–	–	362	250	344	233	272
31 Leather and Leather Products	250	239	367	244	247	218	277	308
32 Stone, Clay and Glass	245	268	319	314	289	307	279	279
33 Primary Metals	366	358	362	370	415	340	376	359
34 Fabricated Metals	319	326	358	368	351	358	326	327
35 Non-electrical Machinery	373	301	382	417	379	486	367	384
36 Electrical Machinery	–	–	–	–	–	–	–	–
37 Transportation Equipment	327	373	341	409	354	429	409	400
38 Instruments	420	–	298	426	480	359	355	–
39 Miscellaneous	337	329	362	426	397	354	344	425

APPENDIX, PART XI
(continued)

SIC Code Number and Industry	Pennsyl- vania	Delaware	Maryland	Ohio	Indiana	Illinois	Michigan	Wisconsin
20 Food	$283	$294	$211	$332	$255	$325	$324	$342
21 Tobacco	255	279	761	278	236	295	185	183
22 Textiles	458	- -	218	226	327	265	250	255
23 Apparel	176	209	159	177	228	280	163	215
24 Lumber and Wood Products	289	265	276	305	287	316	272	267
25 Furniture	321	311	312	331	349	327	306	279
26 Paper	229	315	229	282	284	294	185	258
27 Printing and Publishing	293	338	419	304	286	386	352	311
28 Chemicals	337	353	297	338	327	304	279	260
29 Petroleum and Coal Products	437	435	366	388	445	365	233	340
30 Rubber	354	- -	- -	- -	- -	- -	- -	- -
31 Leather and Leather Products	269	322	270	291	315	315	298	263
32 Stone, Clay and Glass	327	161	173	254	201	258	198	173
33 Primary Metals	323	365	323	354	358	418	294	327
34 Fabricated Metals	324	357	302	297	375	382	325	355
35 Non-electrical Machinery	344	433	389	375	378	390	395	362
36 Electrical Machinery	- -	- -	- -	- -	- -	- -	- -	- -
37 Transportation Equipment	359	341	370	365	341	357	293	319
38 Instruments	417	- -	330	427	- -	360	432	390
39 Miscellaneous	314	233	364	334	332	333	413	262

APPENDIX, PART XI
(continued)

SIC Code Number and Industry	Minnesota	Iowa	Missouri	Kansas	Nebraska	Virginia	North Carolina	South Carolina
20 Food	$344	$304	$373	$459	$313	$253	$111	$169
21 Tobacco	390	418	239	--	--	188	113	--
22 Textiles	278	212	242	--	--	174	125	158
23 Apparel	291	246	290	--	218	209	270	239
24 Lumber and Wood Products	324	278	308	412	282	235	229	204
25 Furniture	353	357	325	425	273	318	312	267
26 Paper	--	302	312	--	--	280	606	281
27 Printing and Publishing	860	290	504	440	421	266	370	349
28 Chemicals	--	380	308	328	--	276	206	113
29 Petroleum and Coal Products	--	468	441	--	--	292	233	--
30 Rubber	--	--	--	--	--	--	--	--
31 Leather and Leather Products	349	317	334	466	354	476	268	280
32 Stone, Clay and Glass	178	195	346	415	360	196	173	232
33 Primary Metals	481	348	453	--	--	309	214	200
34 Fabricated Metals	397	364	400	424	413	323	297	298
35 Non-electrical Machinery	360	427	372	288	--	326	338	353
36 Electrical Machinery	--	--	--	--	--	--	--	--
37 Transportation Equipment	376	388	354	489	473	311	262	314
38 Instruments	--	--	342	--	--	--	--	--
39 Miscellaneous	260	291	338	546	360	265	235	428

APPENDIX, PART XI
(continued)

SIC Code Number and Industry	Georgia	Florida	Kentucky	Tennessee	Alabama	Mississippi	Arkansas	Louisiana	Texas
20 Food	$248	$318	$189	$262	$257	$252	$253	$384	$322
21 Tobacco	112	- -	211	181	411	165	302	342	- -
22 Textiles	150	121	212	160	155	133	188	294	237
23 Apparel	400	300	214	332	257	348	436	400	258
24 Lumber and Wood Products	249	260	273	244	267	307	279	349	307
25 Furniture	339	- -	393	328	327	357	280	422	347
26 Paper	268	- -	333	188	- -	- -	- -	600	- -
27 Printing and Publishing	547	320	497	408	290	394	330	524	510
28 Chemicals	210	237	307	364	210	120	- -	372	295
29 Petroleum and Coal Products	501	- -	373	568	136	540	- -	300	- -
30 Rubber	- -	- -	- -	- -	- -	- -	- -	- -	- -
31 Leather and Leather Products	274	403	319	284	295	361	313	414	365
32 Stone, Clay and Glass	290	218	227	185	294	328	190	257	247
33 Primary Metals	330	463	381	217	304	535	171	460	- -
34 Fabricated Metals	356	468	380	407	418	381	342	517	374
35 Non-electrical Machinery	352	281	341	328	465	564	676	519	505
36 Electrical Machinery	- -	- -	- -	- -	- -	- -	- -	- -	- -
37 Transportation Equipment	319	259	391	387	367	400	400	808	382
38 Instruments	- -	- -	600	- -	- -	- -	- -	- -	- -
39 Miscellaneous	458	- -	362	424	476	578	390	457	455

APPENDIX, PART XII

AVERAGE COST OF MANUFACTURING EMPLOYEES BY REGION, 1900

SIC Code Number and Industry	New England	Middle Atlantic	East North Central	West North Central	South Atlantic	East South Central	West South Central	Average for Regions
20 Food	$496	$556	$529	$520	$310	$420	$449	$516
21 Tobacco	611	407	400	457	302	318	387	390
22 Textiles	385	367	300	342	193	209	191	344
23 Apparel	418	414	386	351	255	302	310	398
24 Lumber and Wood Products	428	446	436	456	280	318	361	396
25 Furniture	506	510	433	476	278	360	365	459
26 Paper	476	450	401	320	246	232	219	440
27 Printing and Publishing	612	648	542	529	426	512	527	588
28 Chemicals	586	613	574	609	224	273	421	457
29 Petroleum and Coal Products	560	593	517	510	423	429	589	556
30 Rubber	469	535	436	398	-	-	-	476
31 Leather and Leather Products	479	437	395	429	310	378	470	440
32 Stone, Clay and Glass	537	521	496	495	306	327	372	496
33 Primary Metals	576	574	595	544	368	380	-	560
34 Fabricated Metals	537	529	519	517	331	429	408	521
35 Non-electrical Machinery	583	578	539	560	434	427	527	560
36 Electrical Machinery	-	-	-	-	-	-	-	-
37 Transportation Equipment	588	556	514	564	434	470	587	534
38 Instruments	517	511	532	660	106	177	91	517
39 Miscellaneous	540	511	459	434	194	370	205	501

APPENDIX, PART XIII

AVERAGE COST OF MANUFACTURING EMPLOYEES BY STATE, 1900

(dollars)

SIC Code Number and Industry	Maine	New Hampshire	Vermont	Massachusetts	Rhode Island	Connecticut	New York	New Jersey
20 Food	$278	$562	$411	$565	$570	$554	$589	$565
21 Tobacco	478	516	518	660	446	561	464	381
22 Textiles	355	394	378	386	391	389	386	405
23 Apparel	270	337	312	436	402	444	451	400
24 Lumber and Wood Products	399	404	348	495	438	481	482	508
25 Furniture	443	425	400	525	614	509	532	533
26 Paper	503	471	537	474	361	448	462	484
27 Printing and Publishing	432	497	439	642	570	619	696	558
28 Chemicals	390	515	714	584	594	601	638	633
29 Petroleum and Coal Products	503	379	353	628	570	624	665	600
30 Rubber	- -	- -	- -	483	424	471	494	566
31 Leather and Leather Products	442	430	420	491	452	513	447	485
32 Stone, Clay and Glass	508	523	578	558	466	508	581	509
33 Primary Metals	587	- -	- -	583	405	573	620	530
34 Fabricated Metals	494	488	423	558	485	533	566	525
35 Non-electrical Machinery	515	505	531	598	564	582	594	577
36 Electrical Machinery	- -	- -	- -	- -	- -	- -	- -	- -
37 Transportation Equipment	546	542	561	594	659	602	564	575
38 Instruments	- -	401	- -	514	534	521	501	529
39 Miscellaneous	478	400	418	554	508	550	559	497

APPENDIX, PART XIII
(Continued)

SIC Code Number and Industry	Pennsylvania	Delaware	Maryland	Ohio	Indiana	Illinois	Michigan	Wisconsin
20 Food	$611	$275	$333	$519	$465	$563	$472	$499
21 Tobacco	356	378	365	364	377	482	384	436
22 Textiles	343	297	272	342	350	223	289	286
23 Apparel	315	260	329	363	301	427	371	338
24 Lumber and Wood Products	423	241	337	428	400	461	433	447
25 Furniture	463	576	469	436	389	506	428	377
26 Paper	415	534	356	384	430	411	368	420
27 Printing and Publishing	569	452	523	545	497	577	491	476
28 Chemicals	580	325	561	637	548	634	489	523
29 Petroleum and Coal Products	515	549	533	531	424	575	476	367
30 Rubber	508	- -	- -	415	- -	531	458	369
31 Leather and Leather Products	413	464	305	387	413	548	421	277
32 Stone, Clay and Glass	492	476	452	466	518	530	472	441
33 Primary Metals	577	533	502	596	576	605	545	628
34 Fabricated Metals	500	499	430	504	493	546	509	487
35 Non-electrical Machinery	569	532	516	536	483	568	514	539
36 Electrical Machinery	- -	- -	- -	- -	- -	- -	- -	- -
37 Transportation Equipment	549	552	534	503	492	566	476	501
38 Instruments	521	- -	579	610	461	543	346	484
39 Miscellaneous	421	432	352	437	447	501	417	382

APPENDIX, PART XIII
(Continued)

SIC Code Number and Industry	Minnesota	Iowa	Missouri	Kansas	Nebraska	North Dakota	South Dakota	Virginia
20 Food	$566	$439	$536	$514	$539	$565	$495	$322
21 Tobacco	451	413	479	393	435	513	473	230
22 Textiles	355	295	371	204	379	- -	- -	246
23 Apparel	363	295	366	286	391	441	288	271
24 Lumber and Wood Products	494	423	413	413	487	254	531	288
25 Furniture	498	408	500	378	397	723	357	293
26 Paper	317	340	315	- -	- -	- -	- -	286
27 Printing and Publishing	548	440	595	406	533	508	442	428
28 Chemicals	512	779	596	449	719	- -	- -	307
29 Petroleum and Coal Products	497	525	543	465	393	- -	423	431
30 Rubber	- -	398	- -	- -	- -	- -	- -	- -
31 Leather and Leather Products	427	401	427	448	500	476	443	309
32 Stone, Clay and Glass	510	457	519	452	457	475	446	290
33 Primary Metals	471	352	587	501	- -	- -	- -	325
34 Fabricated Metals	519	448	555	482	491	633	499	390
35 Non-electrical Machinery	525	497	584	616	544	661	420	483
36 Electrical Machinery	- -	- -	- -	- -	- -	- -	- -	- -
37 Transportation Equipment	548	526	560	624	589	554	664	422
38 Instruments	674	579	703	365	529	- -	- -	- -
39 Miscellaneous	450	357	486	475	466	- -	510	137

APPENDIX, PART XIII
(Continued)

SIC Code Number and Industry	West Virginia	North Carolina	South Carolina	Georgia	Florida	Kentucky	Tennessee	Alabama
20 Food	$401	$253	$256	$312	$351	$489	$459	$289
21 Tobacco	366	207	139	250	532	315	324	375
22 Textiles	291	184	180	210	345	264	212	189
23 Apparel	376	229	175	230	336	291	327	305
24 Lumber and Wood Products	372	234	222	264	341	346	334	269
25 Furniture	400	210	288	319	409	400	351	313
26 Paper	365	– –	– –	105	– –	– –	232	– –
27 Printing and Publishing	455	391	418	415	503	514	546	481
28 Chemicals	414	245	281	215	214	524	406	223
29 Petroleum and Coal Products	476	406	334	413	538	434	394	448
30 Rubber	– –	– –	– –	– –	– –	– –	– –	– –
31 Leather and Leather Products	386	315	325	261	427	402	369	316
32 Stone, Clay and Glass	413	207	240	275	330	384	321	270
33 Primary Metals	434	– –	– –	153	– –	507	311	363
34 Fabricated Metals	542	226	255	271	567	467	403	280
35 Non-electrical Machinery	570	324	365	394	508	469	390	422
36 Electrical Machinery	– –	– –	– –	– –	– –	– –	– –	– –
37 Transportation Equipment	484	410	407	419	508	476	481	437
38 Instruments	– –	– –	– –	135	– –	459	– –	– –
39 Miscellaneous	– –	201	116	260	263	361	445	140

APPENDIX, PART XIII
(Continued)

SIC Code Number and Industry	Mississippi	Arkansas	Louisiana	Oklahoma	Texas
20 Food	$328	$381	$424	$520	$504
21 Tobacco	- -	428	370	363	464
22 Textiles	214	202	a	- -	297
23 Apparel	308	401	266	264	366
24 Lumber and Wood Products	317	323	367	270	427
25 Furniture	81	352	320	454	426
26 Paper	- -	- -	219	- -	- -
27 Printing and Publishing	411	414	541	401	568
28 Chemicals	253	425	410	- -	482
29 Petroleum and Coal Products	535	536	584	444	615
30 Rubber	- -	- -	- -	- -	- -
31 Leather and Leather Products	180	456	433	538	492
32 Stone, Clay and Glass	271	318	256	446	422
33 Primary Metals	- -	- -	- -	- -	- -
34 Fabricated Metals	446	461	280	470	529
35 Non-electrical Machinery	494	518	474	463	591
36 Electrical Machinery	- -	- -	- -	- -	- -
37 Transportation Equipment	524	592	479	467	620
38 Instruments	- -	- -	- -	- -	673
39 Miscellaneous	41	339	112	213	463

APPENDIX, PART XIV

OUTPUT-LABOR RATIOS BY REGION, 1860
(dollars per employee)

SIC Code Number and Industry	New England	Middle Atlantic	East North Central	West North Central	South Atlantic	East South Central	West South Central	Average for Regions
20 Food	$1167	$1388	$1532	$1676	$ 835	$1000	$1472	$1337
21 Tobacco	641	685	581	596	432	508	1019	532
22 Textiles	557	516	532	614	374	421	563	533
23 Apparel	401	368	353	516	421	413	1092	380
24 Lumber and Wood Products	606	648	617	869	611	750	984	663
25 Furniture	558	689	640	737	659	770	601	647
26 Paper	810	811	866	677	1036	835	- -	821
27 Printing and Publishing	755	859	679	747	772	934	915	817
28 Chemicals	1433	1467	1640	1057	477	700	1675	1121
29 Petroleum and Coal Products	2158	1481	1309	4072	1374	1327	9000	1591
30 Rubber	1034	1196	- -	- -	- -	- -	- -	1125
31 Leather and Leather Products	427	602	561	677	549	649	700	514
32 Stone, Clay and Glass	582	593	499	636	476	547	706	573
33 Primary Metals	753	712	691	1258	563	570	781	712
34 Fabricated Metals	717	745	811	928	798	956	1020	761
35 Non-electrical Machinery	847	816	874	770	744	1020	1236	847
36 Electrical Machinery	- -	- -	- -	- -	- -	- -	- -	- -
37 Transportation Equipment	664	683	634	782	589	757	1164	676
38 Instruments	732	942	834	814	- -	- -	- -	843
39 Miscellaneous	852	788	1138	883	739	1271	1795	836

APPENDIX, PART XV

OUTPUT-LABOR RATIOS BY STATE, 1860

SIC Code Number and Industry	Maine	New Hampshire	Vermont	Massachusetts	Rhode Island	Connecticut	New York	New Jersey
20 Food	$710	$928	$785	$1303	$2356	$809	$1586	$1477
21 Tobacco	482	435	473	622	683	715	669	985
22 Textiles	479	531	583	563	566	588	523	514
23 Apparel	255	381	382	417	408	427	387	369
24 Lumber and Wood Products	549	524	512	703	880	671	629	841
25 Furniture	591	463	548	545	706	757	731	594
26 Paper	1020	939	531	827	573	712	806	730
27 Printing and Publishing	739	750	489	793	758	679	901	616
28 Chemicals	1399	848	792	1464	1290	1553	1463	1380
29 Petroleum and Coal Products	3026	1604	1488	1951	2118	3069	1517	2667
30 Rubber	-	-	-	906	1253	1050	1609	816
31 Leather and Leather Products	463	401	578	424	545	465	642	559
32 Stone, Clay and Glass	426	554	876	605	457	524	608	518
33 Primary Metals	705	622	679	778	673	768	847	733
34 Fabricated Metals	780	703	712	746	908	659	756	662
35 Non-electrical Machinery	554	717	1114	871	689	1025	896	893
36 Electrical Machinery	-	-	-	-	-	-	-	-
37 Transportation Equipment	462	679	570	687	754	745	729	680
38 Instruments	769	-	532	942	1150	656	1012	-
39 Miscellaneous	740	610	1129	895	781	843	806	840

APPENDIX, PART XV
(Continued)

SIC Code Number and Industry	Pennsylvania	Delaware	Maryland	Ohio	Indiana	Illinois	Michigan	Wisconsin
20 Food	$1262	$1467	$ 903	$1477	$1146	$1857	$1630	$1679
21 Tobacco	508	925	1947	584	575	876	555	360
22 Textiles	517	367	521	489	585	515	647	809
23 Apparel	363	353	247	339	377	562	276	409
24 Lumber and Wood Products	649	534	646	627	697	732	546	557
25 Furniture	622	520	692	639	570	773	522	549
26 Paper	830	1060	950	881	927	554	729	1011
27 Printing and Publishing	810	796	883	644	622	851	683	580
28 Chemicals	1565	1086	981	1794	897	2659	822	1031
29 Petroleum and Coal Products	1464	1890	1049	1310	1033	1441	1083	1119
30 Rubber	900	- -	- -	- -	- -	- -	- -	- -
31 Leather and Leather Products	568	615	617	547	531	607	616	540
32 Stone, Clay and Glass	650	393	378	532	421	529	498	385
33 Primary Metals	649	789	715	623	734	1062	906	800
34 Fabricated Metals	779	578	700	739	1003	920	868	740
35 Non-electrical Machinery	752	670	538	861	934	839	814	1354
36 Electrical Machinery	- -	- -	- -	- -	- -	- -	- -	- -
37 Transportation Equipment	650	586	699	649	612	644	676	553
38 Instruments	862	- -	2375	756	- -	672	1469	1064
39 Miscellaneous	746	1071	683	1262	730	1042	949	771

APPENDIX, PART XV
(Continued)

SIC Code Number and Industry	Minnesota	Iowa	Missouri	Kansas	Nebraska	Virginia	North Carolina	South Carolina
20 Food	$1432	$1604	$1746	$1982	$1056	$989	$353	$484
21 Tobacco	468	680	595	- -	- -	448	311	- -
22 Textiles	320	512	629	- -	- -	484	283	307
23 Apparel	714	386	540	- -	303	356	398	914
24 Lumber and Wood Products	562	630	932	2062	1403	570	522	596
25 Furniture	599	842	707	957	543	558	575	533
26 Paper	- -	831	524	- -	- -	938	1248	763
27 Printing and Publishing	670	600	864	609	875	518	792	730
28 Chemicals	- -	541	1069	742	- -	919	551	286
29 Petroleum and Coal Products	- -	1425	5038	- -	- -	1406	901	- -
30 Rubber	- -	- -	- -	- -	- -	- -	- -	- -
31 Leather and Leather Products	572	670	694	748	525	556	515	531
32 Stone, Clay and Glass	327	408	565	5020	411	490	351	444
33 Primary Metals	818	780	1307	- -	- -	546	553	453
34 Fabricated Metals	767	780	1016	1096	1434	848	656	823
35 Non-electrical Machinery	510	1207	696	800	- -	726	592	824
36 Electrical Machinery	- -	- -	- -	- -	- -	- -	- -	- -
37 Transportation Equipment	633	640	816	1040	647	553	569	660
38 Instruments	- -	- -	813	- -	- -	- -	- -	- -
39 Miscellaneous	561	478	896	1181	2465	735	550	748

APPENDIX, PART XV
(Continued)

SIC Code Number and Industry	Georgia	Florida	Kentucky	Tennessee	Alabama	Mississippi	Arkansas
20 Food	$1082	$ 587	$ 992	$1156	$ 958	$ 501	$1255
21 Tobacco	335	- -	451	673	675	625	428
22 Textiles	347	252	596	373	354	303	393
23 Apparel	849	450	356	1141	381	796	1073
24 Lumber and Wood Products	651	773	736	750	705	830	896
25 Furniture	824	- -	833	696	662	757	465
26 Paper	1178	- -	869	742	- -	- -	- -
27 Printing and Publishing	980	600	891	943	737	1493	733
28 Chemicals	362	354	2108	1627	452	242	- -
29 Petroleum and Coal Products	1854	- -	1216	2211	1772	2100	- -
30 Rubber	- -	- -	- -	- -	- -	- -	- -
31 Leather and Leather Products	567	582	705	637	550	626	659
32 Stone, Clay and Glass	425	631	520	456	571	703	344
33 Primary Metals	688	1350	695	443	585	715	314
34 Fabricated Metals	641	913	997	902	1113	771	1113
35 Non-electrical Machinery	774	401	958	711	1397	1109	1692
36 Electrical Machinery	- -	- -	- -	- -	- -	- -	- -
37 Transportation Equipment	593	829	769	790	668	765	- -
38 Instruments	- -	- -	1760	- -	- -	- -	763
39 Miscellaneous	995	- -	1330	881	725	1143	650

APPENDIX, PART XV
(Continued)

SIC Code Number and Industry	Louisiana	Texas
20 Food	$1565	$1436
21 Tobacco	1142	- -
22 Textiles	589	496
23 Apparel	1106	331
24 Lumber and Wood Products	1026	997
25 Furniture	653	594
26 Paper	1750	- -
27 Printing and Publishing	827	1003
28 Chemicals	1696	1283
29 Petroleum and Coal Products	9000	- -
30 Rubber	- -	- -
31 Leather and Leather Products	687	799
32 Stone, Clay and Glass	754	500
33 Primary Metals	810	- -
34 Fabricated Metals	1158	731
35 Non-electrical Machinery	1254	944
36 Electrical Machinery	- -	- -
37 Transportation Equipment	1359	798
38 Instruments	- -	- -
39 Miscellaneous	1946	1577

APPENDIX, PART XVI

OUTPUT-LABOR RATIOS BY REGION, 1900
(dollars per employee)

SIC Code Number and Industry	New England	Middle Atlantic	East North Central	West North Central	South Atlantic	East South Central	West South Central	Average for Regions
20 Food	$1191	$1452	$1872	$1282	$ 764	$1210	$1101	$1458
21 Tobacco	958	969	924	1804	1002	1426	924	1056
22 Textiles	660	643	537	584	391	405	524	606
23 Apparel	726	771	740	588	508	555	563	734
24 Lumber and Wood Products	733	785	783	837	569	602	669	720
25 Furniture	935	852	686	766	510	650	650	762
26 Paper	989	894	784	537	611	355	424	885
27 Printing and Publishing	1221	1261	1024	915	747	909	893	1112
28 Chemicals	4009	1648	1589	1654	396	654	1063	1299
29 Petroleum and Coal Products	1412	1417	1309	1231	1091	1120	1487	1360
30 Rubber	1303	954	843	-	-	-	-	1151
31 Leather and Leather Products	678	710	593	561	596	760	739	662
32 Stone, Clay and Glass	829	937	767	759	499	550	602	824
33 Primary Metals	965	1256	1199	844	912	908	672	1178
34 Fabricated Metals	831	873	913	847	670	780	748	874
35 Non-electrical Machinery	940	948	919	939	729	717	928	927
36 Electrical Machinery	-	-	-	-	-	-	-	-
37 Transportation Equipment	801	760	703	701	560	568	645	709
38 Instruments	754	935	814	1375	969	803	1224	883
39 Miscellaneous	938	942	816	784	1586	754	777	907

APPENDIX, PART XVII

OUTPUT LABOR RATIOS BY STATE, 1900
(dollars per employee)

SIC Code Number and Industry	Maine	New Hampshire	Vermont	Massachusetts	Rhode Island	Connecticut	New York	New Jersey
20 Food	$544	$1542	$980	$1368	$1458	$1348	$1574	$1715
21 Tobacco	742	816	721	1041	965	843	1075	1609
22 Textiles	619	614	617	664	696	656	662	703
23 Apparel	477	508	544	800	656	709	885	618
24 Lumber and Wood Products	647	763	634	820	730	828	786	859
25 Furniture	761	655	636	992	849	1029	886	895
26 Paper	1167	1234	1288	916	602	850	908	841
27 Printing and Publishing	964	788	751	1324	974	1088	1387	911
28 Chemicals	1115	1956	3492	1812	1528	1950	1779	1409
29 Petroleum and Coal Products	1091	997	483	1770	1247	1528	1642	1142
30 Rubber	- -	- -	- -	1097	1164	2255	971	992
31 Leather and Leather Products	606	568	579	702	732	755	696	732
32 Stone, Clay and Glass	779	721	832	889	678	813	1266	754
33 Primary Metals	1063	- -	- -	953	810	974	1142	1310
34 Fabricated Metals	739	762	688	906	788	800	931	789
35 Non-electrical Machinery	729	844	949	998	852	896	982	895
36 Electrical Machinery	- -	- -	- -	- -	- -	- -	- -	- -
37 Transportation Equipment	715	663	614	827	897	859	735	774
38 Instruments	- -	672	- -	849	943	690	902	988
39 Miscellaneous	841	777	519	945	947	938	1030	847

APPENDIX, PART XVII
(continued)

SIC Code Number and Industry	Pennsylvania	Delaware	Maryland	Ohio	Indiana	Illinois	Michigan	Wisconsin
20 Food	$1463	$ 695	$ 800	$1845	$2146	$1944	$1249	$1805
21 Tobacco	710	624	1265	890	653	783	976	1045
22 Textiles	615	410	486	602	525	563	492	497
23 Apparel	684	424	583	702	517	868	580	629
24 Lumber and Wood Products	815	402	624	758	735	731	784	858
25 Furniture	764	883	852	735	582	836	636	594
26 Paper	878	1158	742	786	787	761	656	879
27 Printing and Publishing	1095	627	912	990	883	1163	851	826
28 Chemicals	1689	1273	1331	2056	1522	1751	1143	1272
29 Petroleum and Coal Products	1271	1233	2232	1351	919	1521	959	1213
30 Rubber	669	- -	- -	670	- -	1499	761	618
31 Leather and Leather Products	730	874	497	564	614	765	687	442
32 Stone, Clay and Glass	792	741	716	713	710	894	781	740
33 Primary Metals	1269	970	851	1296	880	1136	1004	1543
34 Fabricated Metals	848	705	694	829	896	965	971	901
35 Non-electrical Machinery	939	777	991	919	781	1006	818	878
36 Electrical Machinery	- -	- -	- -	- -	- -	- -	- -	- -
37 Transportation Equipment	793	676	666	692	683	716	716	720
38 Instruments	978	- -	1011	1059	1075	775	775	1826
39 Miscellaneous	830	765	629	806	642	888	809	678

APPENDIX, PART XVII
(continued)

SIC Code Number and Industry	Minnesota	Iowa	Missouri	Kansas	Nebraska	North Dakota	South Dakota	Virginia
20 Food	$1560	$1189	$1365	$1007	$1271	$1561	$1151	$ 743
21 Tobacco	759	667	2767	723	736	712	763	899
22 Textiles	668	472	603	380	310	--	414	424
23 Apparel	553	507	643	497	657	688	514	511
24 Lumber and Wood Products	1025	731	644	651	779	667	860	526
25 Furniture	824	692	789	592	660	762	502	568
26 Paper	553	576	519	--	--	--	--	589
27 Printing and Publishing	1023	759	1011	707	888	951	759	822
28 Chemicals	1463	1624	1756	952	2091	--	--	899
29 Petroleum and Coal Products	1303	1373	1295	895	959	--	519	905
30 Rubber	--	494	--	--	--	--	--	--
31 Leather and Leather Products	625	157	635	642	724	758	676	561
32 Stone, Clay and Glass	738	699	812	699	763	809	680	516
33 Primary Metals	317	565	998	713	--	--	--	877
34 Fabricated Metals	892	796	905	626	746	777	594	720
35 Non-electrical Machinery	886	810	1012	908	756	994	663	688
36 Electrical Machinery	--	--	--	--	--	--	--	--
37 Transportation Equipment	648	683	771	649	646	583	785	584
38 Instruments	1466	683	1391	1442	1030	--	--	1358
39 Miscellaneous	872	556	876	892	1205	--	504	614

APPENDIX, PART XVII
(continued)

SIC Code Number and Industry	West Virginia	North Carolina	South Carolina	Georgia	Florida	Kentucky	Tennessee	Alabama
20 Food	$1023	$ 624	$666	$ 832	$712	$1696	$1112	$ 707
21 Tobacco	1224	1262	405	448	884	1526	993	914
22 Textiles	456	354	405	420	429	519	372	391
23 Apparel	760	437	495	439	547	543	568	589
24 Lumber and Wood Products	741	485	466	608	648	636	585	553
25 Furniture	649	429	599	539	538	804	539	538
26 Paper	722	323	553	630	- -	- -	355	- -
27 Printing and Publishing	734	666	720	727	770	926	985	782
28 Chemicals	1675	653	709	339	328	1935	1402	433
29 Petroleum and Coal Products	954	925	991	1376	1720	972	1400	1247
30 Rubber	- -	- -	- -	- -	- -	- -	- -	- -
31 Leather and Leather Products	794	629	618	520	548	804	667	- -
32 Stone, Clay and Glass	623	333	392	503	454	641	541	916
33 Primary Metals	964	704	769	614	- -	1016	745	459
34 Fabricated Metals	957	455	608	637	815	820	701	923
35 Non-electrical Machinery	1087	679	610	706	889	783	646	838
36 Electrical Machinery	- -	- -	- -	- -	- -	- -	- -	729
37 Transportation Equipment	531	520	496	569	587	594	588	521
38 Instruments	- -	490	- -	1044	- -	1083	- -	563
39 Miscellaneous	- -	584	463	600	443	791	753	648

APPENDIX, PART XVII
(continued)

SIC Code Number and Industry	Mississippi	Arkansas	Louisiana	Oklahoma	Texas
20 Food	$ 744	$ 993	$ 940	$1536	$1359
21 Tobacco	- -	704	986	527	770
22 Textiles	385	288	495	- -	554
23 Apparel	558	641	532	538	589
24 Lumber and Wood Products	637	601	712	444	744
25 Furniture	533	670	600	639	689
26 Paper	- -	- -	424	- -	- -
27 Printing and Publishing	779	748	914	684	951
28 Chemicals	453	1315	1015	- -	1212
29 Petroleum and Coal Products	1685	1201	1672	625	1405
30 Rubber	- -	- -	- -	- -	- -
31 Leather and Leather Products	579	632	647	757	801
32 Stone, Clay and Glass	448	524	427	690	674
33 Primary Metals	- -	- -	672	- -	- -
34 Fabricated Metals	716	604	760	569	773
35 Non-electrical Machinery	740	871	913	835	959
36 Electrical Machinery	- -	- -	- -	- -	- -
37 Transportation Equipment	568	637	614	676	657
38 Instruments	- -	- -	1001	- -	2108
39 Miscellaneous	524	600	824	415	745

APPENDIX, PART XVIII

TOTAL CAPITAL INVESTED IN MANUFACTURING BY REGION, 1860

SIC Code Number and Industry	New England	Middle Atlantic	East North Central	West North Central	South Atlantic	East South Central	West South Central	Total for Regions (000$)
20 Food	9,983,797	65,520,981	43,838,075	10,460,500	11,317,896	7,565,387	1,618,033	150,304.7
21 Tobacco	614,600	2,690,830	555,365	1,103,510	4,574,320	2,917,535	40,200	12,496.3
22 Textiles	101,637,487	38,897,702	2,647,896	1,150,160	6,727,991	4,293,045	1,344,680	156,699.0
23 Apparel	7,330,480	25,038,612	4,605,296	498,860	343,897	790,122	321,520	38,928.8
24 Lumber and Wood Products	12,858,919	29,732,096	25,538,280	4,989,048	7,024,336	6,321,505	3,461,337	89,925.4
25 Furniture	2,745,025	5,888,699	3,760,573	451,695	416,331	391,365	82,030	13,735.7
26 Paper	6,732,360	6,058,766	1,300,253	17,400	558,350	142,600	1,800	14,811.7
27 Printing and Publishing	3,055,850	15,036,350	2,372,924	291,150	365,050	832,250	188,024	22,141.8
28 Chemicals	4,246,220	15,438,586	1,788,325	582,450	3,476,516	1,929,370	334,420	27,795.9
29 Petroleum and Coal Products	6,649,225	15,409,873	3,961,300	1,176,967	1,827,100	2,205,316	45,000	31,274.8
30 Rubber	1,984,000	1,650,000	400	–	–	–	–	3,634.4
31 Leather and Leather Products	19,405,806	35,122,824	7,189,690	1,269,362	2,786,670	3,353,413	755,348	69,883.2
32 Stone, Clay and Glass	4,632,508	15,097,060	2,967,015	506,575	1,393,492	831,627	645,575	26,073.9
33 Primary Metals	13,185,350	57,764,447	9,445,126	2,668,500	3,980,262	5,157,910	56,000	92,257.6
34 Fabricated Metals	12,400,065	14,124,917	4,095,369	1,250,479	1,211,251	1,272,355	513,130	34,867.7
35 Non-electrical Machinery	10,855,505	19,547,057	10,485,024	1,384,200	3,047,943	2,303,760	950,375	48,573.9
36 Electrical Machinery	–	–	–	–	–	–	–	–
37 Transportation Equipment	6,661,835	16,378,411	4,671,347	771,845	2,454,071	1,837,607	842,180	33,617.2
38 Instruments	1,072,000	1,883,700	53,450	7,350	–	3,000	–	3,019.6
39 Miscellaneous	9,653,065	16,163,880	1,563,447	432,250	121,275	241,845	35,563	28,211.4
Total	235,704,097	397,444,791	130,839,155	29,012,301	51,626,751	42,390,012	11,235,215	898,253.0

APPENDIX, PART XIX

TOTAL CAPITAL INVESTED IN MANUFACTURING BY STATE, 1860

SIC Code Number and Industry	Maine	New Hampshire	Vermont	Massachusetts	Rhode Island	Connecticut	New York	New Jersey
20 Food	$ 1,268,820	$ 560,970	$ 754,835	$ 5,830,717	$ 634,200	$ 934,255	$31,622,585	$ 4,771,735
21 Tobacco	3,600	26,200	14,500	244,200	52,300	273,800	1,236,817	335,750
22 Textiles	7,364,680	15,462,380	2,063,050	50,201,977	14,583,500	11,961,900	13,236,056	4,826,550
23 Apparel	400,050	236,880	79,450	3,603,750	401,650	2,608,700	12,268,061	2,762,865
24 Lumber and Wood Products	4,772,740	1,809,811	1,138,535	3,739,923	360,485	1,037,425	12,863,909	1,926,875
25 Furniture	106,217	179,050	149,200	1,892,758	139,900	277,900	3,373,231	253,100
26 Paper	519,100	426,900	139,500	3,696,560	8,400	1,941,900	2,462,246	1,023,500
27 Printing and Publishing	265,400	216,200	90,000	1,982,550	127,100	374,600	8,959,200	267,300
28 Chemicals	260,900	180,400	19,190	2,122,005	198,500	1,465,225	5,384,156	2,368,400
29 Petroleum and Coal Products	991,500	258,000	106,725	3,734,400	792,600	766,000	8,713,050	20,000
30 Rubber	- -	- -	- -	563,000	156,000	1,265,000	775,000	870,000
31 Leather and Leather Products	1,476,434	1,261,273	646,662	14,131,642	273,495	1,616,300	15,924,624	4,095,369
32 Stone, Clay and Glass	352,243	125,190	705,050	2,807,625	250,800	391,600	5,255,629	2,060,034
33 Primary Metals	569,600	425,500	284,600	7,300,950	815,100	3,789,600	12,594,010	5,124,810
34 Fabricated Metals	562,300	450,700	322,150	3,963,850	1,723,875	5,377,190	7,553,530	1,642,400
35 Non-electrical Machinery	714,350	459,600	1,443,200	4,514,355	1,434,300	2,289,700	9,548,742	1,284,300
36 Electrical Machinery	- -	- -	- -	- -	- -	- -	- -	- -
37 Transportation Equipment	856,790	797,950	358,020	2,242,050	183,400	2,223,625	5,050,966	2,836,535
38 Instruments	1,000	- -	1,400	469,800	10,000	589,800	854,750	- -
39 Miscellaneous	93,800	95,625	59,650	3,651,865	1,652,650	4,099,475	9,439,573	1,331,390
Total	20,579,524	22,972,629	8,375,717	116,687,977	23,798,255	43,283,995	167,116,135	37,800,913

APPENDIX, PART XIX
(Continued)

SIC Code Number and Industry	Pennsylvania	Delaware	Maryland	Ohio	Indiana	Illinois	Michigan	Wisconsin
20 Food	$24,144,074	$728,162	$4,254,425	$16,188,863	$8,406,170	$10,914,188	$3,541,590	$4,787,264
21 Tobacco	810,213	35,000	273,050	309,385	48,500	106,630	32,750	58,100
22 Textiles	17,446,596	700,500	2,688,000	1,310,785	779,161	272,550	161,500	123,900
23 Apparel	8,502,946	77,850	1,426,890	3,309,965	371,380	294,980	252,500	376,471
24 Lumber and Wood Products	13,752,602	351,660	837,050	5,638,793	3,072,878	2,359,208	8,169,707	6,297,694
25 Furniture	1,895,368	61,700	305,300	2,253,443	442,780	511,920	326,530	225,900
26 Paper	2,020,220	280,000	272,800	919,150	147,500	54,103	46,500	133,000
27 Printing and Publishing	5,455,950	89,200	264,700	1,312,354	191,120	495,900	216,350	157,200
28 Chemicals	6,897,230	543,000	245,800	1,339,020	80,650	212,550	67,475	88,630
29 Petroleum and Coal Products	5,303,523	177,300	1,196,000	1,966,650	154,900	1,180,000	138,000	521,750
30 Rubber	5,000	- -	- -	- -	- -	400	- -	- -
31 Leather and Leather Products	12,956,006	595,650	1,551,175	3,825,821	605,921	1,014,575	1,019,568	723,805
32 Stone, Clay and Glass	7,128,877	117,200	535,320	1,251,040	279,925	700,765	516,735	218,550
33 Primary Metals	37,155,364	316,100	2,574,163	6,875,440	329,858	898,356	828,500	512,972
34 Fabricated Metals	4,307,962	142,600	478,425	1,363,990	343,927	657,600	1,122,872	606,980
35 Non-electrical Machinery	7,023,815	281,100	1,409,100	4,518,030	1,340,366	2,914,795	1,410,933	300,900
36 Electrical Machinery	- -	- -	- -	- -	- -	- -	- -	- -
37 Transportation Equipment	6,934,910	848,550	707,450	1,964,479	688,990	1,231,948	401,765	384,165
38 Instruments	1,019,950	- -	9,000	42,900	- -	5,400	4,500	650
39 Miscellaneous	5,081,067	27,500	284,350	1,116,208	85,489	178,425	111,025	72,300
Total	167,596,629	5,373,072	19,312,998	55,506,316	17,369,515	24,004,293	18,368,800	15,590,231

APPENDIX, PART XIX
(Continued)

SIC Code Number and Industry	Minnesota	Iowa	Missouri	Kansas	Nebraska	Virginia	North Carolina	South Carolina
20 Food	$ 696,250	$ 3,119,393	$ 6,427,127	$ 134,630	$ 83,100	$ 6,590,065	$ 1,792,486	$ 1,151,655
21 Tobacco	3,200	14,300	1,086,010	--	--	3,889,490	646,730	--
22 Textiles	3,740	107,980	1,038,440	--	--	1,928,713	1,516,850	862,925
23 Apparel	3,400	61,510	425,450	--	8,500	219,347	4,675	44,450
24 Lumber and Wood Products	1,420,620	1,819,940	2,222,648	395,940	129,900	1,546,507	1,058,831	1,292,066
25 Furniture	48,150	151,050	240,295	10,000	2,200	201,270	50,170	6,275
26 Paper	--	12,000	5,400	--	--	154,500	121,850	111,000
27 Printing and Publishing	14,500	117,000	141,550	2,800	15,300	103,600	43,300	18,700
28 Chemicals	--	54,000	527,700	750	--	129,250	2,062,476	945,270
29 Petroleum and Coal Products	--	471,300	705,667	--	--	1,512,600	41,500	--
30 Rubber	--	--	--	--	--	--	--	--
31 Leather and Leather Products	72,025	311,047	837,240	37,150	11,900	1,380,528	466,588	361,265
32 Stone, Clay and Glass	1,500	50,983	434,142	17,700	2,250	654,255	73,287	377,075
33 Primary Metals	25,000	191,150	2,452,350	--	--	3,095,212	220,750	100,000
34 Fabricated Metals	60,375	321,447	853,157	6,000	9,500	922,516	133,620	41,100
35 Non-electrical Machinery	300	217,900	1,154,000	12,000	--	437,897	455,846	812,200
36 Electrical Machinery	--	--	--	--	--	--	--	--
37 Transportation Equipment	11,600	123,495	616,950	18,000	1,800	736,180	494,769	682,205
38 Instruments	--	--	7,350	--	--	--	--	--
39 Miscellaneous	11,500	7,700	409,500	1,750	1,800	94,617	3,300	22,640
Total	2,372,160	7,152,195	19,584,976	636,720	266,250	23,596,547	9,187,028	6,828,826

APPENDIX, PART XIX
(Continued)

SIC Code Number and Industry	Georgia	Florida	Kentucky	Tennessee	Alabama	Mississippi
20 Food	$ 1,761,365	$ 22,325	$ 4,208,321	$ 2,219,883	$ 700,708	$ 436,475
21 Tobacco	38,100	- -	1,975,817	928,218	3,500	10,000
22 Textiles	2,389,503	30,000	1,436,745	1,064,300	1,471,500	320,500
23 Apparel	71,925	3,500	618,090	34,950	46,232	90,850
24 Lumber and Wood Products	1,831,432	1,295,500	1,751,935	1,562,713	1,945,647	1,061,210
25 Furniture	158,616	- -	203,915	90,595	58,650	38,205
26 Paper	171,000	- -	128,100	14,500	- -	- -
27 Printing and Publishing	197,750	1,700	145,375	606,900	51,400	28,575
28 Chemicals	198,520	141,000	163,425	31,000	1,733,845	1,100
29 Petroleum and Coal Products	273,000	- -	1,782,966	205,000	135,000	82,350
30 Rubber	- -	- -	- -	- -	- -	- -
31 Leather and Leather Products	556,489	21,800	1,275,809	1,185,307	528,142	364,155
32 Stone, Clay and Glass	239,875	49,000	248,800	58,550	392,700	131,577
33 Primary Metals	534,300	30,000	3,295,500	1,573,310	275,500	13,600
34 Fabricated Metals	85,915	28,100	533,270	343,315	206,620	189,150
35 Non-electrical Machinery	1,317,000	25,000	91,100	320,200	753,460	1,139,000
36 Electrical Machinery	- -	- -	- -	- -	- -	- -
37 Transportation Equipment	451,742	89,175	767,850	542,825	313,457	213,475
38 Instruments	- -	- -	3,000	- -	- -	- -
39 Miscellaneous	718	- -	173,745	19,325	4,125	44,650
Total	10,277,250	1,737,100	18,803,763	10,800,891	8,620,486	4,164,872

APPENDIX, PART XIX
(Continued)

SIC Code Number and Industry	Arkansas	Louisiana	Texas
20 Food	$ 285,650	$ 474,500	$ 857,883
21 Tobacco	9,000	31,200	- -
22 Textiles	70,000	1,200,300	74,380
23 Apparel	12,500	307,020	2,000
24 Lumber and Wood Products	594,190	1,551,517	1,315,630
25 Furniture	9,800	23,050	49,180
26 Paper	- -	1,800	- -
27 Printing and Publishing	9,800	99,400	78,824
28 Chemicals	- -	328,720	5,700
29 Petroleum and Coal Products	- -	45,000	- -
30 Rubber	- -	- -	- -
31 Leather and Leather Products	130,365	440,015	184,968
32 Stone, Clay and Glass	9,750	614,425	21,400
33 Primary Metals	25,000	31,000	- -
34 Fabricated Metals	41,475	313,950	157,705
35 Non-electrical Machinery	42,500	712,000	195,875
36 Electrical Machinery	- -	- -	- -
37 Transportation Equipment	46,800	712,475	82,905
38 Instruments	- -	- -	- -
39 Miscellaneous	600	24,863	10,100
Total	1,287,430	6,911,235	3,036,550

APPENDIX, PART XX

TOTAL CAPITAL INVESTED IN MANUFACTURING BY REGION, 1900

SIC Code Number and Industry	New England	Middle Atlantic	East North Central	West North Central	South Atlantic	East South Central	West South Central	Total for Regions (000$)
20 Food	103,666,998	543,304,895	411,017,511	191,346,164	37,645,212	52,657,991	120,225,628	1,459,864.4
21 Tobacco	3,710,679	51,028,791	19,642,880	11,280,989	24,202,733	11,486,617	1,094,062	122,446.8
22 Textiles	531,519,929	332,896,600	25,509,858	2,643,898	108,530,461	25,831,372	4,079,578	1,031,011.8
23 Apparel	33,751,080	218,486,241	68,433,220	18,832,716	4,905,932	6,360,000	5,158,267	355,927.4
24 Lumber and Wood Products	63,904,334	144,457,152	232,308,629	88,123,063	74,770,660	59,489,317	65,875,968	728,929.2
25 Furniture	21,026,227	41,397,037	62,837,148	8,997,246	3,502,860	2,855,993	1,212,118	141,828.5
26 Paper	73,670,000	91,366,128	44,674,854	879,051	4,490,897	64,316	29,797	215,175.1
27 Printing and Publishing	34,769,769	157,567,378	70,806,132	32,487,000	8,557,527	8,385,893	6,418,854	318,992.6
28 Chemicals	20,709,248	186,665,717	60,206,638	14,453,012	37,889,897	7,342,620	2,739,118	330,006.1
29 Petroleum and Coal Products	48,760,055	357,606,017	149,210,519	57,197,848	10,707,032	8,912,076	4,673,435	637,066.9
30 Rubber	51,179,767	13,325,439	7,703,814	2,436	– –	– –	– –	72,211.4
31 Leather and Leather Products	88,170,476	139,054,972	71,019,133	20,776,030	14,599,197	11,389,488	4,248,463	349,257.8
32 Stone, Clay and Glass	37,378,811	186,719,905	100,709,755	29,687,647	11,116,621	7,077,885	4,173,839	376,864.4
33 Primary Metals	46,667,432	415,620,809	177,866,989	11,431,843	24,327,680	30,323,028	134,923	706,372.6
34 Fabricated Metals	68,826,944	131,104,328	181,168,351	20,036,870	3,138,871	4,034,519	2,344,639	410,654.5
35 Non-electrical Machinery	140,549,712	378,186,297	217,008,978	24,765,885	13,510,581	12,738,209	6,864,769	793,624.5
36 Electrical Machinery	– –	– –	– –	– –	– –	– –	– –	– –
37 Transportation Equipment	28,202,547	149,600,205	134,063,850	38,154,345	12,327,273	11,815,640	6,903,078	381,066.9
38 Instruments	8,700,545	25,033,591	9,241,668	1,340,566	101,749	42,129	264,621	44,724.8
39 Miscellaneous	79,531,366	117,807,996	63,741,529	6,992,454	899,695	1,272,573	1,082,869	271,328.6
Total (000$)	1,484,695.8	3,681,229.4	2,107,171.5	579,429.0	395,224.9	262,079.6	237,524.1	8,747,354.3

APPENDIX, PART XXI

TOTAL CAPITAL INVESTED IN MANUFACTURING BY STATE, 1900

SIC Code Number and Industry	Maine	New Hampshire	Vermont	Massachusetts	Rhode Island	Connecticut	New York	New Jersey
20 Food	12,647,900	4,207,711	3,377,031	66,445,137	6,783,212	10,206,007	299,413,120	44,757,282
21 Tobacco	134,076	147,199	42,941	2,358,501	121,321	906,641	23,404,521	8,003,163
22 Textiles	35,371,837	40,943,337	6,770,098	286,147,379	98,242,892	64,044,386	103,526,973	82,124,268
23 Apparel	1,817,083	1,441,736	964,172	19,461,598	999,034	9,067,457	152,663,014	10,587,112
24 Lumber and Wood Products	18,475,509	14,076,033	9,737,948	16,358,088	1,520,123	3,736,633	58,854,397	7,206,587
25 Furniture	608,253	832,391	1,166,918	14,002,015	430,067	3,986,583	26,664,732	1,579,079
26 Paper	17,573,681	8,314,163	4,853,806	35,107,479	275,582	7,545,289	56,543,199	6,737,396
27 Printing and Publishing	2,065,662	1,215,426	687,145	24,510,928	1,818,417	4,472,191	103,489,989	6,581,277
28 Chemicals	1,175,145	92,441	772,431	15,360,485	950,678	2,358,068	75,015,885	39,899,534
29 Petroleum and Coal Products	1,646,848	1,560,694	756,776	30,832,656	5,803,310	8,159,771	196,046,130	63,311,421
30 Rubber	- -	- -	- -	26,542,446	9,011,736	15,625,585	4,114,297	8,287,036
31 Leather and Leather Products	7,235,276	10,655,291	844,051	64,931,360	831,109	3,673,389	44,349,662	16,078,346
32 Stone, Clay and Glass	6,267,220	1,768,528	5,779,202	17,316,942	1,758,787	4,488,132	57,142,753	32,218,752
33 Primary Metals	119,714	- -	- -	19,259,520	439,531	26,848,667	19,985,786	32,485,425
34 Fabricated Metals	1,275,796	899,939	934,191	20,552,041	1,977,249	43,187,728	64,934,291	8,157,139
35 Non-electrical Machinery	4,032,950	3,077,707	2,507,813	76,365,668	19,088,970	35,476,604	137,643,303	47,602,934
36 Electrical Machinery	- -	- -	- -	- -	- -	- -	- -	- -
37 Transportation Equipment	2,877,169	2,175,959	1,068,296	12,914,582	1,112,928	8,053,613	47,041,812	11,014,399
38 Instruments	- -	70,275	- -	3,221,165	117,701	5,291,404	14,259,022	4,305,708
39 Miscellaneous	189,738	648,899	192,771	28,684,129	15,426,692	34,389,137	74,844,658	16,743,731
Total (000$)	113,513.9	92,127.6	40,455.5	780,372.1	166,709.2	291,517.3	1,559,937.6	447,680.5

APPENDIX, PART XXI
(Continued)

SIC Code Number and Industry	Pennsyl-vania	Delaware	Maryland	Ohio	Indiana	Illinois	Michigan	Wisconsin
20 Food	163,148,374	4,269,170	31,716,949	75,612,043	38,093,444	205,050,357	28,256,521	64,005,146
21 Tobacco	16,218,401	77,229	3,325,477	9,539,705	826,079	4,109,415	2,852,035	2,315,646
22 Textiles	136,390,778	784,209	10,070,372	6,926,443	6,306,789	4,073,878	3,115,264	5,087,484
23 Apparel	39,066,941	333,286	15,835,888	20,844,517	5,166,512	30,011,403	5,674,722	6,736,066
24 Lumber and Wood Products	70,158,842	757,851	7,479,475	26,660,023	16,751,119	19,960,724	80,369,494	88,567,269
25 Furniture	10,992,136	68,337	2,092,753	12,057,746	9,261,922	14,023,254	15,324,608	12,169,618
26 Paper	22,469,025	2,735,984	2,880,524	11,892,004	5,760,831	5,101,651	5,021,967	16,897,401
27 Printing and Publishing	42,610,574	420,747	4,464,791	21,340,031	6,583,547	28,944,152	7,441,820	6,496,582
28 Chemicals	60,359,667	535,324	10,855,307	20,975,817	3,969,843	17,558,093	15,930,127	1,772,758
29 Petroleum and Coal Products	78,445,162	826,065	18,977,239	37,631,138	8,319,533	78,520,479	16,884,926	7,854,443
30 Rubber	924,106	- -	- -	5,989,129	- -	1,188,595	34,172	491,918
31 Leather and Leather Products	70,185,264	5,387,489	3,054,211	18,620,222	3,834,822	16,159,408	8,353,531	24,051,150
32 Stone, Clay and Glass	88,320,044	610,398	8,427,958	37,377,798	21,931,576	28,621,568	6,375,503	6,403,310
33 Primary Metals	355,906,231	4,207,079	3,036,288	94,511,410	15,440,003	54,816,958	6,495,567	6,603,051
34 Fabricated Metals	52,635,149	118,437	5,259,312	46,552,509	14,415,040	83,450,690	15,896,395	20,853,717
35 Non-electrical Machinery	180,982,069	5,315,825	6,642,166	85,374,393	16,787,109	68,708,659	21,929,992	24,208,825
36 Electrical Machinery	- -	- -	- -	- -	- -	- -	- -	- -
37 Transportation Equipment	79,261,347	3,935,074	8,347,573	26,352,883	30,995,459	41,513,846	22,350,176	12,851,486
38 Instruments	6,370,672	- -	98,189	466,161	83,925	8,343,749	271,028	76,805
39 Miscellaneous	20,444,901	9,735	5,764,971	18,526,844	4,105,125	29,635,705	5,362,193	6,111,662
Total (000$)	1,494,889.6	30,392.2	148,329.6	577,250.5	208,632.4	739,792.8	267,940.0	313,554.4

APPENDIX, PART XXI
(Continued)

SIC Code Number and Industry	Minnesota	Iowa	Missouri	Kansas	Nebraska	North Dakota	South Dakota
20 Food	42,729,568	27,161,206	61,722,991	27,170,072	28,095,042	1,566,557	2,900,728
21 Tobacco	1,224,700	1,264,097	8,011,237	408,086	264,873	23,536	84,460
22 Textiles	1,380,402	605,934	637,587	11,520	7,560	- -	895
23 Apparel	3,524,214	3,138,875	9,946,547	1,024,128	902,507	154,663	141,782
24 Lumber and Wood Products	55,444,660	13,182,611	17,598,706	857,240	694,299	27,275	318,272
25 Furniture	2,578,121	1,255,041	4,360,900	500,725	279,204	12,480	10,775
26 Paper	178,014	225,409	475,628	- -	- -	- -	- -
27 Printing and Publishing	7,900,285	5,719,090	12,099,819	2,519,487	2,885,583	625,902	736,834
28 Chemicals	1,708,684	1,002,269	9,884,144	777,409	1,080,506	- -	- -
29 Petroleum and Coal Products	9,159,577	4,315,450	35,063,247	1,516,869	7,132,380	- -	- -
30 Rubber	- -	2,436	- -	- -			10,325
31 Leather and Leather Products	4,708,285	3,710,129	8,526,214	1,435,180	1,486,690	585,189	
32 Stone, Clay and Glass	4,169,502	5,734,222	15,612,284	1,864,814	1,695,963	191,485	324,343
33 Primary Metals	735,256	367,310	5,066,481	5,262,796	- -	- -	419,377
34 Fabricated Metals	6,136,025	4,414,002	7,561,170	691,837	944,560	92,415	- -
35 Non-electrical Machinery	4,527,902	3,817,766	13,498,372	2,454,209	340,091	85,535	196,861
36 Electrical Machinery	- -	- -	- -	- -	- -	- -	42,010
37 Transportation Equipment	7,057,398	7,601,389	16,136,764	3,202,821	3,798,961	212,153	- -
38 Instruments	85,099	29,700	1,095,634	111,483	18,650	- -	144,859
39 Miscellaneous	2,339,411	1,066,898	2,739,424	549,395	287,496	- -	9,830
Total (000$)	155,587.2	84,613.8	230,037.0	50,358.0	49,914.6	3,577.3	5,341.4

APPENDIX, PART XXI
(Continued)

SIC Code Number and Industry	Virginia	West Virginia	North Carolina	South Carolina	Georgia	Florida	Kentucky	Tennessee
20 Food	10,400,369	5,833,653	5,889,405	4,100,534	10,266,312	1,154,939	29,283,751	13,185,084
21 Tobacco	8,963,213	2,604,792	7,146,288	54,720	83,813	5,349,907	9,451,725	1,852,511
22 Textiles	6,764,517	683,683	34,796,053	40,415,968	25,855,595	14,645	4,289,318	6,384,194
23 Apparel	1,288,962	889,265	847,411	573,177	1,134,846	172,271	3,843,628	1,854,329
24 Lumber and Wood Products	12,428,545	11,556,096	14,950,373	5,890,915	14,421,180	15,523,551	12,988,382	14,854,667
25 Furniture	374,430	538,265	1,109,786	84,436	1,373,796	22,147	1,475,960	1,135,682
26 Paper	2,732,064	964,206	13,628	259,826	521,173	--	--	64,316
27 Printing and Publishing	2,858,686	1,148,439	793,142	681,338	2,537,149	538,773	3,444,221	3,611,072
28 Chemicals	5,934,943	289,717	3,434,694	10,832,570	11,137,986	6,259,987	1,162,375	2,015,519
29 Petroleum and Coal Products	2,929,810	585,562	709,329	964,089	4,362,553	1,155,689	4,921,305	2,409,046
30 Rubber	--	--	--	--	--	--	--	--
31 Leather and Leather Products	5,333,970	5,419,902	1,571,625	90,209	2,152,691	30,800	6,509,828	4,173,992
32 Stone, Clay and Glass	2,751,856	3,996,995	999,240	788,492	2,367,040	212,998	3,081,512	1,989,776
33 Primary Metals	9,590,464	12,810,498	944,208	108,026	874,484	--	4,429,292	5,988,487
34 Fabricated Metals	1,054,362	336,418	345,273	222,779	1,131,109	48,930	2,687,795	853,534
35 Non-electrical Machinery	6,994,659	925,551	1,180,754	449,462	3,678,512	281,643	3,527,246	3,853,222
36 Electrical Machinery	--	--	--	--	--	--	--	--
37 Transportation Equipment	5,324,664	1,557,690	1,515,911	702,796	2,520,141	706,071	5,565,278	2,474,789
38 Instruments	2,201	--	8,749	--	90,799	--	21,130	--
39 Miscellaneous	172,568	--	240,203	150,743	329,619	6,562	526,349	644,402
Total (000$)	85,900.5	50,140.9	76,496.0	66,370.0	84,838.7	31,478.9	97,209.0	67,344.6

APPENDIX, PART XXI
(Continued)

SIC Code Number and Industry	Alabama	Mississippi	Arkansas	Louisiana	Oklahoma	Texas
20 Food	4,972,775	5,216,381	4,622,808	67,583,768	1,674,683	46,344,369
21 Tobacco	182,381	--	20,241	825,308	21,338	227,175
22 Textiles	12,467,073	2,690,787	43,525	1,523,206	--	2,512,847
23 Apparel	399,138	262,905	278,476	3,103,911	58,483	1,717,397
24 Lumber and Wood Products	13,565,756	18,080,512	23,118,850	21,789,939	151,561	20,815,618
25 Furniture	173,607	70,744	195,075	559,007	5,650	452,386
26 Paper	--	--	--	29,797	--	--
27 Printing and Publishing	855,643	474,957	777,748	1,939,830	395,108	3,306,168
28 Chemicals	2,954,831	1,209,895	87,605	2,388,277	--	263,236
29 Petroleum and Coal Products	1,156,854	424,871	842,237	1,989,287	720	1,841,191
30 Rubber	--	--	--	--	--	--
31 Leather and Leather Products	607,722	97,946	195,582	921,197	135,889	2,995,795
32 Stone, Clay and Glass	1,451,835	554,762	540,772	834,653	235,302	2,563,112
33 Primary Metals	19,905,249	--	--	134,923	--	--
34 Fabricated Metals	361,830	131,360	123,180	1,304,788	37,555	879,116
35 Non-electrical Machinery	4,939,129	418,612	432,163	3,584,432	38,650	2,809,524
36 Electrical Machinery	--	--	--	--	--	--
37 Transportation Equipment	2,790,111	985,462	1,137,235	1,554,994	39,750	4,171,099
38 Instruments	20,999	--	--	230,156	--	34,465
39 Miscellaneous	61,443	40,379	15,625	854,764	13,895	198,585
Total (000$)	66,866.2	30,659.7	32,431.1	111,152.3	2,808.8	91,132.-

APPENDIX, PART XXII

CAPITAL-LABOR RATIOS BY REGION, 1900

SIC Code Number and Industry	New England	Middle Atlantic	East North Central	West North Central	South Atlantic	East South Central	West South Central	Average for Regions
20 Food	$ 2277	$ 3412	$ 2912	$ 2603	$ 1475	$ 2259	$ 4848	$ 2939
21 Tobacco	680	716	579	892	833	1178	517	740
22 Textiles	1813	1361	1183	1462	1179	1385	1998	1533
23 Apparel	531	653	545	458	467	465	589	600
24 Lumber and Wood Products	1532	1725	1687	2095	1053	1095	1514	1566
25 Furniture	1435	994	1058	1041	689	919	762	1043
26 Paper	2360	1976	1903	579	1940	328	295	2084
27 Printing and Publishing	1202	1546	1051	1033	1006	1171	880	1249
28 Chemicals	2611	3725	2535	2587	834	731	1951	2298
29 Petroleum and Coal Products	8069	10848	9415	11040	6824	5458	6402	9619
30 Rubber	2586	1977	1423	– –	– –	– –	– –	1998
31 Leather and Leather Products	805	1451	1102	934	1758	1990	1115	1153
32 Stone, Clay and Glass	846	1263	1050	1028	703	650	642	1277
33 Primary Metals	2064	2604	2300	2065	1802	2104	2397	2650
34 Fabricated Metals	1470	1543	1845	1296	929	1113	988	1617
35 Non-electrical Machinery	1757	1936	1480	1378	1564	1151	1853	1712
36 Electrical Machinery	– –	– –	– –	– –	– –	– –	– –	– –
37 Transportation Equipment	1277	1377	1231	996	582	654	562	1195
38 Instruments	1219	1559	1631	1508	1170	843	1838	1525
39 Miscellaneous	1469	1318	2490	941	875	936	1381	1333

APPENDIX, PART XXIII

CAPITAL-LABOR RATIOS BY STATE, 1900

SIC Code Number and Industry	Maine	New Hampshire	Vermont	Massachusetts	Rhode Island	Connecticut	New York	New Jersey
20 Food	$ 1350	$ 2273	$ 1673	$ 2791	$ 2439	$ 1792	$ 3777	$ 3186
21 Tobacco	534	438	558	725	583	683	724	1842
22 Textiles	1641	1576	1796	1814	1914	1958	1415	1583
23 Apparel	398	478	490	559	394	545	676	477
24 Lumber and Wood Products	1670	1710	1565	1309	1345	1454	1595	1431
25 Furniture	900	1043	959	1435	1129	2189	1011	975
26 Paper	3296	3003	3677	2049	519	1827	1945	1806
27 Printing and Publishing	992	1375	858	1195	1099	1491	1603	1281
28 Chemicals	3904	1016	1870	2723	1857	2421	3400	4201
29 Petroleum and Coal Products	5819	4563	859	10423	8411	9179	14691	10348
30 Rubber	--	--	--	2186	2058	4780	1732	2226
31 Leather and Leather Products	859	752	1005	786	931	1435	1044	1157
32 Stone, Clay and Glass	1121	671	974	858	490	716	1178	1292
33 Primary Metals	1900	--	--	2040	2570	2076	2279	2792
34 Fabricated Metals	1503	1007	1319	1312	1093	1605	1633	1048
35 Non-electrical Machinery	1685	1341	1684	1769	1834	1751	1813	1523
36 Electrical Machinery	--	--	--	--	--	--	--	--
37 Transportation Equipment	1058	1238	958	1294	1106	1461	1385	1002
38 Instruments	--	857	--	1217	812	1241	1487	1770
39 Miscellaneous	1020	705	888	1301	1388	1748	1390	1243

APPENDIX, PART XXIII
(Continued)

SIC Code Number and Industry	Pennsylvania	Delaware	Maryland	Ohio	Indiana	Illinois	Michigan	Wisconsin
20 Food	$ 3621	$ 1650	$ 1736	$ 2823	$ 2268	$ 3024	$ 2328	$ 3564
21 Tobacco	552	576	661	674	325	523	451	758
22 Textiles	1225	791	1375	1552	1307	957	874	1143
23 Apparel	663	345	591	669	412	523	403	644
24 Lumber and Wood Products	2048	712	1149	1129	893	934	1966	2678
25 Furniture	1004	1314	781	1219	898	949	1074	1197
26 Paper	1947	4029	1998	1556	2168	1008	1647	3336
27 Printing and Publishing	1549	1079	1025	1214	879	994	994	1136
28 Chemicals	4101	1727	3082	3345	1840	2696	1986	2238
29 Petroleum and Coal Products	6199	5399	27305	7191	4877	13517	8624	6878
30 Rubber	1437	- -	- -	1560	- -	1032	1266	1245
31 Leather and Leather Products	2152	1887	774	849	979	1033	1507	1382
32 Stone, Clay and Glass	1334	857	1130	1058	892	1081	1139	1617
33 Primary Metals	2629	2678	1291	2356	1887	2378	1874	2608
34 Fabricated Metals	1621	779	1099	1633	1408	2056	1697	2193
35 Non-electrical Machinery	2248	2341	1241	1541	1303	1466	1330	1621
36 Electrical Machinery	-	- -	- -	-	-	-	-	- -
37 Transportation Equipment	1515	1099	1075	925	1402	1343	1260	1326
38 Instruments	1624	- -	854	1168	976	1775	681	948
39 Miscellaneous	1196	885	1163	1464	1119	1462	1197	1276

APPENDIX, PART XXIII
(Continued)

SIC Code Number and Industry	Minnesota	Iowa	Missouri	Kansas	Nebraska	North Dakota	South Dakota	Virginia
20 Food	$ 3493	$ 2084	$ 2796	$ 1893	$ 2745	$ 2602	$ 3012	$ 1461
21 Tobacco	613	518	1194	583	468	386	503	697
22 Textiles	1698	1170	1582	295	252	- -	- -	1173
23 Apparel	397	420	520	363	424	543	363	419
24 Lumber and Wood Products	2867	1867	1292	819	943	1436	1315	875
25 Furniture	1186	977	1011	1039	776	1560	490	592
26 Paper	627	716	517	- -	- -	- -	- -	2022
27 Printing and Publishing	1251	922	1039	802	1032	1083	957	1249
28 Chemicals	2625	1209	2936	1701	3832	- -	- -	2972
29 Petroleum and Coal Products	11089	7145	12958	3241	12624	- -	860	4891
30 Rubber	- -	406	- -	- -	- -	- -	- -	- -
31 Leather and Leather Products	1033	998	818	945	1050	1977	1056	1411
32 Stone, Clay and Glass	656	1040	1302	730	845	1285	1389	879
33 Primary Metals	1641	1625	1537	3363	- -	- -	- -	2161
34 Fabricated Metals	1622	1301	1245	756	964	728	1053	902
35 Non-electrical Machinery	1156	1322	1450	1667	1181	1450	1106	2201
36 Electrical Machinery	- -	- -	- -	- -	- -	- -	- -	- -
37 Transportation Equipment	1064	929	1134	524	1356	1226	779	664
38 Instruments	640	1188	1764	1360	666	- -	- -	550
39 Miscellaneous	1166	453	1124	1665	1081	- -	328	634

APPENDIX, PART XXIII
(Continued)

SIC Code Number and Industry	West Virginia	North Carolina	South Carolina	Georgia	Florida	Kentucky	Tennessee	Alabama
20 Food	$ 2005	$ 1133	$ 1481	$ 1556	$ 1249	$ 3284	$ 1913	$ 1242
21 Tobacco	1881	933	684	443	777	1186	1250	606
22 Textiles	1659	1039	1277	1247	472	1535	1449	1345
23 Apparel	695	471	555	381	528	473	497	335
24 Lumber and Wood Products	1408	861	874	919	1770	981	893	1112
25 Furniture	1094	535	603	811	389	1133	786	692
26 Paper	2485	310	2130	1271	– –	– –	328	– –
27 Printing and Publishing	1041	664	812	1016	926	1297	1376	748
28 Chemicals	2897	2590	3618	496	379	1970	1525	553
29 Petroleum and Coal Products	4011	4325	6649	9915	15409	4778	6373	6287
30 Rubber	– –	– –	– –	– –	– –	– –	– –	– –
31 Leather and Leather Products	4308	1627	434	1078	318	2210	2054	1068
32 Stone, Clay and Glass	879	383	472	681	553	776	593	602
33 Primary Metals	1603	1464	4155	2175	– –	1658	2325	2172
34 Fabricated Metals	1089	699	714	1113	612	1331	744	1179
35 Non-electrical Machinery	1284	1087	975	1256	1075	1112	1048	1297
36 Electrical Machinery	– –	– –	– –	– –	– –	– –	– –	– –
37 Transportation Equipment	486	640	553	510	522	868	576	518
38 Instruments	– –	625	– –	1316	– –	919	– –	778
39 Miscellaneous	– –	1207	942	987	104	859	1083	614

APPENDIX, PART XXIII
(Continued)

SIC Code Number and Industry	Mississippi	Arkansas	Louisiana	Oklahoma	Texas
20 Food	$ 1491	$ 1888	$ 5037	$ 2500	$ 5608
21 Tobacco	- -	349	521	395	542
22 Textiles	1233	907	1805	- -	2185
23 Apparel	422	371	696	305	512
24 Lumber and Wood Products	1478	1175	1658	1443	1967
25 Furniture	649	579	887	471	740
26 Paper	- -	- -	295	- -	- -
27 Printing and Publishing	644	749	1011	725	871
28 Chemicals	433	1413	2191	- -	1045
29 Petroleum and Coal Products	10363	8021	6178	1200	6199
30 Rubber	- -	- -	- -	- -	- -
31 Leather and Leather Products	557	679	781	795	1406
32 Stone, Clay and Glass	482	583	619	694	660
33 Primary Metals	- -	- -	2367	- -	- -
34 Fabricated Metals	864	765	1405	395	741
35 Non-electrical Machinery	1014	1286	2026	1137	1795
36 Electrical Machinery	- -	- -	- -	- -	- -
37 Transportation Equipment	502	455	660	585	566
38 Instruments	- -	- -	2001	- -	1188
39 Miscellaneous	792	274	1784	993	849

APPENDIX, PART XXIV

CAPITAL-OUTPUT RATIOS BY REGION, 1900

SIC Code Number and Industry	New England	Middle Atlantic	East North Central	West North Central	South Atlantic	East South Central	West South Central	Average for Regions
20 Food	1.91	2.35	1.56	2.03	1.93	1.87	4.40	2.03
21 Tobacco	.71	.74	.63	.50	.83	.83	.56	.71
22 Textiles	2.75	2.12	2.20	2.50	3.01	3.42	3.82	2.53
23 Apparel	.73	.85	.74	.78	.92	.84	1.05	.81
24 Lumber and Wood Products	2.09	2.20	2.16	2.50	1.85	1.82	2.27	2.13
25 Furniture	1.54	1.17	1.54	1.36	1.35	1.42	1.17	1.39
26 Paper	2.39	2.21	2.43	1.08	3.17	.92	.70	2.32
27 Printing and Publishing	.98	1.23	1.03	1.13	1.35	1.29	.99	1.13
28 Chemicals	.65	2.26	1.60	1.57	2.11	1.12	1.84	1.76
29 Petroleum and Coal Products	5.72	7.65	7.20	8.97	6.26	4.87	4.31	7.32
30 Rubber	1.98	2.07	1.69	- -	- -	- -	- -	1.96
31 Leather and Leather Products	1.19	2.04	1.86	1.67	2.95	2.62	1.51	1.70
32 Stone, Clay and Glass	1.02	1.35	1.37	1.35	1.41	1.18	1.07	1.31
33 Primary Metals	2.14	2.07	1.92	2.44	1.97	2.32	3.52	2.05
34 Fabricated Metals	1.77	1.77	2.02	1.53	1.39	1.43	1.32	1.84
35 Non-electrical Machinery	1.87	2.04	1.61	1.47	2.15	1.60	2.00	1.85
36 Electrical Machinery	-	-	-	-	-	-	-	-
37 Transportation Equipment	1.60	1.81	1.75	1.42	1.04	1.15	.87	1.63
38 Instruments	1.62	1.67	2.00	1.10	1.21	1.05	1.50	1.69
39 Miscellaneous	1.57	1.40	1.70	1.20	.55	1.24	1.78	1.50

APPENDIX, PART XXV

CAPITAL-OUTPUT RATIOS BY STATE, 1900

SIC Code Number and Industry	Maine	New Hampshire	Vermont	Massachusetts	Rhode Island	Connecticut	New York	New Jersey
20 Food	2.48	1.47	1.71	2.04	1.67	1.33	2.40	1.86
21 Tobacco	.72	.54	.77	.70	.60	.81	.67	1.14
22 Textiles	2.65	2.57	2.91	2.73	2.75	2.99	2.14	2.25
23 Apparel	.84	.94	.90	.70	.60	.77	.76	.77
24 Lumber and Wood Products	2.58	2.24	2.47	1.60	1.84	1.75	2.03	1.67
25 Furniture	1.18	1.59	1.51	1.45	1.33	2.13	1.14	1.09
26 Paper	2.83	2.43	2.86	2.24	.86	2.15	2.16	2.15
27 Printing and Publishing	1.03	1.74	1.14	.90	1.13	1.37	1.16	1.41
28 Chemicals	3.50	.52	.54	1.50	1.22	1.24	1.91	2.98
29 Petroleum and Coal Products	5.34	4.58	1.78	5.89	6.75	6.01	8.94	9.06
30 Rubber	-	-	-	1.99	1.77	2.12	1.78	2.24
31 Leather and Leather Products	1.42	1.32	1.74	1.12	1.27	1.90	1.50	1.58
32 Stone, Clay and Glass	1.44	.93	1.17	.97	.72	.88	.93	1.71
33 Primary Metals	1.79	-	-	2.14	3.17	2.13	2.00	2.13
34 Fabricated Metals	2.03	1.32	1.92	1.45	1.39	2.01	1.75	1.33
35 Non-electrical Machinery	2.31	1.59	1.78	1.77	2.15	1.95	1.85	1.70
36 Electrical Machinery	-	-	-	-	-	-	-	-
37 Transportation Equipment	1.48	1.87	1.56	1.56	1.23	1.70	1.89	1.29
38 Instruments	-	1.28	-	1.43	.86	1.80	1.65	1.79
39 Miscellaneous	1.21	.91	1.71	1.38	1.47	1.86	1.35	1.47

APPENDIX, PART XXV
(Continued)

SIC Code Number and Industry	Pennsylvania	Delaware	Maryland	Ohio	Indiana	Illinois	Michigan	Wisconsin
20 Food	2.48	2.38	2.17	1.53	1.06	1.56	1.86	1.97
21 Tobacco	.78	.92	.52	.76	.50	.53	.46	.73
22 Textiles	1.99	1.93	2.83	2.58	2.49	1.70	1.78	2.30
23 Apparel	.97	.81	1.01	.95	.80	.60	.70	1.02
24 Lumber and Wood Products	2.51	1.77	1.84	1.49	1.22	1.28	2.51	3.12
25 Furniture	1.31	1.49	.92	1.66	1.54	1.14	1.69	2.02
26 Paper	2.22	3.48	2.69	1.98	2.75	1.32	2.51	3.80
27 Printing and Publishing	1.41	1.72	1.12	1.23	1.00	.85	1.17	1.37
28 Chemicals	2.43	1.36	2.32	1.63	1.21	1.54	1.74	1.76
29 Petroleum and Coal Products	4.88	4.38	12.23	5.32	5.30	8.89	8.99	5.67
30 Rubber	2.15	- -	- -	2.33	- -	.69	1.66	2.02
31 Leather and Leather Products	2.95	2.16	1.56	1.51	1.59	1.35	2.19	3.13
32 Stone, Clay and Glass	1.68	1.16	1.58	1.48	1.26	1.21	1.46	2.19
33 Primary Metals	2.07	2.76	1.52	1.82	2.14	2.09	1.87	1.69
34 Fabricated Metals	1.91	1.10	1.58	1.97	1.57	2.13	1.75	2.43
35 Non-electrical Machinery	2.39	3.01	1.25	1.68	1.67	1.46	1.63	1.85
36 Electrical Machinery	- -	- -	- -	- -	- -	- -	- -	- -
37 Transportation Equipment	1.91	1.62	1.61	1.34	2.05	1.88	1.76	1.84
38 Instruments	1.66	- -	.85	1.10	.91	2.29	.88	.52
39 Miscellaneous	1.44	1.16	1.85	1.81	1.74	1.65	1.48	1.88

APPENDIX, PART XXV
(Continued)

SIC Code Number and Industry	Minnesota	Iowa	Missouri	Kansas	Nebraska	North Dakota	South Dakota	Virginia
20 Food	2.24	1.75	2.05	1.88	2.16	1.67	2.62	1.97
21 Tobacco	.81	.78	.43	.81	.64	.54	.66	.78
22 Textiles	2.54	2.48	2.62	.78	.81	-	-	2.77
23 Apparel	.72	.83	.81	.73	.65	.79	.71	.82
24 Lumber and Wood Products	2.80	2.55	2.01	1.26	1.21	2.15	1.53	1.66
25 Furniture	1.44	1.41	1.28	1.76	1.17	2.05	.97	1.04
26 Paper	1.13	1.24	1.00	-	-	-	-	3.43
27 Printing and Publishing	1.22	1.22	1.03	1.14	1.16	1.14	1.26	1.52
28 Chemicals	1.79	.74	1.67	1.79	1.83	-	-	3.30
29 Petroleum and Coal Products	8.51	5.21	10.01	3.62	13.17	-	1.66	5.40
30 Rubber	-	-	-	-	-	-	-	-
31 Leather and Leather Products	1.65	6.37	1.29	1.47	1.45	2.61	1.56	2.51
32 Stone, Clay and Glass	.89	1.49	1.60	1.04	1.11	1.59	2.04	1.71
33 Primary Metals	5.18	2.87	1.54	4.72	-	-	-	2.46
34 Fabricated Metals	1.82	1.63	1.38	1.21	1.29	.94	1.77	1.25
35 Non-electrical Machinery	1.30	1.63	1.43	1.84	1.56	1.46	1.67	3.20
36 Electrical Machinery	-	-	-	-	-	-	-	-
37 Transportation Equipment	1.64	1.36	1.47	.81	2.10	2.10	.99	1.14
38 Instruments	.44	1.74	1.27	.94	.65	-	-	-
39 Miscellaneous	1.34	.81	1.28	1.87	.90	-	.65	1.03

APPENDIX, PART XXV
(Continued)

SIC Code Number and Industry	West Virginia	North Carolina	South Carolina	Georgia	Florida	Kentucky	Tennessee	Alabama
20 Food	1.96	1.82	2.22	1.87	1.75	1.94	1.72	1.76
21 Tobacco	1.54	.74	1.69	.99	.88	.78	1.26	.66
22 Textiles	3.64	2.94	3.15	2.97	1.10	2.96	3.89	3.44
23 Apparel	.91	1.08	1.12	.87	.97	.87	.88	.57
24 Lumber and Wood Products	1.90	1.77	1.88	1.51	2.73	1.54	1.53	2.01
25 Furniture	1.69	1.25	1.01	1.51	.72	1.41	1.46	1.29
26 Paper	3.44	.96	3.85	2.02	- -	- -	.92	- -
27 Printing and Publishing	1.42	1.00	1.13	1.40	1.20	1.40	1.40	.96
28 Chemicals	1.73	3.97	5.10	1.46	1.16	1.02	1.09	1.28
29 Petroleum and Coal Products	4.20	4.68	6.71	7.21	8.96	4.92	4.55	5.04
30 Rubber	- -	- -	- -	- -	- -	- -	- -	- -
31 Leather and Leather Products	5.43	2.59	.70	2.10	.58	2.75	3.08	1.17
32 Stone, Clay and Glass	1.41	1.15	1.20	1.35	1.22	1.21	1.09	1.31
33 Primary Metals	1.66	2.08	5.40	3.54	- -	1.63	3.12	2.35
34 Fabricated Metals	1.14	1.53	1.18	1.75	.75	1.62	1.06	1.41
35 Non-electrical Machinery	1.18	1.60	1.60	1.78	1.21	1.42	1.62	1.78
36 Electrical Machinery	- -	- -	- -	- -	- -	- -	- -	- -
37 Transportation Equipment	.92	1.23	1.11	.90	.89	1.46	.98	.99
38 Instruments	- -	1.27	- -	1.26	- -	.85	- -	1.38
39 Miscellaneous	- -	2.07	2.03	1.64	.24	1.09	1.44	.95

APPENDIX, PART XXV
(Continued)

SIC Code Number and Industry	Mississippi	Arkansas	Louisiana	Oklahoma	Texas
20 Food	2.01	1.90	5.36	1.63	4.13
21 Tobacco	- -	.50	.53	.75	.70
22 Textiles	3.20	3.15	3.65	- -	3.94
23 Apparel	.76	.58	1.31	.57	.87
24 Lumber and Wood Products	2.32	1.96	2.33	3.25	2.64
25 Furniture	1.22	.86	1.48	.74	1.07
26 Paper	- -	- -	.70	- -	- -
27 Printing and Publishing	.83	1.00	1.11	1.06	.92
28 Chemicals	.96	1.07	2.16	- -	.86
29 Petroleum and Coal Products	6.15	6.68	3.69	- -	4.41
30 Rubber	- -	- -	- -	- -	- -
31 Leather and Leather Products	.96	1.07	1.21	1.05	1.72
32 Stone, Clay and Glass	1.08	1.11	1.45	1.01	.98
33 Primary Metals	- -	- -	3.52	- -	- -
34 Fabricated Metals	1.21	1.27	1.85	.70	.96
35 Non-electrical Machinery	1.37	1.48	2.22	1.36	1.87
36 Electrical Machinery	- -	- -	- -	- -	- -
37 Transportation Equipment	.88	.71	1.07	.87	.86
38 Instruments	- -	- -	2.00	- -	.56
39 Miscellaneous	1.51	.46	2.17	2.40	1.14

APPENDIX, PART XXVI

PER CAPITA MANUFACTURING VALUE ADDED BY REGION, 1860-1970
(dollars)

Year	New England	Middle Atlantic	East North Central	West North Central	South Atlantic	East South Central	West South Central	Average for Regions
1860	$ 66.6	$ 39.6	$ 15.4	$ 11.8	$ 7.8	$ 7.4	$ 7.5	$ 24.3
1870	109.7	69.5	31.9	27.9	9.1	9.9	8.3	41.7
1880	105.7	66.1	33.5	15.9	8.2	8.0	5.1	36.8
1890	114.2	88.5	56.9	26.2	13.4	14.8	8.8	50.2
1900	142.8	119.1	79.1	34.7	23.8	20.5	14.9	68.2
1910	182.2	149.9	119.3	39.7	42.2	35.0	27.7	93.5
1920	435.3	367.5	330.3	110.6	118.5	74.2	70.7	241.7
1930	396.7	379.2	394.3	140.6	142.5	93.5	78.1	267.6
1940	287.8	264.4	292.3	100.8	113.5	76.9	63.1	194.4
1950	795.7	768.9	980.6	365.0	371.9	300.2	264.8	625.2
1960	1173.6	1131.5	1333.3	655.9	626.6	597.4	524.7	950.6
1970	1773.9	1685.2	2162.6	1205.3	1130.9	1300.3	1024.5	1569.7

APPENDIX, PART XXVII

PER CAPITA MANUFACTURING VALUE ADDED BY STATE, 1860-1970
(dollars)

Year	Maine	New Hampshire	Vermont	Massachusetts	Rhode Island	Connecticut	New York	New Jersey
1860	$ 23.9	$ 51.3	$ 18.7	$ 91.1	$ 115.5	$ 84.5	$ 40.6	$ 48.1
1870	45.4	80.2	43.2	142.2	165.5	132.3	71.7	66.2
1880	42.5	84.0	37.1	129.5	158.3	129.0	73.0	74.2
1890	59.2	87.0	48.7	131.9	143.5	124.6	103.4	77.8
1900	77.9	118.9	74.0	154.6	191.5	170.0	129.5	122.7
1910	106.3	154.3	94.1	196.0	225.1	209.0	165.8	167.7
1920	262.3	377.6	203.7	453.4	547.0	509.7	375.9	442.9
1930	218.7	316.2	214.8	402.6	471.4	501.7	395.1	438.3
1940	179.9	214.0	144.6	275.3	334.0	405.0	247.9	366.4
1950	497.4	663.3	545.2	780.3	776.2	1057.9	708.5	1006.6
1960	715.0	987.0	730.8	1174.7	1082.1	1490.6	1073.4	1411.7
1970	1235.7	1364.8	1250.2	1682.6	1555.5	2365.7	1556.4	2003.6

APPENDIX, PART XXVII
(Continued)

Year	Pennsylvania	Delaware	Maryland	Ohio	Indiana	Illinois	Michigan	Wisconsin
1860	$ 40.8	$ 33.2	$ 21.9	$ 20.9	$ 10.8	$ 11.9	$ 15.9	$ 13.5
1870	76.1	49.4	35.4	38.9	24.6	28.3	38.2	27.5
1880	62.3	49.6	38.6	38.7	22.3	37.3	32.4	30.0
1890	80.3	83.1	59.2	64.7	34.9	71.6	46.4	45.7
1900	114.9	94.8	76.5	84.7	59.9	99.2	58.9	68.0
1910	136.2	108.3	90.0	128.6	90.6	134.5	111.9	104.5
1920	354.7	356.7	222.2	378.7	246.3	297.5	421.0	271.9
1930	356.2	290.1	258.7	434.8	350.9	384.0	426.9	323.2
1940	251.4	207.1	233.2	307.7	283.0	278.8	342.2	218.8
1950	773.9	904.1	621.0	1002.6	974.2	910.2	1160.2	782.4
1960	1139.6	1157.2	864.6	1426.0	1342.6	1255.1	1388.8	1184.3
1970	1876.9	2101.1	1067.9	2271.2	2283.0	2037.3	2282.0	1835.0

APPENDIX, PART XXVII
(Continued)

Year	Minnesota	Iowa	Missouri	Kansas	Nebraska	North and South Dakota	Virginia	West Virginia
1860	$ 8.4	$ 7.6	$ 14.4	$ 14.3	$ 12.8	--	$ 11.2[a]	--
1870	18.4	13.5	44.6	12.0	19.1	$ 5.0	10.7	$ 17.9
1880	23.0	12.0	22.4	7.8	7.7	5.3	11.5	13.4
1890	32.8	17.6	39.4	18.3	20.5	5.1	18.5	14.9
1900	44.0	23.7	47.5	25.2	35.6	8.5	26.5	31.1
1910	61.6	39.8	66.7	38.8	40.2	10.2	45.7	56.6
1920	137.4	92.2	157.1	91.3	86.9	22.8	117.4	136.3
1930	158.0	131.1	214.2	109.2	87.1	27.9	156.9	145.5
1940	111.2	96.4	155.4	66.0	52.5	24.2	141.7	112.9
1950	402.4	353.2	511.8	322.0	204.1	77.8	399.7	440.0
1960	692.1	662.3	897.7	564.4	436.5	140.2	607.9	753.2
1970	1299.0	1320.6	1446.8	1093.4	954.2	279.0	1036.1	1312.3

APPENDIX, PART XXVII
(Continued)

Year	North Carolina	South Carolina	Georgia	Florida	Kentucky	Tennessee	Alabama	Mississippi
1860	$ 6.1	$ 4.7	$ 6.0	$ 9.9	$ 12.5	$ 6.9	$ 5.0	$ 4.1
1870	5.4	5.2	9.5	10.6	17.3	10.4	4.8	3.9
1880	4.7	6.2	7.4	8.8	15.6	7.7	3.7	2.3
1890	8.9	8.8	12.7	18.8	25.6	14.1	11.5	4.9
1900	21.6	17.4	20.4	38.5	30.5	20.1	18.5	10.1
1910	43.0	30.9	32.9	62.1	48.9	34.9	29.2	24.3
1920	161.7	90.5	86.7	124.1	65.6	89.9	81.3	56.2
1930	218.6	91.6	101.3	92.3	90.3	123.4	97.5	53.4
1940	152.9	89.4	90.7	62.2	65.9	109.9	87.3	33.6
1950	457.5	403.8	356.3	158.7	325.2	356.1	337.8	128.9
1960	825.4	719.0	629.4	364.4	647.9	719.5	600.5	322.4
1970	1610.8	1417.5	1179.5	647.8	1379.0	1524.6	1252.9	862.5

APPENDIX, PART XXVII
(Continued)

Year	Arkansas	Louisiana	Texas
1860	$ 3.6	$ 12.1	$ 4.8
1870	3.6	14.8	5.4
1880	2.5	8.9	4.2
1890	7.0	15.8	8.6
1900	14.5	25.9	13.3
1910	25.4	53.8	24.3
1920	55.3	135.6	63.4
1930	50.8	117.3	79.0
1940	34.6	84.6	70.6
1950	168.0	341.3	294.2
1960	421.0	480.0	602.9
1970	1053.3	892.6	1154.2

[a] Includes West Virginia.

APPENDIX, PART XXVIII

AVERAGE COST OF MANUFACTURING EMPLOYEES, SELECTED INDUSTRIES, 1860

Area	Black-smithing	Carriages	Boots and Shoes	Bread	Brick	Carpen-tering
Maine	$348	$253	$228	$362	$135	$435
New Hampshire	310	405	225	337	130	392
Vermont	344	342	310	294	183	231
Massachusetts	410	400	235	370	146	469
Rhode Island	380	342	206	291	142	434
Connecticut	376	435	251	331	161	430
New York	312	348	264	305	129	455
New Jersey	287	358	271	294	164	413
Pennsylvania	266	333	254	285	328	379
Delaware	288	325	277	272	105	398
Maryland	260	347	257	276	113	440
Ohio	299	355	290	315	134	413
Indiana	308	338	310	257	111	366
Illinois	281	363	307	341	193	353
Michigan	239	294	282	318	122	400
Wisconsin	277	378	239	239	96	339
Minnesota	398	445	343	400	63	260
Iowa	318	415	306	270	102	381
Missouri	311	365	330	330	325	445
Kansas	248	700	317	300	423	- -
Nebraska	312	- -	360	197	60	- -
Virginia	241	328	258	315	114	333
North Carolina	222	263	300	- -	159	404
South Carolina	230	320	275	240	121	- -
Georgia	262	327	279	390	272	538
Florida	330	254	371	- -	218	- -
Kentucky	281	407	342	291	112	415
Tennessee	246	410	293	355	105	400
Alabama	273	396	295	- -	244	258
Mississippi	300	436	373	- -	200	323
Arkansas	275	618	350	- -	191	- -
Louisiana	409	684	413	327	189	603
Texas	350	470	308	405	125	404
United States	307	364	251	320	190	430

APPENDIX, PART XXVIII
(Continued)

Area	Cotton Goods	Flour and Meal	Iron Castings	Leather	Lime	Malt Liquors
Maine	$202	$290	$378	$303	$378	$344
New Hampshire	227	303	335	331	468	399
Vermont	209	355	397	323	315	- -
Massachusetts	202	235	377	380	311	414
Rhode Island	202	319	402	375	709	361
Connecticut	189	342	300	367	200	417
New York	183	331	365	294	294	333
New Jersey	186	295	385	312	268	357
Pennsylvania	186	293	348	280	266	323
Delaware	- -	312	351	366	240	- -
Maryland	218	301	328	299	273	310
Ohio	180	322	372	294	159	348
Indiana	231	313	310	- -	308	347
Illinois	- -	352	409	342	277	329
Michigan	- -	338	369	341	238	330
Wisconsin	- -	392	366	326	237	311
Minnesota	- -	358	481	360	283	320
Iowa	- -	342	373	323	274	276
Missouri	180	360	367	285	309	369
Kansas	- -	495	- -	420	- -	392
Nebraska	- -	333	- -	- -	- -	439
Virginia	163	245	335	230	288	339
North Carolina	108	210	237	244	128	- -
South Carolina	138	187	200	272	189	- -
Georgia	148	256	373	240	281	240
Florida	121	- -	463	- -	- -	- -
Kentucky	168	280	445	277	- -	289
Tennessee	156	256	360	250	- -	393
Alabama	151	249	616	277	208	- -
Mississippi	169	239	535	326	120	- -
Arkansas	- -	253	171	293	- -	- -
Louisiana	137	338	464	252	- -	483
Texas	- -	305	- -	305	- -	481
United States	196	315	383	306	287	358

APPENDIX, PART XXVIII
(Continued)

Area	Lumber Sawed	Machinery Steam Engines etc.	Millinery	Printing	Saddlery and Harness	Soap and Candles
Maine	$297	$405	$141	$321	$343	$289
New Hampshire	285	317	227	255	379	371
Vermont	259	353	169	273	312	- -
Massachusetts	302	423	197	457	366	348
Rhode Island	285	449	147	398	353	279
Connecticut	294	479	190	358	304	352
New York	272	376	206	361	320	330
New Jersey	319	394	144	318	378	322
Pennsylvania	263	342	166	348	310	307
Delaware	273	415	141	342	304	360
Maryland	268	389	135	418	313	328
Ohio	281	370	163	308	284	318
Indiana	276	384	151	281	323	365
Illinois	282	408	252	388	324	351
Michigan	271	399	215	351	322	270
Wisconsin	260	369	153	315	309	293
Minnesota	317	- -	120	277	375	- -
Iowa	273	428	147	293	339	240
Missouri	272	373	281	524	361	344
Kansas	417	288	- -	440	1077	394
Nebraska	282	- -	- -	421	300	- -
Virginia	216	329	164	251	303	262
North Carolina	222	338	144	369	303	180
South Carolina	174	356	- -	349	293	240
Georgia	234	366	375	552	361	360
Florida	259	281	- -	320	465	- -
Kentucky	263	341	214	497	332	235
Tennessee	232	326	- -	408	335	440
Alabama	254	502	- -	290	335	- -
Mississippi	304	566	213	383	380	- -
Arkansas	276	755	- -	330	333	- -
Louisiana	276	513	329	470	515	- -
Texas	301	500	- -	510	461	260
United States	287	400	187	376	338	328

APPENDIX, PART XXVIII
(Continued)

Area	Tin, Copper, and Sheet Iron Ware	Wagons, Carts, etc.	Woolen Goods
Maine	$371	$361	$256
New Hampshire	333	397	281
Vermont	345	319	199
Massachusetts	384	452	233
Rhode Island	373	333	253
Connecticut	404	346	252
New York	311	363	235
New Jersey	334	316	243
Pennsylvania	301	368	232
Delaware	387	270	242
Maryland	333	288	228
Ohio	322	327	246
Indiana	369	314	282
Illinois	371	306	272
Michigan	357	274	243
Wisconsin	353	323	257
Minnesota	441	282	- -
Iowa	372	349	197
Missouri	408	313	282
Kansas	390	376	- -
Nebraska	413	473	- -
Virginia	318	272	216
North Carolina	386	261	237
South Carolina	395	277	124
Georgia	375	268	165
Florida	540	486	- -
Kentucky	403	323	236
Tennessee	414	316	247
Alabama	489	316	172
Mississippi	419	333	96
Arkansas	350	325	- -
Louisiana	542	438	112
Texas	468	341	179
United States	361	354	237

APPENDIX, PART XXIX

AVERAGE COST OF MANUFACTURING EMPLOYEES, SELECTED INDUSTRIES, 1900

Area	Bicycle Repairing	Black-smithing	Book-binding	Boots and Shoes	Bread and other Bakery	Brick and Tile
Maine	$405	$453	$415	$414	$433	$414
New Hampshire	409	516	397	414	497	385
Vermont	393	433	243	363	401	371
Massachusetts	518	616	438	473	483	435
Rhode Island	457	577	413	210	499	- -
Connecticut	497	578	445	414	534	410
New York	478	603	441	389	509	410
New Jersey	443	538	348	390	523	353
Pennsylvania	411	504	397	340	440	390
Delaware	319	408	- -	- -	516	326
Maryland	328	416	362	323	372	302
Ohio	426	468	388	314	435	367
Indiana	428	451	385	248	396	331
Illinois	467	555	395	485	462	408
Michigan	402	547	322	346	440	332
Wisconsin	378	433	275	328	352	369
Minnesota	405	469	461	355	405	387
Iowa	399	428	318	339	392	387
Missouri	458	460	409	347	435	355
Kansas	396	413	- -	- -	366	347
Nebraska	400	462	- -	315	419	383
North Dakota	479	452	- -	- -	350	449
South Dakota	290	449	710	- -	556	410
Virginia	296	304	269	179	371	285
West Virginia	355	386	- -	- -	366	335
North Carolina	263	244	- -	353	282	191
South Carolina	275	236	- -	- -	309	211
Georgia	297	281	- -	264	341	204
Florida	341	360	- -	- -	320	258
Kentucky	328	373	237	246	356	274
Tennessee	310	363	- -	- -	438	255
Alabama	304	249	- -	- -	310	229
Mississippi	270	285	- -	- -	402	221
Arkansas	385	332	- -	- -	395	249
Louisiana	397	406	480	365	320	250
Oklahoma	200	424	- -	- -	383	364
Texas	426	418	- -	- -	481	266
United States	436	497	418	414	463	353

APPENDIX, PART XXIX
(Continued)

Area	Carpen- tering	Railroad Cars and Construction and Repairs	Clothing (men's factory)	Cooper- age	Cotton Goods	Flouring and Grist Mill
Maine	$532	$527	$214	$364	$316	$489
New Hampshire	504	535	282	385	330	444
Vermont	463	573	276	305	256	428
Massachusetts	622	601	427	469	351	531
Rhode Island	521	620	- -	- -	334	471
Connecticut	618	606	386	511	333	426
New York	669	518	474	472	298	516
New Jersey	635	522	366	485	342	510
Pennsylvania	576	554	421	453	360	484
Delaware	587	601	- -	- -	373	362
Maryland	503	511	327	421	251	424
Ohio	557	528	329	407	263	501
Indiana	517	535	218	372	228	476
Illinois	570	538	390	429	- -	520
Michigan	525	514	250	372	- -	505
Wisconsin	482	533	261	404	232	508
Minnesota	519	553	296	509	- -	583
Iowa	476	536	226	377	- -	410
Missouri	487	570	276	371	- -	515
Kansas	480	622	188	429	- -	512
Nebraska	539	578	- -	495	- -	521
North Dakota	576	539	- -	- -	- -	535
South Dakota	562	681	- -	- -	- -	528
Virginia	392	498	165	217	228	416
West Virginia	355	482	326	449	- -	492
North Carolina	365	482	172	215	169	210
South Carolina	338	468	213	226	168	251
Georgia	355	505	181	242	195	194
Florida	469	508	- -	363	- -	173
Kentucky	461	516	257	247	208	426
Tennessee	443	518	214	322	201	472
Alabama	338	482	244	296	178	172
Mississippi	456	527	- -	- -	203	131
Arkansas	429	625	- -	281	- -	263
Louisiana	479	581	190	356	- -	165
Oklahoma	461	606	- -	- -	- -	488
Texas	595	604	245	349	258	566
United States	573	553	376	401	286	478

APPENDIX, PART XXIX
(Continued)

Area	Foundry and Machine Shop	Furniture Factory Product	Manufac- tured Ice	Hosiery and Knit Goods	Iron and Steel	Milli- nery
Maine	$483	$380	$- -	$201	$- -	$268
New Hampshire	478	393	- -	317	- -	300
Vermont	487	363	- -	374	- -	255
Massachusetts	554	480	- -	314	557	379
Rhode Island	527	586	- -	294	- -	334
Connecticut	549	484	554	349	525	379
New York	550	482	631	339	565	338
New Jersey	523	511	514	243	470	309
Pennsylvania	528	426	578	270	558	281
Delaware	474	- -	446	212	473	226
Maryland	480	440	541	175	482	275
Ohio	492	390	517	248	586	252
Indiana	447	355	472	349	560	230
Illinois	530	456	486	274	579	280
Michigan	483	385	- -	231	477	240
Wisconsin	503	328	- -	221	633	223
Minnesota	482	393	- -	265	429	257
Iowa	459	344	457	- -	- -	225
Missouri	548	434	563	- -	539	263
Kansas	575	332	486	- -	- -	221
Nebraska	515	344	- -	- -	- -	255
North Dakota	661	- -	- -	- -	- -	327
South Dakota	426	- -	- -	- -	- -	206
Virginia	460	286	425	214	317	243
West Virginia	537	352	494	- -	513	237
North Carolina	343	190	327	171	- -	232
South Carolina	436	- -	326	206	- -	246
Georgia	386	265	343	166	249	294
Florida	470	- -	407	- -	- -	339
Kentucky	424	363	439	- -	477	245
Tennessee	361	299	461	143	273	327
Alabama	384	292	332	- -	339	297
Mississippi	467	- -	356	- -	- -	258
Arkansas	479	315	375	- -	- -	289
Louisiana	498	334	421	- -	- -	221
Oklahoma	473	- -	559	- -	- -	197
Texas	542	400	494	- -	- -	296
United States	520	408	495	292	543	287

APPENDIX, PART XXIX
(Continued)

Area	Lime and Cement	Leather	Distilled Liquors	Malt Liquors	Lumber and Timber	Lumber, Planing Mill Products
Maine	$427	$391	$- -	$- -	$385	$474
New Hampshire	- -	397	- -	662	395	429
Vermont	315	459	- -	- -	327	370
Massachusetts	537	482	756	812	439	552
Rhode Island	406	465	- -	756	352	483
Connecticut	421	503	560	811	389	523
New York	452	425	429	758	400	485
New Jersey	444	492	426	790	433	532
Pennsylvania	391	407	532	640	411	471
Delaware	- -	425	271	668	243	415
Maryland	328	343	512	644	243	411
Ohio	433	446	535	662	386	462
Indiana	348	405	475	576	380	416
Illinois	465	506	568	630	381	503
Michigan	426	392	- -	612	425	381
Wisconsin	339	426	566	494	437	378
Minnesota	451	197	- -	488	472	407
Iowa	481	- -	- -	592	375	415
Missouri	355	533	261	600	333	508
Kansas	364	- -	- -	- -	301	452
Nebraska	- -	- -	- -	657	346	440
North Dakota	- -	- -	- -	- -	250	- -
South Dakota	619	- -	- -	393	511	419
Virginia	258	353	228	483	282	351
West Virginia	369	338	381	458	343	430
North Carolina	114	287	172	- -	212	244
South Carolina	- -	200	155	- -	196	296
Georgia	246	224	204	428	229	310
Florida	- -	- -	- -	- -	310	388
Kentucky	339	397	503	554	328	387
Tennessee	303	299	312	451	306	386
Alabama	227	433	339	314	244	326
Mississippi	- -	240	- -	- -	288	314
Arkansas	200	250	277	- -	298	320
Louisiana	- -	335	- -	602	328	367
Oklahoma	373	- -	480	- -	220	449
Texas	329	318	326	606	391	500
United States	406	434	466	653	369	444

APPENDIX, PART XXIX
(Continued)

Area	Masonry	Mineral and Soda Waters	Plumbing	Printing and Publishing	Saddlery and Harness	Slaughtering and Meat Packing
Maine	$565	$408	$549	$361	$445	$516
New Hampshire	503	387	527	459	464	- -
Vermont	478	435	534	405	438	- -
Massachusetts	557	504	608	694	564	477
Rhode Island	424	511	545	652	571	515
Connecticut	529	484	592	611	510	456
New York	625	550	650	664	506	508
New Jersey	578	516	560	559	472	531
Pennsylvania	534	388	558	533	429	531
Delaware	638	345	464	392	438	572
Maryland	628	356	497	496	323	471
Ohio	549	464	551	491	387	456
Indiana	514	408	501	437	428	433
Illinois	580	494	695	495	458	503
Michigan	512	410	508	447	452	497
Wisconsin	512	371	459	438	399	412
Minnesota	569	375	585	481	416	447
Iowa	508	387	514	386	401	418
Missouri	637	454	633	547	469	466
Kansas	525	365	507	353	444	439
Nebraska	508	474	612	470	481	491
North Dakota	662	637	622	439	484	470
South Dakota	564	521	464	390	446	- -
Virginia	444	333	440	439	365	426
West Virginia	428	345	449	418	286	508
North Carolina	253	265	476	354	270	- -
South Carolina	- -	181	338	380	427	- -
Georgia	384	242	381	429	218	317
Florida	459	336	530	441	480	- -
Kentucky	487	394	437	452	430	415
Tennessee	354	411	449	480	398	391
Alabama	402	361	412	445	374	- -
Mississippi	225	324	400	374	460	- -
Arkansas	296	309	485	359	474	- -
Louisiana	605	362	521	610	492	- -
Oklahoma	550	415	434	367	530	- -
Texas	611	384	593	501	461	434
United States	564	464	591	532	445	480

APPENDIX, PART XXIX
(Continued)

	Tinsmith- ing, Copper- smithing, etc.	Tobacco (cigars & cigarettes)	Ship & Boat Building (wooden)	Watch, Clock & Jewelery Repair
Maine	$528	$466	$548	$458
New Hampshire	487	515	720	509
Vermont	373	504	- -	481
Massachusetts	547	636	610	612
Rhode Island	550	412	702	625
Connecticut	597	553	493	628
New York	552	428	582	581
New Jersey	528	430	550	568
Pennsylvania	491	336	466	540
Delaware	497	375	534	648
Maryland	365	321	491	492
Ohio	423	333	438	517
Indiana	431	364	468	535
Illinois	485	470	512	559
Michigan	436	352	424	517
Wisconsin	396	406	503	467
Minnesota	443	424	542	563
Iowa	449	378	353	502
Missouri	483	460	696	537
Kansas	499	385	- -	441
Nebraska	525	429	- -	527
North Dakota	622	513	- -	515
South Dakota	506	464	- -	438
Virginia	418	226	522	543
West Virginia	467	365	381	451
North Carolina	360	210	476	407
South Carolina	390	324	- -	374
Georgia	340	334	271	530
Florida	559	498	521	519
Kentucky	390	288	462	469
Tennessee	432	498	233	614
Alabama	399	475	347	655
Mississippi	487	- -	636	484
Arkansas	454	423	- -	659
Louisiana	439	339	426	552
Oklahoma	469	363	- -	547
Texas	521	440	600	648
United States	486	396	542	559

Bibliography

BOOKS

Bishop, J. Leander. *A History of American Manufactures* (Philadelphia: Edward Young and Co., 1864).

Bolles, Albert S. *Industrial History of the United States* (Norwich, Conn.: The Henry Bill Publishing Co., 1881).

Burns, Arthur F. *Production Trends in the United States Since 1870* (New York: National Bureau of Economic Research, 1934).

Caves, Richard. *Trade and Economic Structure* (Cambridge: Harvard University Press, 1960).

Clark, Victor S. *History of Manufactures in the United States*, 3 vols. (New York: McGraw-Hill for the Carnegie Institution, 1929).

Coxe, Tench. *A Statement of the Arts and Manufactures of the United States for the Year 1810* (Philadelphia: A. Cornman, 1814).

Davis, Lance E., Richard A. Easterlin, William N. Parker, et al. *American Economic Growth* (New York: Harper & Row, Publishers, 1972).

Fite, Gilbert C., and Jim E. Reese. *An Economic History of the United States* (Boston: Houghton Mifflin Co., 1973).

Frickey, Edwin. *Production in the United States, 1860-1914* (Cambridge: Harvard University Press, 1947).

Friedman, Milton, and Anna Jacobson Schwartz. *A Monetary History of the United States, 1867-1960* (Princeton University Press, 1963).

Hays, William L., and Robert L. Winkler. *Statistics: Probability, Inference, and Decision,* Vol. 2 (New York: Holt, Rinehart and Winston, Inc., 1970).

Hession, Charles, and Hyman Sardy. *Ascent to Affluence* (Boston: Allyn and Bacon, Inc., 1969).

Hughes, Jonathan. *Industrialization and Economic History* (New York: McGraw-Hill Book Co., 1970).

Kirkland, Edward C. *Industry Comes of Age: Business, Labor, and Public Policy, 1860-1897* (New York: Holt, Rinehart and Winston, Inc., 1961).

Lebergott, Stanley. *Manpower in Economic Growth: The American Record Since 1800* (New York: McGraw-Hill Book Co., 1964).

Martin, Robert F. *National Income of the United States, 1799-1938* (New York: National Industrial Conference Board, 1939).

Neter, John, and William Wasserman. *Fundamental Statistics for Business and Economics* (Boston: Allyn and Bacon, Inc., 1966).

North, Douglass C. *The Economic Growth of the United States, 1790-1860* (Englewood Cliffs, N.J.: Prentice-Hall, Inc., 1961).

―――. *Growth and Welfare in the American Past* (Englewood Cliffs, N.J.: Prentice-Hall, Inc., 1966).

Nourse, Hugh O. *Regional Economics* (New York: McGraw-Hill Book Co., 1968).

Ohlin, Bertil. *Interregional and International Trade* (Cambridge: Harvard University Press, 1933).

Peterson, John M., and Ralph Gray. *Economic Development of the United States* (Homewood, Ill.: Richard D. Irwin, Inc., 1969).

Rees, Albert. *Real Wages in Manufacturing, 1890-1914* (Princeton: Princeton University Press, 1961).

Ricardo, David. *The Principles of Political Economy and Taxation* in *The Works and Correspondence of David Ricardo,* P. Sraffa, ed. (Cambridge, England: Cambridge University Press, 1951).

Robertson, Ross. *History of the American Economy,* 3d ed. (New York: Harcourt Brace Jovanovich, Inc., 1973).

Samuelson, Paul A. *Economics,* 9th ed. (New York: McGraw-Hill Book Co., 1973).

Shannon, Claude E., and Warren Weaver. *The Mathematical Theory of Communication* (Urbana: The University of Illinois Press, 1964).

Shaw, William H. *Value of Commodity Output Since 1869* (New York: National Bureau of Economic Research, 1947).

Siegel, Sidney. *Nonparametric Statistics* (New York: McGraw-Hill Book Co., 1956).

Taussig, Frank W. *The Tariff History of the United States,* 6th ed. (New York: G. P. Putnam's Sons, 1914).

Taylor, George R. *The Transportation Revolution, 1815-1860* (New York: Holt, Rinehart and Winston, 1951).

Temin, Peter. *Iron and Steel in Nineteenth Century America: An Economic Inquiry* (Cambridge: MIT Press, 1964).

Theil, Henri. *Economics and Information Theory* (Amsterdam: North Holland Publishing Co., 1967).

ARTICLES

Clark, Victor S., "Manufacturing Development During the Civil War," in *The Economic Impact of the American Civil War,* Ralph Andreano, ed. (Cambridge: Schenkman Publishing Co., Inc., 1967).

David, Paul A., "The Growth of Real Product in the United States Before 1840: New Evidence, Controlled Conjectures," *Journal of Economic History,* June 1967, pp. 151-197.

Easterlin, Richard A., "Interregional Differences in Per Capita Income, Population, and Total Income, 1840-1950," in *Trends in the American Economy in the Nineteenth Century,* Conference on Research in Income and Wealth, Studies in Income and Wealth, Vol. 24 (Princeton: Princeton University Press, 1960).

——— , "Regional Income Trends, 1840-1950," in *American Economic History,* Seymour Harris, ed. (New York: McGraw-Hill Book Co., 1961).

Engerman, Stanley L., "The Antebellum South: What Probably Was and What Should Have Been," in *Agricultural History,* January 1970, *The Structure of the Cotton Economy of the Antebellum South,* William N. Parker, ed.

Estle, Edwin F., "A More Conclusive Regional Test of the Heckscher-Ohlin Hypothesis," *Journal of Political Economy,* December 1967, pp. 886-888.

Gallman, Robert E., "Commodity Output, 1839-1899," in *Trends in the American Economy in the Nineteenth Century,* Conference on Research in Income and Wealth, Studies in Income and Wealth, Vol. 24 (Princeton: Princeton University Press, 1960).

——— , "Gross National Product in the United States, 1834-1909," in *Output, Employment, and Productivity in the United States after 1800,* Conference on Research in Income and Wealth, Studies in Income and Wealth, Vol. 30 (New York: Columbia University Press, 1966).

——— , "Trends in the Size Distribution of Wealth in the Nineteenth Century: Some Speculations," in *Six Papers on the Size Distribution of*

Wealth and Income, Conference on Research in Income and Wealth, Studies in Income and Wealth, Vol. 33 (New York: Columbia University Press, 1969).

Horowitz, Ann and Ira, "Entropy, Markov Processes and Competition in the Brewing Industry," *Journal of Industrial Economics,* July 1968, pp. 196-211.

Horowitz, Ira, "Numbers-Equivalents in U.S. Manufacturing Industries: 1954, 1958 and 1963," *Southern Economic Journal,* April 1971, pp. 396-408.

Hunter, Louis C., "The Heavy Industries," in *Growth of the American Economy,* Harold F. Williamson, ed. (New York: Prentice-Hall, Inc., 1951).

Kuznets, Simon S., "National Income Estimates for the Period Prior to 1870," in *Income and Wealth of the United States, Trends and Structure,* Simon S. Kuznets, ed. (Cambridge, England: Bowes & Bowes, 1952).

Moroney, John R., and James M. Walker, "A Regional Test of the Heckscher-Ohlin Hypothesis," *Journal of Political Economy,* December 1966, pp. 573-586.

Niemi, Albert W., Jr., "The Development of Industrial Structure in Southern New England," *Journal of Economic History,* September 1970, pp. 657-662.

———, "Structural and Labor Productivity Patterns in United States Manufacturing, 1849-1899," *Business History Review,* Spring 1972, pp. 67-84.

———, "Structural Shifts in Southern Manufacturing, 1849-1899," *Business History Review,* Spring 1971, pp. 79-84.

Parker, William N., and Franklee Whartenby, "The Growth of Output Before 1840," in *Trends in the American Economy in the Nineteenth Century,* Conference on Research in Income and Wealth, Studies in Income and Wealth, Vol. 24 (Princeton: Princeton University Press, 1960).

———, "Slavery and Southern Economic Development: An Hypothesis and Some Evidence," in *Agricultural History,* January 1970, *The Structure of the Cotton Economy of the Antebellum South,* William N. Parker, ed.

Poulson, Barry W., "Estimates of the Value of Manufacturing Output in the Early Nineteenth Century," *Journal of Economic History,* September 1969, pp. 521-525.

Rezneck, Samuel, "Light Manufactures," in *Growth of the American Economy,* Harold F. Williamson, ed. (New York: Prentice-Hall, Inc., 1951).

Siegenthaler, Jurg K., "A Scale Analysis of Nineteenth Century Industrialization," *Explorations in Economic History*, Fall 1972, pp. 75-108.

Uselding, Paul J., "Factor Substitution and Labor Productivity Growth in American Manufacturing, 1839-1899," *Journal of Economic History*, September 1972, pp. 670-681.

Weiss, Thomas, "The Industrial Distribution of the Urban and Rural Workforces: Estimates for the United States, 1870-1910," *Journal of Economic History*, December 1972, pp. 919-937.

Wright, Gavin, "Economic Democracy and the Concentration of Agricultural Wealth in the Cotton South, 1850-1860," in *Agricultural History*, January 1970, *The Structure of the Cotton Economy of the Antebellum South*, William N. Parker, ed.

GOVERNMENT DOCUMENTS

U.S. Bureau of the Census, *A Compendium of the Seventh Census* (Washington, D.C.: Senate Printer, 1854).

————, *Eighth Census of the United States, 1860, Manufactures* (Washington, D.C.: Government Printing Office, 1865).

————, *Eleventh Census of the United States, Manufacturing Industries*, Part I (Washington, D.C.: Government Printing Office, 1895).

————, *Eleventh Census of the United States, Report on Real Estate Mortgages* (Washington, D.C.: Government Printing Office, 1895).

————, *Historical Statistics of the United States, Colonial Times to 1957*, (Washington, D.C.: Government Printing Office, 1960).

————, *Ninth Census of the United States, Industry and Wealth*, Vol. III (Washington, D.C.: Government Printing Office, 1872).

————, *Tenth Census of the United States, Manufactures of the United States* (Washington, D.C.: Government Printing Office, 1883).

————, *Twelfth Census of the United States, Manufactures*, Part I, Vol. VII (Washington, D.C.: Government Printing Office, 1902).

————, *Twelfth Census of the United States, Manufactures*, Part II (Washington, D.C.: Government Printing Office, 1902).

————, *1963 Census of Manufactures, Industry Descriptions* (Washington, D.C.: Government Printing Office, 1966).

U.S. Congress, House, *Domestic Exports, 1789-1883*, House Miscellaneous Document No. 2236, 48th Congress, 1st Session, 1883-1884 (Washington, D.C.: Government Printing Office, 1884).

————, Joint Economic Committee, *Hearings*, Part 2, "Historical and Comparative Rates of Production, Productivity and Prices," 86th Congress, 1st Session, 1959 (Washington, D.C.: Government Printing Office, 1959). Testimony of Moses Abramovitz, pp. 411-433, and Raymond Goldsmith, pp. 230-279.

Index